Apple Pro Training Series
Final Cut Pro X 10.4
Professional Post-Production

Brendan Boykin

Apple Pro Training Series
Final Cut Pro X 10.4
Brendan Boykin
Copyright © 2019 by Brendan Boykin
Updated for Final Cut Pro X v10.4 June 2018

Peachpit Press
www.peachpit.com
Peachpit Press is an imprint of Pearson Education, Inc.
To report errors, please send a note to errata@peachpit.com.

Apple Series Editor: Laura Norman
Editor: Bob Lindstrom
Senior Production Editor: Tracey Croom
Production Coordinator: Maureen Forys, Happenstance Type-O-Rama
Technical Editor: Noah Kadner
Copy Editor: Darren Meiss
Proofreader: Scout Festa
Compositor: Cody Gates, Happenstance Type-O-Rama
Indexer: Valerie Perry
Cover Illustration: Paul Mavrides
Cover Production: Cody Gates, Happenstance Type-O-Rama

ISBN 13: 978-0-13-517173-8
ISBN 10: 0-13-5171733
1 18

Contents at a Glance

Table of Contents

Lesson 1
Getting Started

Editing is storytelling. It's choosing from a sometimes vast array of video and audio clips and assembling them into a coherent experience that can educate, excite, motivate, or move viewers. Built on that fundamental truth of video editing, Final Cut Pro X enables a rich workflow that permits you to approach editing as a storyteller, rather than an equipment technician. The goal of this book is to guide you through that creative workflow, structuring and refining a complete storytelling project from start to finish. Along the way, you'll learn features and acquire skills to realize high-quality editorial results using Final Cut Pro.

For the new editor, Final Cut Pro will help you tell your story without the technical frustrations you may have experienced with other video editing systems. For the seasoned editor, Final Cut Pro can reinvigorate your editing creativity with unique features such as the innovative Magnetic Timeline 2, which encourages you to experiment with your story and make complex editorial changes while eliminating the necessity to micromanage individual clips and their relationships.

GOALS

▶ Download and prepare lesson media files

▶ Understand basic Final Cut Pro workflow

Welcome to Final Cut Pro X.

Learned from a Legacy

Just as offline digital editing once revolutionized traditional splice-and-tape techniques, Final Cut Pro aims to take digital editing to the next level. As cutting-edge programming, Final Cut Pro uses the power of 64-bit architecture and every cycle of the CPUs and GPUs to realize breathtaking performance. When combined with an iMac Pro, Final Cut Pro dramatically accelerates a professional editing workflow.

As an editing suite, Final Cut Pro is the foundation of an experience that naturally carries you from one creative choice to the next, rather than becoming mired in technical tasks. In addition to its powerful editing capabilities, Final Cut Pro incorporates flexible meta-data tools that help you organize the increasing quantity of media an editor must organize in today's digital world. And when editing is completed, you're able to distribute your final projects to whichever format or platform your client or audience requires. The result is a forward-looking application that removes conventional stumbling blocks so that all editors can create and share their stories using the highest-quality software and hardware available.

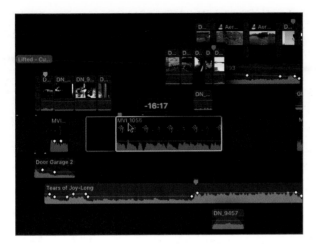

All clips synchronized with a primary storyline clip follow along without clip collisions in the Magnetic Timeline 2.

Reference 1.1
Using This Book

This book is available in multiple formats. The electronic versions may include enhanced content such as:

▶ Glossary: Click/tap words that appear **glossary styled** to review the term's definition.

▶ Keyboard shortcuts: Click/tap keyboard shortcuts (such as **Command-Z**) to jump to Appendix A, which includes an abridged list of over 300 commands that you may assign to keyboard shortcuts.

▶ Links: Click/tap links to view internal and external cross-referenced information sources.

> **NOTE** ▶ Due to technical differences between various ebook formats and platforms, some of the digital features described are not available in all formats.

1.1-A Performing the Exercises

The exercises in this book build on each other from Lesson 1 to Lesson 8. You are advised to complete each exercise (starting with Exercise 1.1.1 in this lesson) before attempting the next exercise, and to move through each lesson before proceeding to the next.

1.1-B Verifying Your Progress with Checkpoints

At the conclusion of major exercises and lessons, you'll find a checkpoint reference. These checkpoints are the author's version of the completed exercise, which you can compare with your version. Refer to Appendix C for more details on downloading and using this learning tool.

Exercise 1.1.1
Downloading the Source Media Files

The source media files you'll use throughout the book are available for download from Peachpit Press. They are organized into zip-compressed files that automatically unzip after download unless you have changed your browser's preferences.

To download these files, you must register your purchase on peachpit.com in order to access the online content:

1   Go to www.peachpit.com/register.

2   Sign in or create a new account.

3   Enter the ISBN: 9780135171738.

4   Answer the questions as proof of purchase.

5   The Lesson Files can be accessed through the Registered Products tab on your Account page. Click the Access Bonus Content link below the title of your product to proceed to the download page.

6   Click the lesson file links to download them to your computer.

   After downloading the zip files from the website, you are ready to proceed with the following exercise.

   NOTE ▶ After redeeming your access code, that code is saved in your Peachpit.com account. You may log in to your Peachpit.com account to re-download the zip files later, if necessary.

Exercise 1.1.2
Preparing the Source Media Files

After downloading the zip files, you will place the files into a folder that you may create in any location you have permission to access. Examples of an accessible location to which you may read/write files are: the desktop, home folder, or Movies folder. If you have an external volume you'd like to use, ensure that the volume is set up in a supported format such as HFS+, that you have read and write permissions for the volume, and that the volume is on a fast storage device such as a 7200 RPM hard disk or solid-state disk with a minimum 10 GB of available storage space.

1   In the Dock, click the Finder icon to open a Finder window.

The Finder is an application used to navigate your Mac computer's filesystem.

2   Choose where you'd like to store the downloaded media.

Every video production begins with the acquisition of media files. You start this process for the exercises in this book when you download the book's media files. Because you will need to access those files to complete the exercises, you should gather and organize them in a media folder.

If you aren't sure where to create the media folder, a great folder location to use for training purposes is your desktop. If you currently store your Desktop and Documents folders on your iCloud Drive, you must select a local folder—such as your Movies folder—to store this book's lesson files and any Final Cut Pro libraries you may create.

3   In the Finder window, navigate to your chosen storage location, such as the desktop.

4   Choose File > New Folder.

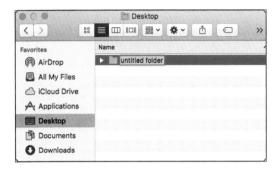

A new, untitled folder is created with its name highlighted, ready to be renamed.

5   Type *FCP X Media*, and press Return.

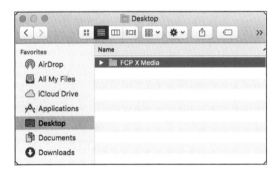

The FCP X Media folder appears, ready to store the downloaded files. To do so, you'll open a second Finder window so you can drag the media files to the newly created FCP X Media folder.

6   Choose File > New Finder Window.

A second Finder window appears.

7 Choose Go > Downloads.

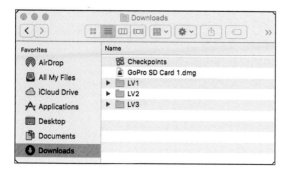

The second Finder window displays the Downloads folder contents.

8 For convenience, arrange the two windows side by side on the desktop.

9 From the Downloads folder, drag the following files/folders to the FCP X Media folder: Checkpoints, GoPro SD Card 1.dmg, LV1, LV2, and LV3.

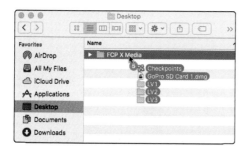 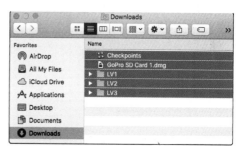

After moving the files to the FCP X Media folder, you may verify the move by clicking the disclosure triangle to the left of the FCP X Media folder and viewing the folder's contents.

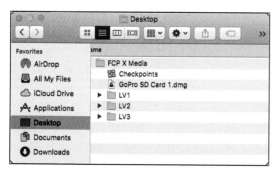

NOTE ▸ If any of the files/folders end with the extension .zip, double-click the file to unpack its contents.

10 Close both Finder windows.

Throughout this book, the exercises will reference the FCP X Media folder and its contents. You'll need to remember where you saved the folder when accessing its contents within Final Cut Pro.

Reference 1.2
Introducing the Job and the Workflow

All books need a story, and in this book two production companies, H5 Productions and Ripple Training, recorded **sound bites** and **B-roll** for a video about aerial cinematography. As an editor, you've agreed to cut a 1:30- to 2-minute vignette for them about H5's owner and helicopter pilot, Mitch Kelldorf, and his passion for flight and film.

In the first four lessons of this book, you will edit a first version "rough cut" using the same real-world workflow that thousands of Final Cut Pro editors follow. At the end of Lesson 4, you will export your rough cut to "show to the client."

The rough cut at the conclusion of Lesson 4

Starting in Lesson 5, you'll implement the client's suggested changes and insert additional material. You'll finesse the rough cut with additional edits, and then move into the sweetening tasks of adding titles, effects, and speed changes. Finally, you'll turn your attention to refining the audio mix before you examine the share options for exporting the project.

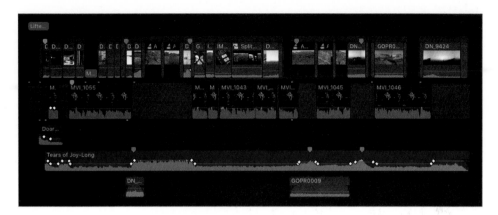

The finished edit at the conclusion of Lesson 8

Lesson 10 describes "sub-workflows" you can use to replace or supplement your editing workflow. Among these are techniques for synchronizing clips recorded in a dual-system setup, used often in HD-DSLR setups, and editing clips recorded in a multicamera scenario.

1.2-A Learning the Workflow

When you look at the Final Cut Pro editing workflow from the 30,000-foot level, you see three phases: import, edit, and share.

During the import phase—sometimes referred to as ingest or transfer—you process source media files into clips. Then, those clips are stored and organized in preparation for the edit phase.

Organizing clips within an event

The edit phase—where you'll spend most of your time with Final Cut Pro—is when the magic begins. This phase comprises several sub-workflows, including trimming clips down to the best material, adding graphics, and mixing the audio.

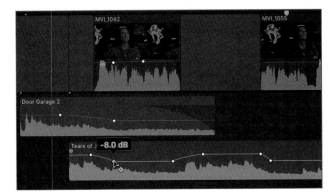

Adjusting audio keyframes

The share phase is when you prepare your finished editing project for distribution to various online hosts or clients, for playback on a variety of devices, and for final archiving.

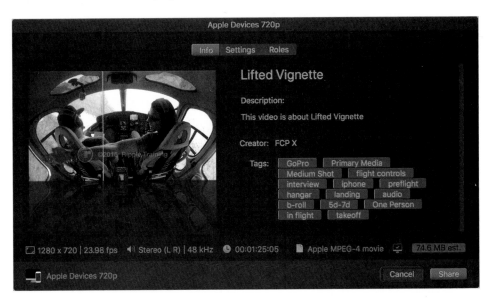

Entering metadata for export

That's the high-level Final Cut Pro workflow within which you will build your stories. As you continue through this book, you'll learn the many tools and techniques, the buttons and keyboard shortcuts, you'll use again and again during your editing workflow. So as you begin this editing odyssey, start by committing one keyboard shortcut to memory: **Command-Z**. If you click a button or press a key and don't get the expected result, just press **Command-Z**. Then, try the edit again. Don't be afraid to experiment. Final Cut Pro is built to encourage exploration of all your editing options and all your creativity.

Lesson Review

1. Define the three post-production workflow phases in Final Cut Pro.
2. Describe the device recommendations for storing source media files.
3. Describe the volume formatting and access recommendations for a media storage device.

Answers

1. Import: The process of ingesting and storing your story's source media files, and organizing the clips that represent those source files. Edit: The creative process of assembling, trimming, and effecting clips to tell a story. Share: The export process of outputting your completed story for various distribution platforms and formats.
2. Media files should be stored on a fast storage device such as a 7200 RPM or greater hard disk or a solid-state disk.
3. A media storage volume should be formatted in a supported format like HFS+ and be read and write accessible.

Lesson 2

Importing Media

You perform the Final Cut Pro post-production preflight, or pre-edit, during the import phase of your workflow. Devoting some time to **media management** and clip organization at the beginning of your editorial process pays off heavily during the later phases of an edit. As part of the import process described in this lesson, you will bring media files into the application as clips that you'll use for your project. Before you start the import process, however, you must be familiar with the clip organization structure of Final Cut Pro.

Reference 2.1
Understanding Clips, Events, and Libraries

The Mac operating system, macOS, uses nested folders on a storage volume—such as a hard disk—as containers in which you store, manipulate, organize, and share content.

Files are enclosed in a folder stored on a volume.

GOALS

▶ Define the clip, event, and library containers

▶ Understand the differences between managed and external media files

▶ Create a camera archive

▶ Import files using Media Import and the Finder

13

Similarly, Final Cut Pro uses specialized clip, event, and library containers to store and organize your media.

Clips are enclosed in an event stored in a library.

2.1-A The Clip Container

After acquiring source media files, such as those you downloaded in the previous lesson, you will import them into Final Cut Pro for editing. The import process creates a clip inside Final Cut Pro that represents each source media file. Each clip varies in its contents: Some combine audio and video content, others contain only video or audio. Think of each clip simply as a container. To edit a video file, you must import the file into Final Cut Pro. Final Cut Pro places the file's contents into a clip container.

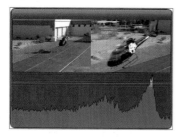

The clip container references
a source media file.

2.1-B The Event Container

Clips within Final Cut Pro are virtually organized into larger containers called events. Events may contain a wide variety of clips, but are best utilized to organize clips that have one or more common elements. A common element could be interviews, shots for a movie scene, or stock footage. The event container can include a varied cornucopia of clips or a narrowly defined selection of clips. It's up to you to define the specifics of event containers.

The event container holds multiple clip containers.

▶ **What Should Go into an Event?**

Events may store whichever clips you choose. Some editors like to create one event, throw all available clips into that event, and later go "gold digging" to find the nuggets. Other editors prefer to create multiple events, each one storing clips grouped by acquisition date, camera card, scene of the movie, or a subtopic within a documentary edit. Your events could represent a combination of those options because only you define the contents of your events.

Before you decide what to place into your events, remember that an event in Final Cut Pro is a virtual storage container. You may move and reorganize the clips within events to help you quickly locate your editing content. What is hidden from view is the powerful media management that Final Cut Pro performs under the hood as you import and organize files into those events. Events work in conjunction with the larger library container to define the virtual and physical locations where your source media files are stored.

2.1-C The Library Container

A library is the largest content container in Final Cut Pro. Libraries allow you to bundle your events and thousands of clips for powerful yet simple management of your projects. Libraries facilitate the easy handoff of a project or multiple projects to another editor or production colleague. You need at least one library open to edit your project, and you may simultaneously open as many as you want.

The library container bundles events together.

In Lesson 9, you'll further explore the media management settings and tools that apply to clips, events, and libraries. Those tools allow you to move, copy, and organize the source files within Final Cut Pro. For now, you'll start importing clips, and see how Final Cut Pro handles your media when using the default media management settings.

Exercise 2.1.1
Creating a Library

Because all the clips you'll edit are contained inside an event, and an event is contained inside a library, you'll need to create a library before you can import media. You can save a library on any accessible and supported local or network volume.

1   From the Dock or the Applications folder, open Final Cut Pro by clicking the application's icon.

If this is your first time opening Final Cut Pro, a "What's New in Final Cut Pro X" window appears.

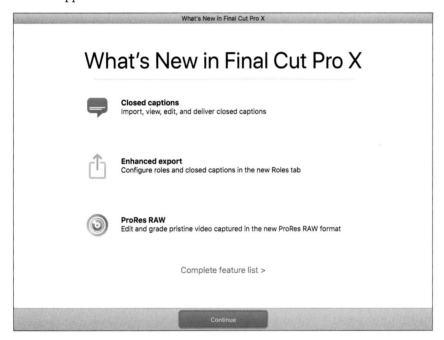

This window lists features that are new to the most recent update of Final Cut Pro. You'll explore several new features and many others in this book. You can learn additional information about all Final Cut Pro features at the Final Cut Pro X Help webpage.

2   If necessary, click Continue.

The Final Cut Pro main window fills your screen, ready to edit.

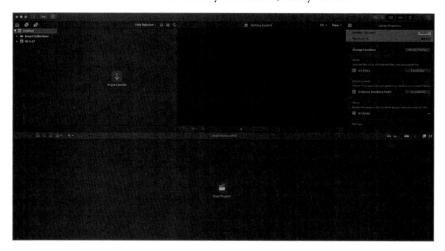

The Libraries sidebar lists the open libraries in Final Cut Pro. If this is the first time you've opened Final Cut Pro, an "Untitled" library appears.

If you've previously opened Final Cut Pro, you may have other libraries listed. Because you'll be starting a new edit using this book's media, you should create a new library.

NOTE ▶   If you've used earlier versions of Final Cut Pro X, a dialog may appear asking if you want to update your existing libraries. You may choose not to update at this time; however, choosing to update or not won't affect your ability to complete this book's exercises.

3   Choose File > New > Library.

A Save dialog appears asking where to store your library. You can save a library container to any available, supported storage device (ideally a high-speed local or network volume).

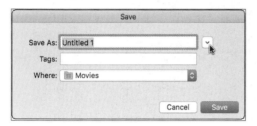

4   To display Finder options, click the disclosure triangle next to the Save As field. Navigate to the same location in which you saved the FCP X Media folder.

NOTE ▸   In Lesson 1, you downloaded and moved the media to a new folder named FCP X Media, which you created at one of the suggested locations: an external volume, the Movies folder, or the desktop.

5   In the Save As field, enter *Lifted*, and click Save.

In the Libraries sidebar to the left, you will see a new library, Lifted, that automatically contains an event named for today's date. You also have one library that was created when you first opened Final Cut Pro. Let's close that library, and any others you may have, to protect their contents.

6 Control-click (or right-click) the unwanted library, and from the shortcut menu, choose Close Library.

7 Using the same method, close any additional libraries you may have listed beyond the Lifted library.

Closing existing libraries protects their contents while you are working with the materials used in this book. And don't worry, you'll later learn how to open existing libraries.

In the Libraries sidebar, look at the default contents in the Lifted library. They include a folder and a single event with the current date as its name. You'll learn more about the organizational power of Smart Collections in Lesson 3, but for now, you'll focus on getting media files loaded into the Lifted library's event. Because you will import media from one of this project's GoPro cameras into that event, rename the event to something more descriptive.

8 In the Lifted library, click the text label of the event. When the text label switches to a text entry field, enter *GoPro*, and press Return.

The event is renamed. You've created a new library and prepared an event to receive the source media files as clips.

Exercise 2.1.2
Preparing to Import Camera Source Files

For this exercise, you will mount a cloned SD card that you downloaded in Lesson 1. This clone will simulate a physical camera SD card.

1   Press **Command-H** to hide Final Cut Pro and return to your desktop.

2   Locate the FCP X Media folder you created in Lesson 1.

3   Inside the FCP X Media folder, double-click the **GoPro SD Card 1.dmg** file.

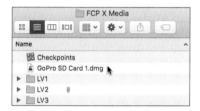

In a moment, a removable volume icon will appear on your desktop. This software card simulates a physical camera card connected to your computer.

NOTE ▶   If another application opens when a card is inserted, press Command-Q to quit the application.

4   To return to Final Cut Pro, click its Dock icon.

Final Cut Pro remained in the background, awaiting your return. Depending on your system configuration, the Media Import window may already be open for you.

5 If Media Import did not open automatically, click the Media Import button.

Before you import any media, you'll examine the Media Import interface.

Reference 2.2
Using the Media Import Window

The Media Import window presents a unified interface for ingesting source media files into Final Cut Pro. The Media Import window specifies where source media files reside and how their clip representations are cataloged within a library's event(s). You can edit these clips into a project to begin your post-production workflow.

Final Cut Pro is designed to get you editing quickly by minimizing technical barricades. The Media Import window has four panes: sidebar, Viewer, Browser, and import options.

▶ Sidebar: To the left, the sidebar lists available devices (cameras, volumes, and favorites) as import sources.

▶ Viewer: Previews the source media file selected in the lower Browser.

▶ Browser: Displays the source media files available for import from the device selected in the sidebar.

▶ Import options: Specifies the virtual and physical locations of clips and source media files during import, along with transcoding and analysis options.

The sidebar is the first pane you see when you open the Media Import window. It includes a list of Final Cut Pro–compatible devices.

When you select a device in the sidebar, the device's media files appear in the lower Browser pane, which has two available views: filmstrip and list.

Toggle to display list view

Toggle to display filmstrip view

NOTE ▶ The available view options depend upon the selected device type.

Source media files that appear in the Browser are ready for previewing in the Viewer and for importing. You needn't worry about configuring additional settings. If Final Cut Pro can access the file to preview it, you can import it.

Once you've selected which media files to import, you can turn your attention to the import options. The media management features of Final Cut Pro ensure that you know where the clips you're about to import will be stored. You have access to incredibly powerful, user-configurable options with just a few clicks.

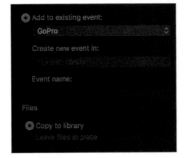

Select the library event to virtually
organize clips and media management
options to physically store files.

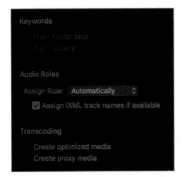

Select the desired metadata and
transcoding options to apply during import.

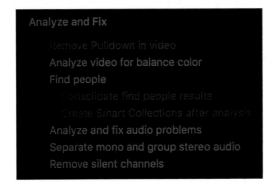

Select clip analysis and repair options.

After setting the import options, Final Cut Pro ingests the source media files as clips that appear in the main window's Browser, ready for editing. When you combine the 64-bit architecture of Final Cut Pro and macOS with Mac hardware, you have virtually instantaneous editing access to the clips, even at 4K resolution, while the import is still underway. Forget same-day editing. This is same-hour editing.

> ▶ **Codecs? Frame Rate? Aspect? What?**
>
> These are some of the specifications that describe media files, much as "US Letter" is a specification that describes paper trimmed to 8.5 x 11 inches. These three terms define the mathematical compression applied to each frame, the frames per second recorded, and the pixel size, square or rectangular.

Exercise 2.2.1
Creating a Camera Archive

Before you start importing, you should perform one very important process: Back up your source media. The Create Archive command allows you to clone your source media device within the application that Final Cut Pro will manage and catalog. Although some editing workflows allow you to back up your source media files outside the application, the purpose of Create Archive is to ensure that you have a backup of your original source media files, just in case. We've all deleted a file at some point that we wished we could get back.

1   From the Cameras section of the list, select the GOPRO1 camera card.

The contents of the card appear in the Browser area. Before you start previewing the media files, you should begin the backup process.

2   Below the sidebar, click the Create Archive button.

A dialog asks you to name the new archive and choose a save location. Be sure to choose a meaningful name for the archive. It could be the name of the client, scene, project name, project number, or any combination of metadata that will later help you distinguish this archive from every other archive.

3   For this exercise, type *Heli Shots-GoPro* to describe the files as the helicopter shots from the GoPro SD Card 1.

4   If necessary, click the disclosure triangle button to display the rest of the Finder options.

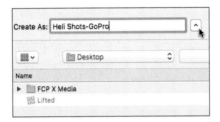

You have the option to add the camera archive to the Favorites section of the left side-bar for convenient access. For now, leave this option deselected.

5   Navigate to the location of your FCP X Media folder, and click the New Folder button.

6   Enter *Lifted Archives* as the new folder name. In the New Folder dialog, click Create; and in the previous dialog, also click Create.

A timer appears next to the GOPRO1 card in the sidebar. You may proceed with the importing process before the archive has completed.

▶ Why Should I Create Camera Archives?

Final Cut Pro imports source files from a variety of camera formats. For the most efficient import process, the Media Import window uses the source camera metadata. The metadata is stored among several files of the camera card/magazine, or is embedded in the media files. Some of the external files are hidden when viewing the source files in the Finder, so if you drag the source files from the card to your computer, you will not be copying all the associated metadata. As a result, in some cases, the source files will not be recognized by the Media Import window at all. Best practice is to clone your camera card/magazine using the Create Archive function. Creating an archive, rather than dragging files from the camera, preserves the camera metadata and volume structure, and allows Final Cut Pro to recognize the source format.

▶ Where Should I Store Camera Archives?

The libraries that contain your clips should be stored on a media volume that is physically separate from your Macintosh HD volume. Ideally, the media volume is a RAID (redundant array of independent disks) volume, often referred to as a protected volume. A RAID is a group of disks bound together by hardware or software that presents those disks as a single volume. A RAID may be configured to provide data redundancy or bandwidth performance or a combination of both. If the media volume is your only secondary volume, storing the camera archives on the media volume maintains everything on one volume, which helps you to keep your editing project consolidated. However, keeping all the parts of your editing project on one unprotected (non-RAID) volume also creates a single point of failure. A best practice is to store your camera archives on a protected volume separate from your libraries.

Reference 2.3
Importing Source Media from a Camera

The Media Import window accesses a camera's source media files, as you learned when creating an archive or clone of the camera card/magazine as a backup. However, creating an archive is not the same as importing files to your library. The archive is merely a backup of the original content. Now it's time to import the media files as clips into a library event for use in Final Cut Pro.

You'll begin by learning how to navigate the filmstrip representations of each media file. The mouse or trackpad is not the only way, or even the fastest way, to navigate Final Cut Pro. The techniques you learn here will apply throughout the rest of the application and your entire editing workflow. They will also help you use Final Cut Pro more efficiently.

▶ **Command Editor**

Final Cut Pro has over 300 customizable keyboard commands that you can assign using the Command Editor window (Final Cut Pro > Commands > Customize).

For more information on using the Command Editor, see the "Assigning Keyboard Shortcuts" section of **Appendix A**.

Exercise 2.3.1
Navigating Within a Filmstrip Preview

As an independent editor, you may spend hours poring over source media files. Using keyboard commands to move through those materials may save only seconds at a time, but those seconds can compound into hours over the life of a complex editing project.

1   With the simulated SD card still mounted, select it from the Cameras section at the top of the sidebar.

At the lower-right of the Browser pane, you can toggle the source file's display view: filmstrip or list. Let's start with the filmstrip view to get your first taste of skimming.

2   Click the Filmstrip View button, if necessary.

The source media files from the cloned SD card are displayed as thumbnails, which you can use to quickly skim a file's contents.

3   Move your pointer across a file's thumbnail to skim the media.

A preview of the file's contents appears in the thumbnail and in the Viewer pane above the thumbnails. The preview also plays the audio track if one is included in the file. You may also play the file in real time.

4   With the pointer placed over a thumbnail, click the thumbnail, and then press the Spacebar.

The Spacebar initiates real-time file preview. Pressing the Spacebar again pauses the preview.

5   Press the Spacebar again to pause playback, and then move your pointer across the thumbnail.

Two indicators appear on the thumbnail: the skimmer at the pointer and the playhead where playback stopped. You'll learn how these indicators affect previewing and editing clips in later lessons.

You've already seen how you can skim a source media file to quickly preview its contents. For a longer duration file, real-time playback may be too slow and skimming may be too fast. Using the keyboard shortcuts enables you to have precise playback control. The keyboard shortcuts for playback are referred to as the J K L keys.

6   Skim to the start of **GOPR0003**, and then press **L** to start playback.

The clip plays forward at normal speed.

7   Press **K** to pause, and then press **J** to play the file in reverse.

8   Press **J** again.

The playhead moves in reverse at two times the normal speed. You can press **J** up to six times, increasing the search rate with each keypress. You can increase forward playback speed by pressing **L**.

9   Press **L** a couple of times. The file plays forward, moving faster with each keypress. Press **K** to pause.

You will later learn additional navigation controls. Now that you can navigate the thumbnail previews, however, you'll learn more about the filmstrip view options.

2.3.1-A Expanding the Filmstrip View

Although filmstrip view defaults to displaying thumbnails, you may open up those thumbnails into an expanded filmstrip preview that allows you finer control over the skimmer when reviewing longer files.

1 In the Media Import window, click the Clip Appearance button.

The stopwatch icon and the associated slider control allow you to change the display time scale. The time notation to the right indicates the length of playback time each filmstrip frame represents. The leftmost value, All, represents each source media file as one frame. That is, all frames of the source file are represented by a single frame per file.

2 Drag the slider until the time is set to 1s.

Each frame in the filmstrip now represents one second of source media.

NOTE ▸   When the frames representing a file extend beyond a line of frames, the edges of the line appear torn. The file's filmstrip continues on the next line.

3   Drag the slider to the left until All appears, returning the Browser to displaying one frame per file.

Exercise 2.3.2
Importing Files from a Camera Card

In the following exercises, you'll explore some import methods in Final Cut Pro. You'll import media files from a GoPro camera used to shoot extra helicopter B-roll, and then import a batch of files, including an interview with the pilot and the bulk of the B-roll files.

1   With the GOPRO1 SD card still selected in the sidebar, in the Browser, click in an empty gray area outside any file thumbnails. With no files selected, an Import All button is visible.

If you wanted to import all the source media files into an event as clips, you would click the Import All button. Alternatively, you could import only specific media files, ignoring any not-so-great shots.

2   Select the **GOPR0003** thumbnail.

The thumbnail is highlighted by a yellow border to indicate that the file is selected. You could import this file immediately by clicking the Import Selected button. But first, you have more files to select.

3   Click the **GOPR0006** thumbnail.

GOPR0006 is selected, and **GOPR0003** is deselected. As in macOS, you can hold down the Shift or Command modifier keys when clicking to select multiple items.

4   While holding down the Command key, click **GOPR0003** again to select both files.

Command-clicking allows you to select individual non-contiguous files, whereas Shift-clicking **GOPR0003** would also include **GOPR0005** in your selection. For the Lifted project you'll be editing, you want to import all six GoPro files.

5   In the Browser section of the Media Import window, click in the empty gray area to deselect all files.

You have indicated to Final Cut Pro that you want to import all the files on the GOPRO1 SD card. Now, you'll turn your attention to the last pane of the window, Import Options.

▶ **Importing Ranges Within a Camera File**

At times, you may want to import only sections of a media file. These sections are known as **range selections**, or ranges. They allow you to import only the desired portions of a source media file. You have multiple ways to set a single range within a filmstrip preview:

▶   Cue the skimmer or playhead to the desired frame, and then press **I** to mark a start point. Then cue after the final desired frame and press **O** to mark an end point.

▶   Position the mouse pointer over the desired start point, and then drag to the desired end point. The duration information displays as you drag.

A source media file may contain useable media in multiple sections. Additional range selection methods allow you to mark and import more than one range within a file:

▶   Cue the skimmer or playhead to the start of the next desired range within the file, and then press **Command-Shift-I** to mark the additional start point. Then, cue after the final desired frame and press **Command-Shift-O** to mark the end point of the additional range.

▶   Position the mouse pointer over the desired start point, and then Command-drag to the desired end point. The duration information displays as you drag.

NOTE ▶   Depending on the camera/video file format, range selection within a file may not be available.

Importing Ranges Within a Camera File *continued*

When marking ranges, you may need to view the source timecode from the media file. The Skimmer Info window, which appears above the skimmer, displays the file name and the source timecode. You may toggle the Skimmer Info window's show/hide status in the View > Browser menu, or by pressing **Control-Y**.

If you mark a range or ranges within a file and then decide to import only one range or the entire file, you may clear one range or all ranges:

▶   To clear a selected range, press **Option-X**.

▶   To clear all ranges, select a range of the file and press **X**.

Reference 2.4
Choosing Media Import Options

The Media Import Options pane guides you through three important areas of Final Cut Pro clip and media management:

▶   The virtual storage location of clips within the interface

▶   The physical storage location of those clips' source media files on accessible volumes

▶   The available transcoding and analysis automations

2.4-A Choosing Virtual Storage

The top section of Import Options defines the clip organization within Final Cut Pro. Because a source media file must be accessible as an event clip to be available for editing, the options here enable you to add clips to an existing event or create a new event for the clips. Let's first look at the "Add to existing event" option.

When you select "Add to existing event," the pop-up menu lists the events available in the open libraries. You may place a clip in any event inside any library.

When you select "Create new event in," a name field enables, as does a pop-up menu for choosing a library in which to store the event. The naming convention you use for events is completely up to you. The event's name may be as simple as the client's name, the current editing project, or a barcode number assigned to the raw media.

This section of the pane defines which event in the library will contain the imported clips. This is a virtual storage assignment that allows you to start organizing your clips for editing within Final Cut Pro. Let's turn our attention to where the source media files for those clips will be physically stored.

2.4-B Choosing Physical Storage

To simplify this discussion, just remember two fundamental facts about Final Cut Pro libraries:

▶ Libraries can be physical containers storing source media files.

▶ Libraries also can be virtual containers referencing source media files stored outside the library.

Clips in Final Cut Pro may represent source media files physically stored inside the library, or may represent links that point to source media files stored in physical locations separate from the library. The location of media files is determined when you choose to use either **managed media** or **external media**.

Managed media is the simplest solution for a single user, a mobile editor, or when archiving. You instruct Final Cut Pro to physically copy imported media files inside a selected library. And because you created the library earlier, you've already defined where on a volume the library and its media are stored and managed by Final Cut Pro.

Although managed media is simple to use, using external media might be the best practice for managing media within your workflow. When you're using externally referenced media, source files are stored outside the Final Cut Pro libraries. External media management is recommended for workflows where the source media files are shared among multiple users or applications because multiple editors can access the source media files without interrupting other workflows. Using external media also keeps libraries small, which translates to faster and easier sharing when passing a library to another user with the same media storage access.

When importing source media files from a volume rather than a camera card, the second media storage option, "Leave files in place," is available. Also known as "Edit in place," this option does exactly what it suggests. No source media files are copied or moved during import, which leaves the files as external media outside the library.

> **NOTE ►** You'll learn more about internally managed and externally referenced media in Lesson 9, "Managing Libraries."

2.4-C Generating Keywords and Assigning Audio Roles

Depending on your pre-edit organizational methods, you may spend a significant amount of time organizing your media files in the Finder. The Media Import options include two ways to tighten up your organizational efforts. Additionally, using production audio that supplies iXML is another organizational time-saver.

▶ From Finder tags: Create and assign clips to Keyword Collections respective to the macOS tags assigned to those clips.

▶ From folders: Replicate an existing folder structure at the Finder level within the event using keywords.

▶ Assign iXML: Assign roles to audio tracks based on track metadata.

2.4-D Using Transcode and Analysis Options

More Media Import options are available in the Transcoding area. Selecting one or both of the transcode options creates an additional source media file for the clip.

▶ Create optimized media: Generate an Apple ProRes 422 version of the source file— a benefit for compositing, multiple effects, and reducing processing loads.

▶ Create proxy media: Generate an Apple ProRes 422 (Proxy) version of the source file with embedded audio—a compressed yet easy-to-process codec that allows you to store more source files on a volume.

Selecting analysis options can further automate clip sorting within the event, analyze clips to identify a specific technical aspect of a clip, and perform a nondestructive repair of a detected audio error.

NOTE ▶ You may apply transcoding and analysis options to one or more clips during the edit phase of your workflow.

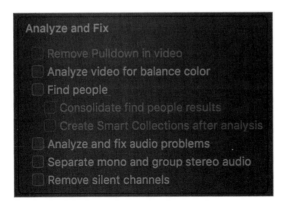

▶ Remove Pulldown in video: Applies to source media files recorded in a special frame-cadence format.

▶ Analyze video for balance color: Create a one-click neutralizing correction averaged across the clip's duration.

▶ Find people: Analyze the clip for shot composition and facial detection.

▶ Consolidate find people results: Average the "Find people" results based on two-minute sections of a clip.

▶ Create Smart Collections after analysis: Aggregate the results of the "Find people" analysis into a dynamic collection.

▶ Analyze and fix audio problems: Nondestructively repair serious audio issues such as ground-loop hum or background rumble.

▶ Separate mono and group stereo audio: Define how source audio channels are combined or separated.

Clip-sorting options, such as those in the Keywords category, rely on existing or newly created metadata. You will learn more about metadata in Lesson 3, "Organizing Clips."

Exercise 2.4.1
Applying Media Import Options

Now that you're familiar with the Media Import options, you'll continue to import the camera clips. You created the library and an event for this editing project in Exercise 2.1.1. Now, you'll add source media files as clips.

1   If necessary, from the "Add to existing event" pop-up menu, choose the GoPro event in the Lifted library.

You've instructed the import process to create clips in the GoPro event to represent those source media files. Now you will see where Final Cut Pro will store the source media.

2   For Files, notice that "Copy to library" is chosen.

These source media files will become managed media files within the Lifted library, and the source media files will be copied from the SD card to the GoPro event stored in the Lifted library. Because they will be managed media files, your only concern is whether you placed the library on a volume with enough free space to store all the managed media.

3   Deselect any other transcode, keyword, or analysis options. Click Import All.

NOTE ▶ Your Media Import Options pane should match the settings chosen in the Reference 2.2 section for this import exercise.

The media files for this part of the course do not need to be analyzed by any of these automation tools. As with the transcode options previously discussed, you may analyze any clip at any time. Doing the analysis during import is optional.

As you start the import, notice that:

▶   The Media Import window closes automatically when the import process is underway.

▶   The clips appear in the Browser with a small stopwatch that disappears after a clip is imported.

▶   You can start skimming and editing the newly imported clips.

When the import process completes, a notification appears on your display.

4   Click the Eject button to dismiss the notification and eject the simulated SD card used in the exercise.

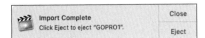

Reference 2.5
Import Files from a Volume

If you are collaborating with someone else on a project, at some point you will need to import files handed to you on a volume or emailed/FTP'd to you (rather than accessing an original camera card containing media). Or you may receive a breaking news clip shared through the cloud. Like any other file for import, the received file must be in a format that Final Cut Pro can read and play.

NOTE ▶ See Appendix B of this book and the Supported Formats section of the Apple Final Cut Pro Support webpage for complete and current information on supported file formats.

The import from a volume process starts much like importing content from the SD card:

▶ Mount the volume.

▶ In Final Cut Pro, click the Media Import button.

▶ Select your source device in Media Import's left sidebar.

▶ Navigate to the desired file(s) in the Browser.

▶ Select the files for import.

▶ In the Media Import Options pane, the process is the same with an additional media storage option available.

A difference between volume and camera import will be visible in the Browser pane: Importing from a volume displays files in list view by default.

2.5-A Leaving Files in Place

When you imported content from the SD card, the "Copy files" option was your only choice. Final Cut Pro required that you copy the media files from the SD card into an attached volume. This requirement is a good thing. If the files were not copied, the result-ing clips would go **offline** when you ejected the camera card. The offline state would have occurred because the clip within Final Cut Pro would still be referencing the source media files on the now-removed SD card.

How an offline media file appears in Final Cut Pro

When you import source media files from a volume, Final Cut Pro gives you the option to copy or not to copy those source files. You would copy the source media files if they were stored, for example, on a borrowed volume you had to return before you were finished editing. Copying is also a preferred choice when you import media from a shared storage volume to a portable volume to make your project portable.

The second option, "Leave files in place," does not copy the source files, but simply references them at their current locations. This external media option is very useful in a shared storage environment of multiple users. It allows an editor to use the same source media files as other editors within the same workgroup without creating redundant copies on the server.

Beyond the slight difference in media management options, importing from a volume is as easy as importing from a camera.

> ▶ **Using Symlinks**
>
> When you're using external media, the source media files are not copied into the library. Instead, **symlinks** (simulated files) are created inside the library that refer to the externally stored source media files. That external location may be anywhere on any accessible volume. Using external media files is a best practice for an editor in a multiuser environment.

Exercise 2.5.1
Importing Existing Files from a Volume

In this exercise, you will import files processed and organized outside of Final Cut Pro: the source **B-roll** and **sound bite** files you will need for the vignette. They were copied from their source camera memory card and manually organized. This scenario reflects a very common import scenario in many genres and workflows—the importing of file/archive footage or of shared media.

1 Click the Media Import button, or press **Command-I**.

The Media Import window opens. You will be importing from the downloaded files.

2 Starting in the sidebar, navigate to the location of the FCP X Media folder created in Lesson 1.

This location is either an external volume, your Documents folder, or your desktop. The necessary media is in the FCP X Media folder. Selecting your home folder in the sidebar is one possible starting point.

3   Double-click the FCP X Media folder to open it and locate the LV1/LV Import folder. Then, open the LV Import folder to display its contents and the contents of its subfolders.

The media files have been sorted by folder. You can take advantage of this organizational structure in Final Cut Pro.

4   Select the LV Import folder.

Now you need to set some import options.

5   At the top of the Import Options pane, select "Create new event in," and from the pop-up menu, choose the Lifted library. Type *Primary Media* as the event name.

Remember, you can set up the event and library to organize your media however you wish. Unlike the previous import, this time during import you will reference external media that is left in place. Because you have constant access to the volume where the media files reside, you do not need to copy the source media.

6   In the Files category, select "Leave files in place."

Another difference from the previous import method is that you will import a folder of media files. Final Cut Pro can import the metadata of the Finder folder structure using keywords. Keywords are metadata tokens applied to a clip. Keywords later may be used to quickly sort and find distinct or related (or unrelated) clips. This feature is very handy when your library contains a few hundred or a few thousand clips.

NOTE ▶ Creating keywords from macOS tags is covered in Lesson 5.

7   From the Keywords category, select "From folders" and deselect "From Finder tags."

NOTE ▶ The command applies keywords only when a folder is selected for import. Importing selected files within the folder will not apply keywords.

8   Deselect all other transcode and analysis options, and then click Import Selected.

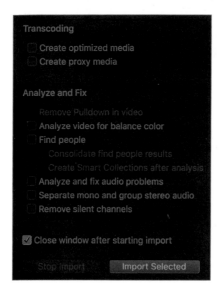

The Media Import window closes, and the new event appears in your Lifted library.

NOTE ▶ If necessary, dismiss a notification that the clips were successfully imported.

9   Click the disclosure triangle next to the Primary Media event to display its contents.

The folder you selected, and its enclosed folders, were converted into keywords. Choosing the "From folders" import option copies the Finder folder structure into the event.

NOTE ▶   You will learn more about using keywords, along with other metadata techniques, in Lesson 3.

▶ **Dragging from the Finder or Other Apps**

Final Cut Pro events accept files that you drag directly from the Finder or other applications. But you do need to know how media import options are handled in these cases. When you're dragging files directly into Final Cut Pro, the import preferences control such issues as managed and external media status, transcoding, and analysis options.

The import preferences are found in the Final Cut Pro > Preferences menu.

Dragging from the Finder or Other Apps *continued*

This list of import preferences should look familiar. Because dragging an item to an event in a library is understood as an import operation, these import options manage the details. Notice that the top section of the Media Import Options pane is missing. The library and event are defined by which item you drag to in the Libraries sidebar.

The pointer identifies which of the media storage options is active and allows you to override those options.

▶   When an item is dragged to an event, a Keyword Collection in an event, or the Browser, and the "Copy to library storage location" option is selected, the pointer displays a plus sign inside a circle.

▶   When an item is dragged to an event, Keyword Collection, or the Browser, and the "Leave in place" option is selected, the pointer displays a hooked arrow.

▶   If the pointer indicates a copy, you can override it and perform a "Leave in place" import by holding down Command-Option before releasing the mouse button.

▶   If the pointer indicates a "Leave in place" import, you may override it and perform a copy import by holding down Option before releasing the mouse button.

You've now imported the source media files into Final Cut Pro. You should feel good knowing that you can create a library and some events for getting media into Final Cut Pro. Although you could start editing right away with these imported files, the resulting clips could be numerous and unorganized. In Lesson 3, you will organize these imported clips for faster recall of particular clips.

Lesson Review

1. Which of these three is the largest container: clip, event, or library?

2. Describe possible organizational criteria for sorting clips and projects into events.

3. Name and describe the built-in command for backing up camera media files.

4. Where should you store camera archives?

5. What two views are available in the Media Import window, and when are the two views available?

6. What setting on the Zoom slider in filmstrip view allows you to see each file as a single thumbnail?

7. What keyboard shortcuts or modified-skimming keys let you mark multiple range selections within a clip?

8. In the Media Import Options pane, which of these two sections sets media files as managed or external?

A   B

9. Fill in the blank: With the "Create optimized media" option selected, Final Cut Pro X transcodes imported media to the _____ codec.

10. When dragging files from the Finder to an event, where do you set the option to copy (or not copy) the files into the library?

11. You are about to import source media files grouped into various folders. Which Media Import option must be selected to replicate the folder structure within an event?

Answers

1. The library is the largest of the media containers.

2. The criteria are whatever you choose: a scene of a film, a segment of a news-magazine show, a webisode, stock footage, raw media from an SD card, all versions of the projects, and so on. An event is a flexible storage container that can be as all-encompassing or as granularly compartmentalized as your raw media and projects.

3. The Create Archive command creates a clone of your source media device, preserving the folder structure and metadata along with the source media files.

4. You may store camera archives anywhere; however, to reduce the chance of a single-point failure taking down an entire editing job, store your camera archives on a volume physically separate from the media storage volume you use for editing.

5. Filmstrip and list view. The two views are available when importing from a recognized camera card file structure; otherwise, only the list view is available in the Browser of the Media Import window.

6. All. The setting defines the time length represented by each thumbnail of the clip.

7. The keyboard shortcuts are Command-Shift-I and Command-Shift-O. Holding down Command while skimming a clip also marks additional ranges.

8. B. "Copy to library" creates managed media; "Leave files in place" creates externally referenced media.

9. Apple ProRes 422

10. Final Cut Pro > Preferences and select the Import pane.

11. From folders

Lesson 3
Organizing Clips

With the 64-bit architecture of Final Cut Pro X and macOS, you could start editing before the import process is complete. Whether you chose managed media or external media, Final Cut Pro will start you off by referencing the source files at their current storage locations. If you chose to copy, Final Cut Pro will auto-switch to the copied version when it is imported. You've already noticed that Final Cut Pro has organized some clips in your Libraries sidebar. However, most editors need to perform a little more pre-edit organization. With a thousand or so clips, the long-form editor must be organized for maximum efficiency. When you divert time to digging for a clip, it breaks your editing rhythm and halts your storytelling momentum.

The metadata underpinning of Final Cut Pro is the key to efficient, creative editing. This lesson explores the possibilities of organizing your clips within the application. These additional pre-edit steps will make the application work for you and help in getting your story told.

Reference 3.1
Introducing the Libraries Sidebar, the Browser, and the Viewer

In Lesson 2, you imported media into events located inside a library. You discovered that the source media files, as represented by clips within an event, could be stored internally (managed) or externally (referenced) in relation to their library. Whether your media is managed or referenced, your focus should now shift to using the clips within the Final Cut

GOALS

► Apply keywords to a clip and clip ranges

► Search and filter clips by keywords

► Add notes and ratings to a clip

► Create Smart Collections

► Detect people and composition within clips

► Understand and assign roles

Pro interface, and not so much at the Finder level outside the application. Final Cut Pro includes tools that enable you to manage clips and their storage locations entirely within the app, which frees you to concentrate on the actual editing. An efficient editing work-flow depends on accessing the right clip at the right creative moment. To find those clip gems, you'll utilize three areas in the upper half of the interface: the Libraries sidebar, the Browser, and the Viewer.

In the Libraries sidebar you'll find open libraries and their associated events. After importing clips and applying a couple of enabled analysis tools, Final Cut Pro creates metadata about each clip along with collections of clips that share the same metadata. You may utilize this metadata to parse and group clips in your own way to fit your personal editing workflow.

These collection containers display their contents in the Browser, which is where you skim, select, and mark ranges of clip content. The Browser includes a powerful set of fea-tures to sort and organize clips within collections. The Browser also may be used to create complex collections you can store for later use.

In the Viewer, your story will come to life. All the metadata wrangling you will do is based on what you can see (and hear) in the Viewer. The Viewer displays a clip's contents when you skim the clip in the Browser. When you press the J K L keys, the result is shown in the Viewer. Final Cut Pro allows you to change the layout so that the Viewer moves to a second display with a larger viewing area. And by incorporating features of macOS and Apple TV to your workflow, you may wirelessly push the Viewer's display to an even larger display.

You will utilize all three of these areas to enhance your clips with metadata. Remember, although these organizational steps aren't required for editing in Final Cut Pro, being able to find, track, and share your finished project based on metadata is leaps and bounds faster than the traditional approach of cramming as much clip info as possible into the filename or into a few columns of additional information.

Reference 3.2
Using Keywords

Keywords are applied to clips to decrease your clip search times and to speed up the storytelling process. Your choice of keywords can be fairly generic to help you locate a wide range of content. In fact, a keyword so granular that it describes only one clip may be a wasted keyword. In that case, a simple clip name change may be preferable to applying a keyword.

You may apply a keyword to an entire clip or to only a range within a clip. You create a range by marking a selection within a clip using the pointer or keyboard shortcuts. If a clip's contents started with a helicopter takeoff and ended with a helicopter landing, you might apply three keywords to the single clip:

▶ Helicopter: Applied to the entire clip

▶ Takeoff: Applied to the start of the clip

▶ Landing: Applied to the end of the clip

You may apply as many keywords as you wish to a clip. When applying a keyword, the keyword ranges may overlap. This gives you incredible sort and sift capabilities without media management nightmares. A keyword is not a traditional subclip, is not a nested clip, and best of all, does not involve duplicating a clip as in other applications. Final Cut Pro links those keywords to one source media file. And no matter how granular you do get with a keyword in segmenting the content of a clip, you always have access to the entire source media file during the edit.

When a keyword is manually applied, a blue stripe appears along the top of the clip's filmstrip.

The keyword also appears in the list view when the clip's details are displayed by clicking the clip's disclosure triangle.

You may quickly create a selection based on the keyword by selecting the keyword shown under the clip in list view, or by clicking the blue stripe at the top of the clip's filmstrip.

An *analysis keyword* is a keyword added to a clip based on the analysis options chosen during import. In the Import Options pane and the Import preferences pane, you can enable these analysis tools during import; however, you may specifically request an analysis later in your edit workflow.

Whether manually or automatically generated, the keywords organize your clips into Keyword Collections stored in the Libraries sidebar. Keyword Collections are virtual folders that display clips or ranges of clips that have the same keyword. In the next few exercises, you will see that keywording is a huge step toward harnessing the power of metadata to make an efficient edit.

Exercise 3.2.1
Keywording a Clip

In Lesson 2, you imported a folder of source media files from a volume. During that import, you assigned keywords to the clips based on their presence in that folder and subfolders. As a result, your Lifted library lit up with additional items when Final Cut Pro assigned keywords to those clips. Let's review some of those keywords and learn how you can create your own.

1   In the Libraries sidebar, select the Lifted library's Primary Media event.

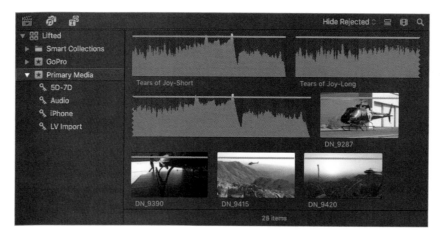

Selecting the event instructs Final Cut Pro to display the clips associated with that event.

2   In the Browser, click the Filmstrip View button, if necessary.

3   To ensure that you are seeing the same clip order pictured in this exercise, from the Clip Appearance and Filtering pop-up menu, choose Group By > None and Sort By > Name.

Choosing Group displays an event's clips with no sub-groupings, whereas choosing Sort organizes an event's clips alphabetically.

4   Drag the Zoom slider to All.

Adjusting the Zoom slider to All displays one thumbnail per clip.

5   In the lower part of the Browser, look at the notation text, which appears in one of two formats.

If a clip is selected, the notation text shows the number of clips
selected from all the clips in the event, plus the selection's duration.

When no clips are selected, the notation text displays the total number of clips in the event.

This text describes the overall contents of the selected library item. Currently, from a total of 28 clips, you may have selected one clip. The total duration of one or more selected clips is displayed. To see as many of the 28 clips as possible, you'll make a slight change to the Browser's display options.

6   Click the Clip Appearance and Filtering button, and in the pop-up menu, deselect Waveforms, if necessary.

7   Drag the Clip Height slider to the left to reduce the thumbnail height. Resize the thumbnails to the minimum height at which clip names remain visible and the thumbnail contents are recognizable.

8   To see even more clips, drag the divider bar between the Browser and the Viewer to the right.

Another option to see more clips is to hide the Libraries sidebar.

9   In the Browser, click the "Show or hide the Libraries sidebar" button.

You now have more room, but you need to see the Libraries sidebar for this exercise.

10 Click the "Show or hide the Libraries sidebar" button to display the Lifted library's contents.

▶ Workspaces

After arranging the size of the Browser and Viewer and making the sidebar visible, you may save this custom arrangement as a workspace. Custom workspaces are transportable to different desktops and portables and to individual users.

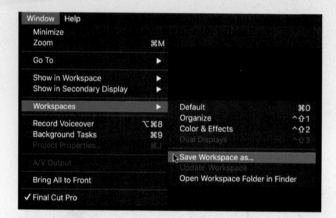

Final Cut Pro includes preset workspaces to remove interface distractions during certain tasks. For example, the Organize workspace hides the Timeline, thereby yielding more screen real estate to the Browser and Viewer. You can quickly toggle between the Browser and Timeline views without changing workspaces by clicking the "Show or hide the Browser" and "Show or hide the Timeline" buttons to the right in the toolbar.

3.2.1-A Adding a Keyword to One or More Clips

Your Primary Media event contains 28 clips, and the Keyword Collections listed within the event contain subgroupings of those event clips. Final Cut Pro created these collections based on the folders that you imported in Lesson 2. These collections are helpful, but you should create additional collections for finer subgroupings.

1   In the Libraries sidebar, select the 5D-7D Keyword Collection to view its contents.

The Browser updates to display the 23 clips associated with the 5D-7D keyword, a mixture of B-roll and interview clips. To quickly find the interview clips (which you'll be using in Lesson 4), let's create a Keyword Collection that references them.

2   Within the 5D-7D Keyword Collection, click to select the first on-camera sound bite of Mitch, the owner and pilot of H5 Productions.

3   To select the remaining sound bite clips, you can use a combination of Shift-click and Command-click to select all of Mitch's sound bites.

The Browser recognizes your selection of six clips with a total running time of just over 2 minutes and 47 seconds. You'll find this information notated at the bottom of the Browser.

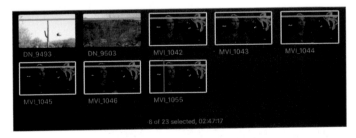

To group these clips into a separate Keyword Collection, you will assign a keyword in the Keyword Editor.

4 In the toolbar, click the Keyword Editor button.

The Keyword Editor HUD (heads-up display) opens.

The Keyword Editor already contains two keyword tokens: 5D-7D and LV Import. This demonstrates the power of metadata within Final Cut Pro: You may attach as many keywords as you want to a clip. The end result is that a single clip may appear in several Keyword Collections without the need to actually duplicate the clip on the volume. To see this feature in action, you will apply an additional keyword to these sound bites.

5 In the Keyword Editor, type *Interview* and press Return.

Not only did the the Interview token appear in the Keyword Editor, but you also gained a collection in the Primary Media event.

6 In the Libraries sidebar, select the newly created Interview Keyword Collection.

The Browser updates to display the six clips assigned to the Interview keyword. Later, when you start the edit in Lesson 4, the Interview Keyword Collection will be your go-to source for these sound bites.

7 Take a moment to explore the other Keyword Collections in the Primary Media event. Look for the following:

▶ The number of clips within each Keyword Collection

▶ The clips that appear in each Keyword Collection

3.2.1-B Removing a Keyword

Did you notice that the LV Import Keyword Collection contains all 28 clips? This Keyword Collection functions the same as selecting the event itself. Because this duplication is not necessary, let's remove the keyword LV Import from all 28 clips. Fortunately, you do not have to do this one clip at a time.

1 In the Primary Media event, Control-click the LV Import Keyword Collection.

2 From the shortcut menu, choose Delete Keyword Collection, or press **Command-Delete.**

The Keyword Collection is removed; however, the clips remain in the event and the other collections. Just as you may freely add keywords to a clip, you can also freely delete keywords.

3.2.1-C Adding Clips to a Keyword Collection

The end result of the following exercise is the same as adding the Interview keyword to sound bites, as you did earlier. However, in this exercise you'll first create the Keyword Collection, and then drag the clips into it to assign the keyword.

1   In the Libraries sidebar, Control-click the Primary Media event, and from the short-cut menu, choose New Keyword Collection.

An untitled Keyword Collection is created.

NOTE ►   If the shortcut menu lists different commands, such as Cut and Copy, Control-click the event's single-star icon instead of the text.

2   To name the collection, type *B-roll*, and press Return.

Of course, this Keyword Collection is currently empty. An easy way to add clips to this collection and assign the B-roll keyword is to drag clips into it.

3   In the event, select the 5D-7D Keyword Collection.

4   In the 5D-7D Keyword Collection, click the first B-roll clip, and then Shift-click the last B-roll clip.

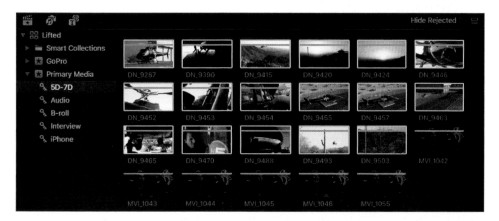

You have selected every clip in the collection that does not contain Mitch's interview.

5   Drag the selected clips to the B-roll Keyword Collection in the Libraries sidebar. When the B-roll Keyword Collection is highlighted, release the mouse button.

6   Confirm that the clips received the B-roll keyword by selecting the B-roll Keyword Collection.

The 17 clips appear in both collections without duplicating any source media files. So you can now search clips by keyword for B-roll, Interview, or the 5D-7D camera type. Later, you will learn to perform complex searches using multiple terms.

3.2.1-D Adding Keywords Using Shortcuts

In Final Cut Pro, you often have more than one way to achieve similar results. In this exercise, you will use a combination of shortcuts in the Keyword Editor to apply more keywords to clips.

1   In the Keyword Editor HUD, click the Keyword Shortcuts disclosure triangle.

Your keyword shortcuts may already be populated. That's OK. You will clear them all before proceeding. You may clear the shortcuts at any time without altering existing keywords or collections. However, modifying keywords in the uppermost field will change previous clip assignments.

2   Delete each keyword shortcut field's contents to clear all the existing shortcuts. Click the token in the shortcut field, and press Delete.

Using the previous figure as an example, you can click the interview token to the right of the Control-1 (^1) button. With the token selected, press Delete.

NOTE ▶   Do not click the Control-0 (^0) button or press the shortcut because doing so will erase the keywords assigned to the currently selected clip.

3   Starting with Control-1 (^1), enter the following keywords:

▶   Control-1 *B-roll*

▶   Control-2 *Hangar*

▶   Control-3 *Preflight*

▶   Control-4 *Takeoff*

▶   Control-5 *In Flight*

▶   Control-6 *Landing*

▶   Control-7 *Flight Controls*

Your Keyword Shortcuts section now looks like this:

Using these new shortcuts, you may quickly apply their associated keywords to one or more clips at once.

4   With the 5D-7D collection selected in the Libraries sidebar, skim and then select
DN_9390, **DN_9446**, and **DN_9452**.

These are B-roll clips, but they are also preflight clips. You can use keyboard shortcuts
to quickly apply the Preflight keyword to them.

5   Press Control-3, or in the Keyword Editor HUD, click the shortcut button (^3) to tag
these B-roll clips with the Preflight keyword.

The clips' assigned keywords now include Preflight. Because this is the first time
you've applied the Preflight keyword, a Preflight Keyword Collection appears in the
Libraries sidebar under the Primary Media event.

6   Using the following matrix, assign keywords to the clips using the specified Keyword
Collections:

NOTE ▸ To remove an undesired or inadvertently applied keyword to a clip, in the
upper field of the Keyword Editor HUD, select the keyword's token and press Delete.

Keyword Collection: 5D-7D

Clip	Hangar	Preflight	In Flight	Flight Controls
DN_9287		X		
DN_9390	X	X		
DN_9415			X	
DN_9420			X	
DN_9424			X	
DN_9446		X		
DN_9452		X		
DN_9453		X		X

Keyword Collection: 5D-7D (continued)

Clip	Hangar	Preflight	In Flight	Flight Controls
DN_9454		X		X
DN_9455		X		
DN_9457		X		
DN_9463		X		
DN_9465	X	X		
DN_9470	X	X		
DN_9488	X	X		
DN_9493			X	
DN_9503			X	

Now that you've added keywords to the 23 5D-7D clips, you still have three clips acquired on an iPhone that need keywords.

7   In the Primary Media event, select the iPhone Keyword Collection. Using the following table, assign keywords to the three iPhone clips within the collection.

Keyword Collection: iPhone

Clip	Hangar	Preflight	In Flight	Flight Controls
IMG_6476			X	X
IMG_6486			X	
IMG_6493			X	X

That takes care of most of the clips in the Primary Media event. But remember, you imported GoPro clips into the GoPro event. For these clips, you'll use two more keywords, which you can add manually in the Keyword Editor and/or create keyword shortcuts for.

8   In the Libraries sidebar, select the GoPro event. Using the following table as a guide, assign keywords to these clips within the collection.

Event: GoPro

Clip	Runup	Hover	Takeoff	In Flight	Landing
GOPR0005		X	X		
GOPR0006	X	X	X		
GOPR0009					X
GOPR1857				X	
GOPR3310			X	X	

Assigning too many keywords to a clip is very easy to do. You can assign as many key-words as you want, but at a certain point, adding more keywords isn't an efficient use of your time. Each editing job will vary in its need for general keywords and detailed levels of keywords. Final Cut Pro allows you to determine the most useful number of keywords.

Exercise 3.2.2
Keywording a Range

In Exercise 3.2.1, you applied keywords to clips. Keywording is not limited to the clip's entire duration. Keywords also may be applied to ranges within a clip. You may overlap as many keywords as required to further describe the ranges of a clip.

1   In the Libraries sidebar, select the B-roll Keyword Collection.

2   Select the **DN_9287** clip, and skim the clip to review its contents.

   NOTE ▸ You'll deal with the needed color correction in a later lesson.

   This clip could have two possible ranges: the helicopter sitting on the ramp, and the helicopter taking off. You will use keywords to identify the two ranges. Let's start with the takeoff portion.

3   Skim the **DN_9287** clip again, looking for a point just before the helicopter takes off. You'll see a slight camera movement at this point in the clip.

4   With the skimmer placed just before the takeoff, press **I**.

Pressing I sets the start of the range selection known as range start. Setting a range start automatically sets a range end at the last frame of the clip. As the takeoff portion of the clip continues to the end of the clip, you can use the range as-is. Let's save that range by assigning it the Takeoff keyword. Earlier, you created keyboard shortcuts for several keywords, including Control-4 for Takeoff.

5   Press Control-4 to assign the Takeoff keyword to the selected range.

6   In the Libraries sidebar, select the Takeoff Keyword Collection, and then skim the **DN_9287** clip.

The keyword is assigned to the marked range, which is now filed in the Takeoff Keyword Collection in the Primary Media event. Notice that the "sitting on the ramp" portion of the clip is not visible. In the Browser, you see only about 12 seconds of takeoff content from the clip, or what is called a **subclip** that matches the selected Keyword Collection.

NOTE ▶ The amount of a clip's content that is visible in the Browser is dependent on several settings that you'll learn about later. The first setting, the selected Keyword Collection, may display all of a clip, a range or ranges within a clip, or none of a clip.

7   Select the B-roll Keyword Collection to see the entire duration of the **DN_9287** clip.

Now, you will mark a range and keyword that range to flag the start of this clip as "on the ramp" content. Start by removing the current range selection on the clip.

8   With the takeoff range selected in **DN_9287**, press **X** to mark the whole clip.

Marking the clip sets, or in this case resets, the start and end points at the full-length of the clip available. Because the start point is now set at the beginning of the clip, you need to set the end point.

9   In clip **DN_9287**, skim to just before the helicopter takes off, and press **O** to set the range end point.

The range selection is about 18 seconds long, as indicated at the bottom of the Browser. You'll keyword this as the ramp range.

10   In the Keyword Editor, type *Ramp*, and press Return.

Did you notice that the keywords 5D-7D, B-roll, and Preflight were assigned to this entire clip in the previous exercises, yet they are not visible in the Keyword Editor HUD? When you are working with a clip range, the keywords applied to other ranges or the entire duration of the clip do not appear in the Keyword Editor. But you do have a way to display all of a clip's keywords all the time.

3.2.2-A Viewing Keywords in List View

In list view, all the keywords applied to a clip are visible when you are viewing the event or a collection that is not limiting the clip to a range.

1   In the Libraries sidebar, select the Primary Media event so you are able to review all the event's clips and their assigned keywords.

2   In the Browser, toggle the Browser to list mode. If necessary, click the disclosure triangle for clip **DN_9287**.

Notice that some of the keywords are on the same line, which indicates that those keywords occupy the same content of the clip. You may verify that by referencing the start and end points to the right.

Carefully review the values for the start and end points for the applied keywords. Although you may see multiple applied keywords at once in the list, you are not necessarily viewing all the clip's source media.

3   Select the Ramp Keyword Collection. Select the "5D-7D, B-roll, Preflight" keyword line listed under the clip, and then skim the filmstrip to verify that you do not see the takeoff.

4   Check the start and end points for the same line of keywords compared to the **DN_9287** line's start and end points.

The ranges are different. Right now, you are restricted to seeing the range as defined by the Ramp Keyword Collection, which is why the clip's start and end points and the Ramp keyword's points are the same.

5   In the Libraries sidebar, select the B-roll Keyword Collection, and in the Browser, skim the **DN_9287** clip again.

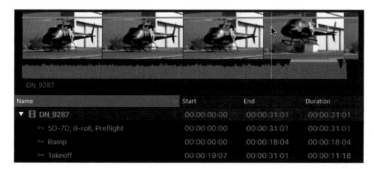

You are now skimming the full duration of the source material represented by the clip. Glance at the clip's start and end points, and note that they now mirror the B-roll keyword's start and end points.

Although this exercise may feel like Final Cut Pro minutiae, it demonstrates an important concept to understand before performing the next exercise: When you start editing, you have no subclip limits; but when looking at a clip in the Browser, the applied keywords, metadata, and the active Keyword Collection do restrict you to only the subclipped content.

You need to apply the two keywords, Ramp and Takeoff, to another clip. The same actions appear in clip **DN_9463**: The helicopter is on the ramp and then takes off.

6   Create two ranges within **DN_9463**, applying the same two keywords, Ramp and Take-off, to the appropriate ranges.

▶ **Tight or Loose?**

When creating what is commonly referred to as subclips in Final Cut Pro, you do not need to worry about setting precise start or end points. When you use the sub-clip in the edit, you will have access to all the source material represented by the original clip. There are no "subclip limits" within the duration of the project clip.

Exercise 3.2.3
Adding Notes to a Clip

Keywords are great, but as mentioned earlier, they should be used in a purposefully generic way to create Keyword Collections that reference more than one clip. The unique details describing a clip's contents may be added to a clip's metadata using the Notes field. The Notes field is accessible in the list view of the Browser, and in the Info inspector.

1   In the Libraries sidebar, select the B-roll Keyword Collection, if necessary.

You are looking at the clips you tagged with the B-roll keyword in Lesson 2.

It would be useful if some of the B-roll clips had descriptive text associated with them. Such a text is searchable, allowing you to filter your event down from hundreds, if not thousands, of clips to the single clip you need for your edit.

2 Switch the Browser to list view, if necessary, and then locate **DN_9390**.

3 Skim the clip to review its content.

This clip starts in black with the hangar door closed. The door starts opening as Mitch, the pilot, walks over to the helicopter to preflight the camera. That's a lot of descriptive information to add to the clip, but Final Cut Pro will allow you to do so. Let's append a shorter description to the clip's Notes field.

4 In the list view, scroll right in the list to locate the Notes column.

Because you will be using this column repeatedly, you may want to reposition the column closer to the Name column.

5 Drag the Notes column header to a location closer to the Name column.

Now you can visually pair the clip and its ranges to their respective notes. Not only can you apply notes to an entire clip in Final Cut Pro, you can also apply notes to a clip's keyword ranges.

6 At the intersection of the Notes column and the **DN_9390** row, click to display a text pointer.

7 In the text field, type *Hangar door opens; Mitch enters L crossing R to preflight camera,* and then press Return.

If you can't view all the entered text, you could drag the right edge of the Notes column to the right to expand the width of the column. Or you could open the Info inspector to review, and modify as necessary, the details about the selected Browser clip.

3.2.3-A Viewing the Info Inspector

As with many Apple applications, Inspector or Info panes display clip details. And these details include more than you probably want or need to know about the clip while editing. In the present case, the Info inspector provides an alternative text field in which to review the note you applied.

1   In the Browser, verify that **DN_9390** is selected.

2   Click the Inspector button (an icon of slider controls), if necessary, to open the Inspector.

The Inspector presents information in subpanels, accessed via buttons at the top of the Inspector.

3   Click the Info button to open the Info inspector.

Here you can see basic and detailed information about the selected clip, including its name and some format details. Below the Name field is the Notes field in which you can review the notes you previously entered. You can also use this field to modify or enter new information about the clip.

4   Change the Notes field to read, *Hangar door opens; Mitch L-R; camera preflight*. Press the Tab key to update the note metadata while advancing to the next text field.

5   Now that you've learned two ways to enter notes metadata, you can use either method
to enter clip metadata as follows:

▶   **DN_9420**: *Sunset through helicopter windows*

▶   **DN_9424**: *Flying into the sunset*

▶   **DN_9446**: *Getting in; tilt-up to engine start*

▶   **DN_9452**: *CU engine start*

▶   **DN_9453**: *Pan/tilt Mitch and instrument panel*

▶   **DN_9454**: *Flipping switches; pushing buttons*

▶   **DN_9455**: *High angle (HA) Mitch getting in helicopter*

▶   **DN_9457**: *HA helicopter starting; great start up SFX*

As you can see, your notes can be as generic or as detailed as you want or need
them to be.

▶   **Assigning Notes to Clip Ranges**

You just finished applying notes to the entire clip. But don't forget that you also can
apply notes to clip ranges. One potential use for notes is to enter interview notes or
even text transcriptions of the interview within that clip.

Reference 3.3
Assigning Ratings

Just when you thought that keywords and notes were all you needed, Final Cut Pro
includes more metadata tools to further organize your clips. One of those tools is the ratings system.

The green stripes indicate favorite ranges.

Ratings—which include three statuses: Favorites, Unrated, and Rejected—may be used in conjunction with other metadata tools or as a stand-alone system. The concept is simple. Every clip in an event starts out as Unrated. As you review a clip in the Browser, you may rate the clip as a Favorite, Rejected, or Unrated. Also, as you did when adding keywords, you may rate a range within a clip. Some editors use the ratings rather than keywords. And other editors blend the two features to enable complex searches that locate the exact clip needed for the edit.

Documentary editors are often handed hours or days of interviews to sift, sort, and craft into the spine of a sound bite–driven story. One approach to sifting interviews involves marking usable sound bites. This process of marking sound bites with potential story-telling power is known as pulling selects. Traditionally, pulling selects involved finding an appropriate sound bite, and then immediately editing the select into a project or timeline. Although Final Cut Pro allows this style of editing, let's explore other potential steps between finding the sound bite and making a project edit. Skimming, pitch correction, and ratings in Final Cut Pro can make this time-consuming process both fast and efficient.

Exercise 3.3.1
Applying Ratings

In Exercise 2.5, you imported the interview clips. As with any imported media, they included usable and non-usable content. In this exercise, you will use the ratings system to pare down those interview clips, creating a searchable group of sound bites.

1   In the Lifted library, under the Primary Media event, select the Interview Keyword Collection.

The Browser displays the interview clips. Note that these interview clips were edited from a longer, continuous clip to limit their file sizes for the purposes of this book. Although the clips have been slightly pre-trimmed, they still include extraneous material for you to remove.

▶ **Breaking Down the Interview in the Field**

File-based camera technology allows you to instantly start and stop recording. Although the term "speed" is still used by cinematographers and videographers to indicate a camera appropriately recording a scene, digital cameras are recording scenes from the moment that recording begins. And in some cases, when using pre-record settings, they start a few seconds before recording begins. Considering this instantaneous response, your editing workflow may benefit from the camera operator placing a quick stop/start cycle between interview answers. A quick double-punch of the camera's Record button automatically forces each interview question and answer into its own clip, Using this simple pre-edit process at acquisition may be a quick way to jump-start your edit.

NOTE ▶ As with any change to your workflow, test this method from start to end before committing to using it on a project.

2 If necessary, set the Browser to list view.

You need to access the clip's metadata during this process.

3 If necessary, click the Name column header until the clip list is alphabetized in ascending order.

4 In the Browser, select **MVI_1042**.

The clip's filmstrip appears, ready for you to skim, mark, and rate the clip.

5   The playhead is already cued to the start of clip, so press the **Spacebar** or the **L** key to play the clip from the beginning.

The clip opens with Mitch at the start of a great statement, "Flying is something I've had a passion for since I was a little kid."

6   Cue the playhead to just before Mitch says, "Flying is."

You could skim back to this point, click with the pointer, or press the J K L keys to locate the playhead at that point; but once you are in the neighborhood, you'll need to use the frame-by-frame navigation controls to precisely locate the start point.

7   To search frame by frame, press the **Left** and **Right Arrow** keys.

Tapping the Left Arrow key steps the playhead backward one frame at a time. Pressing the Right Arrow key moves the playhead forward one frame at a time. You may also hold down either of those keys to play the clip backward or forward at one-third speed.

You are about to set the start point of the select. This point does not have to be frame accurate at the moment, but a little care now can go a long way later in the edit. Look for a frame where Mitch's eyes are open and his mouth is closed.

8   When the playhead is cued to the desired start point, press **I**. That start point should be at timecode 01:31:15:20.

▶ **Editing in Timecode Language**

Timecode is a media address or coordinate system that allows a director/producer to communicate the location of specific material desired for an edit. In the previous step, the timecode 01:31:15:20 gives you an exact range start location for **MVI_1042**. You'll find that as you skim or play a clip, the timecode display indicates the skimmer's or playhead's location within the clip.

▶ 01:31:15:20

The timecode display shows the desired frame's address as 1 hour, 31 minutes, 15 seconds, and 20 frames. This number is recorded by the camera and locked to that specific frame. The timecode for start and end points are included in the text for reference. Skim within the Browser clip until the timecode for the range start appears in the display, and press **I** to set a start point. Skim the Browser clip again to locate the range end timecode, and press **O** to set an end point. In many contemporary projects, you may find yourself acting as director, producer, and editor. The exact moment to start and end a clip will be entirely up to you.

Now you'll find an end point. Mitch finishes the sentence with "a little kid," but launches immediately into his next thought. Although marking the select does not require frame-accurate precision, take a few moments to examine the clip before executing the next step.

9   Start playback by pressing the **Spacebar**. Stop the playhead by pressing the **Spacebar** again after Mitch says "kid" and before he starts his next sentence.

One frame of pause occurs here. You want to cue the playhead at least one frame before that "silent" frame to avoid any extraneous audio samples at the end of the silent video frame. You'll trim away the frames after the playhead.

10   When the playhead is cued, press **O** to mark the end point of the range. Your end
point should be marked at 01:31:18:19.

You may want to take a moment to review the range you marked. Pressing L or the
Spacebar would play back the clip material inside and outside the selection. A different keyboard shortcut allows you to play only the marked range.

11   Press the **/** (slash) key to play back the selected range.

If you need to adjust the range, you may skim to the desired frame, then press the
appropriate key, **I** or **O**, to set the updated point. Alternatively, you may drag an edge
of the range to the new frame.

With the new range marked, you are ready to pull this select. The Favorite status of
the rating system is great for doing so, and it requires only a simple key press.

12   Press **F** to set the marked range as a favorite.

A green stripe appears along the top of the clip's filmstrip within the range to identify
it as a favorite. You will also find new metadata added in the list view.

13   In the list view, click the disclosure triangle next to **MVI_1042** to display the clip's tags.

A new tag, Favorite, appears in the list below the keywords that were applied automatically by Final Cut Pro. You'll use the Notes field to add some topical words for
later searching.

14 Click the text field at the intersection of the Favorite row and the Notes column, and then type *passion when kid*. Press Return.

You've identified that range, so now you'll move on to the next clip, **MVI_1043**.

NOTE ▶ Between Notes and Start, drag the column header divider to the right to open more space for the Notes column.

15 With **MVI_1043** selected in the list, locate the start of the phrase "One thing that is interesting."

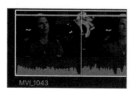

Mitch mutters an extended "uhhh" here. Leave that in for now. You may use the J K L keys and/or the Left and Right Arrow keys in addition to the Skimmer to find the desired start point.

16 With the playhead cued before Mitch says, "Uhhh. One thing," press **I** to mark the start point for the range at 01:34:23:18.

17 To set the end point, cue to after Mitch says, "Frame of what we're shooting. So..."

This is another tricky point to set because Mitch quickly continues with the next sentence, but keep the "So" in the clip for now.

18 Press **O** to mark the end point at 01:34:41:21, and then press **/** (slash) to review your selection. Press **F** to rate this sound bite as a favorite.

19 In the Notes column for this favorite, type *imagery technical pilot framing.*

This clip has another possible sound bite at its end. Let's also mark that as a favorite.

20 Find and mark a start point before Mitch says, "As I'm technically" at 01:34:49:17.

21 Find and mark an end point after Mitch says, "experiencing. So..." at 01:34:57:00.

22 Press **F** to mark this range as a favorite.

Before you apply a note to this favorite and mark the rest of the sound bites, you should understand additional ratings commands, such as how to remove a rating.

► **Favorites Aren't Always Favorites**

Some editors have observed that a favorite is not necessarily going to become a used sound bite, so applying a Favorite tag is too strong a descriptor. Other editors have suggested that the Favorite rating process yields lots of favorites with no real ranking of strong versus weak sound bites. However, actual workflow analysis indicates that pulling selects using favorites generally results in the same number of clips as does a traditional approach to choosing selects. And while a traditional select method deletes clips that are no longer considered selects, a favorite clip may just as easily be removed from the Timeline, while remaining a favorite for later recall.

3.3.1-A Unrating a Favorite

How do you clear a favorite? You unrate it. Remember, every clip is imported as unrated. While this default rating will come in handy when sorting and filtering later, let's experiment with a clip to see it in action.

1   In the Libraries sidebar, select the GoPro event.

2   In the Browser, select the **GOPR1857** clip, and press **F** to favorite this clip.

The green favorite stripe appears at the top of the filmstrip.

To remove this favorite rating, you simply unrate the clip by pressing **U**. But let's explore unrating a range in a bit more detail. You currently have the entire clip rated as a favorite, but the second half of the clip has unwanted content depicting passengers holding an iPhone and iPad. Let's unrate that superfluous section.

3   Using the **I** and **O** keys, set a range that includes the iPhone and iPad users intruding on the shot. Your range should start around 37:21 and continue to the end of the clip.

4   Press **U** to unrate that range's content.

The green stripe is removed from the range.

3.3.1-B Rejecting Clips

Maybe you want to be more assertive in marking a portion of a clip's contents as unusable. The Rejected rating is what you need, and it's appropriately assigned to the **Delete** key. But don't fear, you are not about to delete clips or source media files, just hide them from view.

> **NOTE ▶** The **Delete** key may also be known as the Backspace key or the "big Delete" key. In this book, **Delete** key does not refer to the small Forward Delete key found on full-sized or extended keyboards.

1   With **GOPR1857**'s unrated range selected, press Delete.

The rejected range is hidden from view.

2   Skim to the end of **GOPR1857**, and you will find that the iPhone and iPad section is gone.

The Browser defaults to hiding rejected portions of clips. Let's reconfigure the Browser to display all ratings.

In the Browser, a filter pop-up menu is currently set to Hide Rejected.

3   In the filter pop-up menu, choose All Clips.

Now the range you rejected a moment ago reappears with a red stripe across the top of its filmstrip. Also, in the list view, notice that the **GOPR1857** clip has a listing for a rejected range.

4   In the Browser's list view, click the **GOPR1857** clip's listing.

What if you wanted to unrate that rejected portion because you changed your mind? First, you would need to select the previously marked range. The listed ratings will help you do so.

5   In the list view for **GOPR1857**, select the Rejected rating.

The filmstrip range is marked for the duration of the Rejected rating. Alternatively, clicking the red stripe in the clip's filmstrip will also select the Rejected range.

6   Press **U** to unrate this range in the clip.

The Rejected rating in the list view is removed.

As you saw in the previous steps, rejecting a clip or a range of a clip does not delete the clip because you were able to unrate the rejected range. Pressing the **Delete** key simply assigns a rejected rating. With the Browser set to filter out rejected clips/ranges, your Browser is visually freed of distractions, allowing you to focus on finding the story.

Exercise 3.3.2
Customizing a Favorite

In addition to adding metadata in the Notes field, you may rename the favorite text tag for each subclip you create. This change will not affect the clip's name. This is only a metadata change within Final Cut Pro.

1   In the list view of the Interview Keyword Collection, locate the Favorite tags for clip **MVI_1043**.

Earlier in this lesson, you marked two Favorite ranges. Now you'll modify the metadata of both favorites.

2   Click the "Favorite" text next to the first listed favorite.

NOTE ▶ Clicking toward the first letter of the tag selects the field for editing.

3   In the text field, type *image in the frame*, and press Return.

4   Replace the second favorite text with *technically flying in awe.*

Just like that you've added more custom clip metadata that will pay off during your edit.

3.3.2-A Adding More Metadata

Now it's time to customize the remaining interview metadata. The following table lists the start and end points for favorite ranges you should apply to each sound bite. You will also find notes to apply to each favorite. If you wish, you may also customize the Favorite tag for each subclip. Use the list or filmstrip views, or the Inspector, to complete this exercise.

1   In the Primary Media event, select the Interview Keyword Collection.

2   Mark a Favorite range for the clips listed in the following table.

Keyword Collection: Interview

Clip	Start	End	Notes	Result
MVI_1044	Start of clip	opener for me 01:35:48:00	new discovery	MVI_1044
MVI_1045	Every time we maybe 01:36:33:16	see or capture 01:36:43:06	crest reveal don't know capture	MVI_1045
MVI_1046	At the end of the day 01:37:51:00	adventure I went on 01:38:06:21	wow look what I saw	MVI_1046
MVI_1055	The love of flight 01:42:49:03	uh, so (end of clip)	really the passion is	MVI_1055

▶ **Pasting Timecode**

In a collaborative environment, you may work with a producer, reporter, client, or assistant editor who provides a log or select sheet. This sheet lists the acquired clips by name and/or timecode along with a brief description of the clips' contents. In the case of interview clips, the log may include paraphrased notes or even a full transcription of the interview subject's audio. When a sound bite is selected from the log, you may add more notes to the log or create a separate log that describes each desired sound bite. The sound bite log entry includes the filename, the in-cue of the audio, and the associated timecode for the start of each sound bite. The in-cue, often abbreviated as "IC," states the two or three words spoken or audio heard for the start of the sound bite at the given timecode. Each sound bite log entry also includes the out-cue, or "OC."

Final Cut Pro allows you to copy/paste that timecode data to ensure efficient and accurate recreation of the logged metadata within the app. From a source text document, copy a timecode entry using the standard copy shortcut, **Command-C**. With the destination clip selected in the Final Cut Pro Browser, click the timecode display beneath the Viewer, and then press the Paste keyboard shortcut, **Command-V**. The Browser clip will cue the playhead to the entered timecode. You can then press **I** or **O** to set the appropriate start/end point type.

If you'd like to try copying/pasting timecode, the preceding table is available in the folder you downloaded in Lesson 1. The specific file is FCP X Media > LV3 > **Exercise 3.3.2-A Table 1.pdf**. Also, the Notes entry for each favorite is included for copying/pasting.

Reference 3.4
Search, Sort, and Filter

Whether you use keywords, ratings, notes, or a combination of the three to add information about clips, you are already well on your way to enjoying the metadata backbone of Final Cut Pro. For years, editors have tried to cram as much metadata as possible into a clip's filename, sometimes with befuddling results. With Final Cut Pro, we are at the point where a clip's name may actually become irrelevant during the edit.

The search, sort, and filter features allow an editor to quickly find a clip based on camera metadata, Final Cut Pro metadata, and user-added metadata. Here are a few of examples of each metadata type:

Camera	Final Cut Pro	User
Frame rate	People detection	Ratings
Frame size	Shot detection	Notes
Recording date	Analysis keywords	Keywords

3.4-A Sorting Clips

The Filter pop-up menu provides fast ways to sort your clips, including:

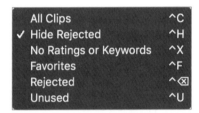

▶   All Clips: Displays all clips in the selected library, event, or collection

▶   Hide Rejected: Displays only clips rated as favorite or unrated

▶   No Ratings or Keywords: Displays clips that are unrated or do not have any keywords

▶   Favorites: Displays only clips rated as favorite

▶   Rejected: Displays only clips rated as rejected

▶   Unused: Displays clips that are not used in the open project

The Filter pop-up menu defaults to Hide Rejected. This setting helps you hide the distraction of unusable content, while continuing to display the good-to-great content. Every editing project may require several approaches to find the best B-roll and sound bites. One editor may start by removing the unusable Rejected content. Or, as you have already done in this lesson, you might begin by keywording the interview clips and then rating the sound bite selects as favorites. Either approach results in a selection of the best clips.

3.4-B Searching Metadata

The search field in the Browser, accessed via the magnifying glass, allows you to perform basic text searches.

The text entered in this field searches against the following metadata fields:

▶ Clip name

▶ Notes

▶ Reel

▶ Scene

▶ Take

▶ Markers

3.4-C Applying Filters

But there is more to the search field. Clicking the Filter HUD button at right of the search field allows you to set additional search criteria by clicking the Add Rule (+) button. Here is a breakdown of the rule categories and criteria available in this HUD:

▶ Text: See the preceding section "Searching Metadata."

▶ Ratings: Displays clips that are favorited or rejected

▶ Media: Displays clips that include video with audio, video only, audio only, or still images

▶ Type: Displays items that are auditions, synchronized, compound, multicam, layered graphic, or projects

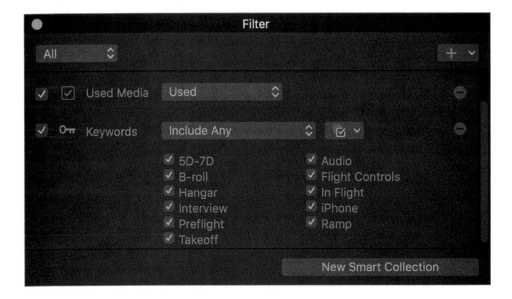

▶ Used Media: Displays both used and unused clips in the open project

▶ Keywords: Displays clips that contain all, any, or none of the selected keywords

▶ People: Displays clips that contain all or any of the selected analysis keywords

▶ Format: Displays clips that include text that matches the Reel, Scene, Take, Audio Output Channels (number), Frame Size, Video Frame Rate, Audio Sample Rate, Camera Name, or Camera Angle fields

▶ Date: Displays clips in which the content was created or the clip was imported on a certain date or within a date range

▶ Roles: Displays clips according to assigned roles

Most of these filter rules allow you to perform inverse or negative searches of the set criteria (is not, does not include, and so on). Also, the Filter window itself offers a rule with two settings: The pop-up menu at the upper-left permits you to choose All or Any.

▶ All: All active criteria must be met for a clip to be displayed in the results.

▶ Any: If a clip matches any of the criteria, the clip will be displayed as a search result.

NOTE ▶ Setting the menu to Any typically yields more results than filtering by All.

3.4-D Creating Smart Collections

Smart Collections are dynamic collections, unlike the static Keyword Collections. Keyword Collections are collections only if you manually add the same keyword to multiple clips, while Smart Collections automatically gather clips that meet all or some criteria you set.

For example, when applying analysis keywords, Final Cut Pro adds keywords to the clips based upon an analysis of their content. Then, Final Cut Pro creates Smart Collections to organize the analysis results. Although this automation is turned off by default, you may activate it at any time during your workflow.

Smart Collections may be created for automatic organization at the event or library level. New clips imported to an event automatically appear in the event's Smart Collections with matching criteria. This automation reduces the time and energy spent on organizing within events. Through the use of a template library or event, an editor can save time by presetting Smart Collections on empty events.

The power and efficiency of the Filter window comes together with the New Smart Collection button at the lower-right of the window.

Clicking the New Smart Collection button creates a Smart Collection, a saved version of the Filter HUD's search parameters.

The collection appears in the Libraries sidebar, assigned to the event. You may alter the criteria of the collection by double-clicking the Smart Collection's icon in the library.

Each new library includes a preset folder of Smart Collections. Clips from any event within the library automatically appear in the library's Smart Collection with matching criteria.

You may create additional library Smart Collections by clicking the New Library Smart Collection button. This button appears in the Filter window when searching a selected library.

Exercise 3.4.1
Filtering an Event

Now that you have a few ratings, keywords, and notes applied to some clips, you are almost ready to edit. But you're only *almost* ready because you still need to search, sort, and filter your clip metadata to find the favored sound bites and B-roll gems among hundreds or thousands of clips.

1   In the Libraries sidebar, select the Primary Media event.

You are going to use the Filter HUD tools to zero in on those clips you'll need while editing—specifically, iPhone clips of the flight controls.

2   In the Browser, from the Filter pop-up menu, choose All Clips.

3   In the Browser, click the magnifying glass to reveal the search field and Filter HUD button. Click the Filter HUD button.

4   In the Filter HUD, click the Add Rule (+) button, and choose Keywords while watching the Browser's contents.

The rule may be interpreted as, "Display all clips containing any of the keywords selected below." Let's see what happens when you change just one small parameter.

5   In the Filter HUD, change the Keywords pop-up menu to Include All.

All the Browser clips disappear because no clip meets the criteria of having all the selected keywords.

6   In the Keywords rule, deselect all checkboxes except the Flight Controls and iPhone keywords.

Your search returns two clips: the only two clips from an iPhone and showing the flight controls. You have created a search that filters the contents of two Keyword Collections. If you wanted to save this search as a Smart Collection, you would proceed by clicking the New Smart Collection button, and naming the Smart Collection in the event. You'll create and keep a different Smart Collection in a moment, so you are not required to save this search as a collection.

Look back at the lists of metadata types, filters, and rules presented in Reference 3.4. By using a combination of these items, you can create very complex searches to quickly sift your event or library, and find the clip you need based on the metadata associated with those clips. Remembering a clip's name is unnecessary when the metadata identifies a clip by its content.

3.4.1-A Finding Orphaned Clips

With all these great Keyword Collections created, finding the clip you need is simple. However, a simple problem was created as well: the orphaned clip, which is a clip lost between Keyword Collections. The clip is still in the event, but does not appear in the more finely grouped collections because the clip was not assigned a keyword. The Filter pop-up menu allows you to identify any orphaned clips so you may assign it appropriate keywords or ratings for later retrieval.

1 If necessary, clear the search field by clicking the X.

2 In the Libraries sidebar, select the Lifted library.

3 From the Filter pop-up menu, choose "No Ratings or Keywords."

One clip appears in the Browser, **GOPR0003**. This is one of the GoPro clips you previously imported. You'll mark the takeoff portion with a keyword so it is no longer an orphaned clip.

4 Mark a range that includes the takeoff and exiting the frame.

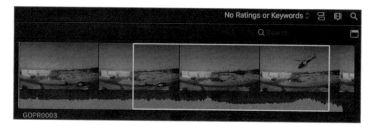

5 Assign the range to the Takeoff Keyword Collection in the GoPro event by dragging the selected range into the respective event's collection.

NOTE ▶ Drag the range to the GoPro event's Takeoff Keyword Collection.

You now have two clips in the Browser. Because you marked a range within a larger clip, these two clips represent the leftover media before and after the range you just keyworded. They are visible because the filter pop-up menu is still set to "No Ratings or Keywords." Because you have keyworded the best content from this clip, you may ignore these remnants by changing the Filter pop-up menu.

6 From the Filter pop-up menu, choose Hide Rejected.

▶ **Using Inter-Library Copying**

As you've learned, source media files needn't be duplicated when placed in multiple collections, even when those collections are within the same library. However, dragging a Browser clip from an event of one library to an event in another library does display a media management dialog with some additional options.

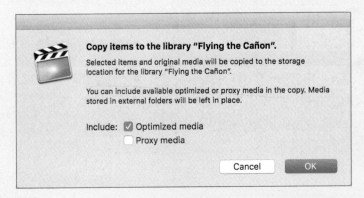

You'll learn more about media management options in Lesson 9.

Exercise 3.4.2
Working with Smart Collections

With all the searching, sorting, and filtering power available in Final Cut Pro, you have the tools to create complex searches you can save for later reference during an edit. But saving a search as a collection is not the end of the story. Saved search collections are Smart Collections that automatically contain any clip in the event or library that matches the collection's search criteria.

To see this in action, let's compare the content of the Primary Media event's Audio Keyword Collection to the Lifted library's Audio Only Smart Collection. Then, you'll import a sound effect and review the two collections.

1 Switching to filmstrip view, review the contents of the Lifted library's Audio Only Smart Collection.

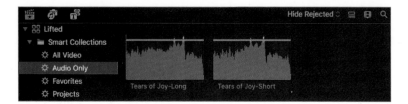

The collection currently references two music clips. Now, onto the Keyword Collection.

2 In the Primary Media event, review the contents of the Audio Keyword Collection.

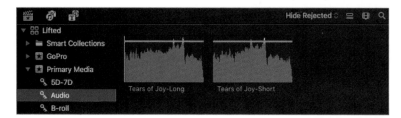

At the moment, both collections refer to the same two clips. Now, you'll import the additional audio file.

3 In the Libraries sidebar, select the Primary Media event.

4 To the left of the toolbar, click the Media Import button.

5   In the Media Import window, navigate to the FCP X Media folder you previously downloaded for this book.

6   Inside the FCP X Media folder, navigate to the LV1 > LV SFX folder, and then select the **Helicopter Start Idle Takeoff** audio file.

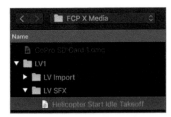

7   Set the Import Options pane as shown in the following figure with all other keyword, transcoding, and analysis options deselected. Click Import Selected.

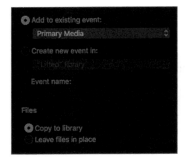

The import is performed very quickly, so you can immediately verify the results.

8   Click between the Audio Keyword Collection and the Audio Only Smart Collection while noting the differences in the Browser.

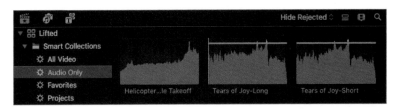

NOTE ▶   If you missed step 3, and left the Audio Keyword Collection selected while importing, the contents of the two collections will not vary when performing step 8.

The audio-only sound effect clip you imported was automatically placed into the Audio Only Smart Collection. So with some pre-post planning, you could create a series of Smart Collections in a library template that would auto-collect clips based on a wide range of metadata.

Exercise 3.4.3
Creating a Library-Wide Smart Collection

Let's create a Smart Collection that will pay off late in your edit phase. When the edit deadline is fast approaching, an editor needs quickly to find clips that are not currently used in the edited project, and that have not been rejected. You have several ways to find these results, but creating a Library Smart Collection will help you quickly find a clip meeting that criteria and execute an edit with that material.

1   With the Lifted library selected, open the Filter HUD by clicking the magnifying glass to toggle the search field, and then click the Filter HUD button.

The Filter HUD appears. You'll create a last-minute "what B-roll hasn't been used yet" search.

2   From the Add Rule (+) pop-up menu, choose Used Media.

3   Choose Unused from the pop-up menu.

It's not impressive until you start scrolling through the results and add a few more criteria to the HUD. As it is a Library Smart Collection, you are seeing results from the GoPro and Primary Media events, and right now, none of these clips are used in an editing project. Notice that Mitch's interview clips are included in the results. Let's kick them out of this search.

4   With the Filter HUD still open, add the Keywords rule to the filter criteria.

At its default, this Keywords rule is set to "include all" mode. Let's thin the herd by limiting the rule to one or two keywords.

5   In the Keywords rule, set the batch select pop-up menu to Uncheck All.

6   Next, select only the Interview keyword.

Now you see only Mitch's interview clips in the Browser. You actually want the inverse of this selection.

7   In the Filter HUD, change the Keywords pop-up menu to Does Not Include Any.

Mitch's interview clips are removed from the results. The results are closer to B-roll only, but notice three audio-only clips are in the results.

8   In the Keywords rule, select the Audio keyword.

You don't exactly have the desired results because only two of the music clips were removed. The remaining sound effect was not assigned the Audio keyword. You'll add a different criteria rule to remove the remaining sound effect and any other audio-only clip that is imported.

9   In the Filter HUD, add a Media Type rule, and in the pop-up menus, set the Media rule to read "Is Not Audio Only."

NOTE ▸ You may need to scroll down in the Filter HUD to see the Media rule.

You now have a smart search built that looks across all events in the library that qualify as B-roll even though not all the clips were keyworded as B-roll. Used in combination with the sifting options, the results may be narrowed to favorites or at least to hide the rejected segments of the unused B-roll. As the clips are edited into a project, the amount of unused media in this search will shrink.

10   Save this search by clicking the New Library Smart Collection button.

In the Libraries sidebar, the collection appears as Untitled.

11   Rename the new collection *Unused B-roll*, and press Return.

Utilizing the available metadata enables you to create complex searches against all of a library's media; and that's without renaming, duplicating, or moving clips. As new clips are imported that match the collection's filter criteria, the clips automatically join the collective.

Exercise 3.4.4
Detecting People and Shot Composition

Some analysis tools can create their own Smart Collections. One tool that performs two types of analyses is Find People, and you can apply it at any time during your workflow. This tool is extremely sophisticated, although the results may appear obvious in this exercise. The goal is to understand how to access the analysis tools on existing clips and the potential results when performing a Find People analysis.

For this exercise, you will perform a Find People analysis. What you need to know is that you should also select the "Create Smart Collections after analysis" option. Without the Create Smart Collections option selected, the results will not be automatically visible.

1   In the Primary Media event, select the Interview Keyword Collection, then switch to list view, if necessary.

2   In the Browser, select clips **MVI_1042** through **MVI_1055**.

3   Control-click any one of the selected clips, and from the shortcut menu, choose "Analyze and Fix."

A dialog appears with very familiar options.

4   In the "Analyze and Fix" dialog, select both "Find people" and "Create Smart Collections after analysis," and click OK.

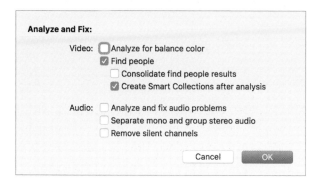

When a background task such as an analysis is underway, a progress report appears to the left in the toolbar.

The Background Tasks indicator showing the progress is actually a button you can click to display more information.

5   In the toolbar to the left, click the Background Tasks button.

The Background Tasks HUD appears with more details about the tasks that Final Cut Pro is performing behind the scenes.

As the analysis progresses, a People folder appears in the Primary Media event.

6   Click the disclosure triangle to display the contents of the People folder.

In its analysis of the selected clips, Final Cut Pro determined that the clips were framing the subject as a medium shot, and that the clips contained only one person. Here's a list of the possible results when performing a Find People analysis:

Framing	People
Close Up Shot	One Person
Medium Shot	Two Persons
Wide Shot	Group

These analysis keywords are huge timesavers when a deadline is approaching. Suppose you need one more B-roll clip that is a single wide shot of the interview subject standing next to the helicopter in the hangar recorded on the 5D. You can find it thanks to the user, camera, and Final Cut Pro–applied metadata. That's the sweet spot when editing with Final Cut Pro. You can think about the story, not the clip.

Reference 3.5
Roles

Roles are an additional, even stronger set of metadata controls available in Final Cut Pro. Roles are categorized as either Media Roles, defining a clip's audio/visual content to the editor and editorial collaborators, or Caption Roles, visually defining a clip's audio content to the audience. We'll discuss Caption Roles in Lesson 8; let's focus now on Media Roles. The Media Roles enable **grouping** inside an editing project. Roles may be used to modify Timeline playback, to organize similar clips within the Timeline, and to create **stems** on export. They allow you to aggregate items such as the primary language audio into one role and the secondary language audio into another role, and then in two simple clicks you can audition one while disabling the other.

> **NOTE ▶** Media Roles, like keywording, yield greater benefits the earlier you add them to your workflow.

Media Roles are available in two types: Video and Audio. Some default roles are created for you in every library. In the Role Editor, you can adjust the color coding for each role, and add roles and subroles to this list.

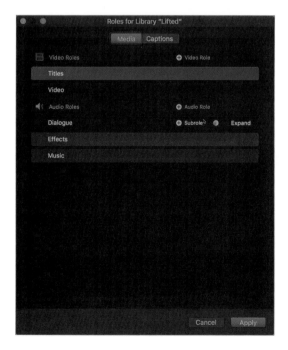

Subroles are specialized subsets of a role assigned to a clip. Each role has a default subrole. You may utilize these default subroles or add additional subroles and assign them customized names. For example, under the Dialogue role, you may want to create a subrole for the primary distribution language and additional subroles for secondary distribution languages. Then, when you're ready to distribute your finished edit, you will be able to quickly switch from the audio intended for the primary audience to an alternative audio track intended for another audience.

Exercise 3.5.1
Assigning Roles

Roles, when assigned to Browser clips, carry over into editing. Roles may assist during the edit, for example, by allowing you to disable all sound bite audio when you need to focus on ambient sounds. By merely deselecting one checkbox you've got the **mix-minus** you need. In the Browser or during the edit, you can assign roles to a clip or a batch selection of clips. Before you start assigning roles, let's look at how to create them.

1   Choose Modify > Edit Roles to open the Role Editor.

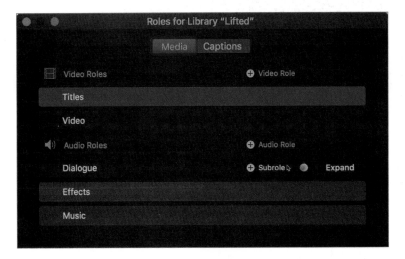

For this editing project, you will be utilizing the Video, Titles, Dialogue, Music, and Effects roles. During the edit, you will also isolate the natural, or ambient, sound recorded by the cameras' onboard microphones. These "nats" audio clips add to the realism and help draw the viewer into the visuals. The nats will be treated separately from any sound effects added later.

2   In the Role Editor, click the Add Audio Role (+) button to add an audio role.

The new role appears, ready for a new name.

3   Rename the role *Natural Sound*, and press Return. Click Apply.

The Natural Sound role automatically receives a subrole, "Natural Sound-1," and is ready for use. With the roles set up, you have several ways to assign them to batches of clips. Let's start by using a menu command.

4   In the Libraries sidebar, select the Lifted library's Audio Only Smart Collection.

5   In the Browser list view, select the Helicopter sound effect. Because this is a sound effect, assign the Effects role to the clip.

6   Choose Modify > Assign Audio Roles > Effects.

NOTE ▶ If you skim any clip while en route to the Modify menu, the sound effect is deselected, thereby causing the Effects menu item to dim.

To see that the clip received the role assignment, check the Inspector.

7   Open the Inspector, if necessary, by clicking the Inspector button, or by pressing **Command-4**.

8   Click the Info button to open the Info inspector, if necessary.

The Info inspector displays some basic metadata about the selected clip.

9   Verify that the Audio Roles pop-up menu is set to Effects-1.

Although you assigned the Effects role, Final Cut Pro automatically assigned the default Effects subrole, Effects-1.

3.5.1-A Assigning Additional Roles

You're now ready to assign additional roles. Leave the Info inspector open—you can assign roles and verify their assignment in the Inspector.

1   In the Audio Only Smart Collection, select the two music clips, **Tears of Joy-Long** and **Tears of Joy-Short**.

In the Info inspector, the top portion recognizes that you are inspecting two items. The audio roles are currently set to Dialogue-1.

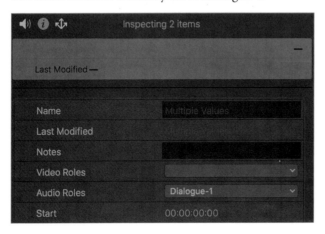

2   Using the Audio Roles pop-up menu in the Inspector, assign the two clips to the Music role by choosing Music-1 subrole from the pop-up menu.

With the music clips, only one role is needed because the clips are audio only. Let's look at the B-roll clips, which are assigned Video and Audio roles.

3   In the Libraries sidebar, select the Unused B-roll collection, which includes clips from both events.

4   In the Browser, select one clip, and then press **Command-A** to select all the B-roll clips.

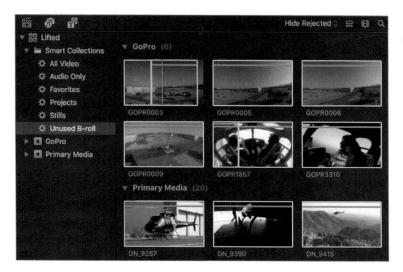

The Inspector recognizes that you are about to modify multiple clips. All the selected clips automatically received the Video Role assignment of Video, but the Audio Role is set to Dialogue-1.

5   In the Info inspector, from the pop-up menu, choose the Natural Sound-1 subrole to assign the desired audio role to the selected clips.

Let's also take this opportunity to get granular with the metadata. Since you have all the B-roll clips selected, you can create and assign a B-roll Video subrole.

6   In the Info inspector, from the Video Roles pop-up menu, choose Edit Roles to open the Roles Editor.

You will be adding a subrole to the Video role.

7   With the pointer over the Video role click the Add subrole button.

8   Rename the subrole B-roll, and press Return. Click Apply to close the window.

9   To assign the new Video subrole to the selected Browser clips, from the Video Roles pop-up menu in the Inspector, choose B-roll.

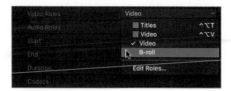

You have one more role assignment to verify for the interview clips. You will also process these as a batch.

10   In the Libraries sidebar under the Primary Media event, select the Interview collection.

11   In the Browser, select one of the interview clips, and then press **Command-A** to select all the clips in the collection.

12   In the Info inspector, verify that Video and Dialogue-1 are selected.

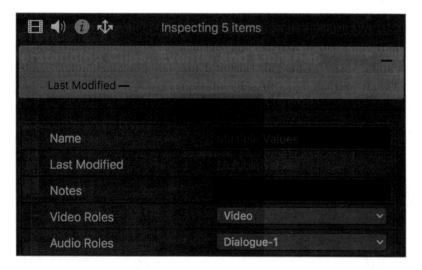

That's all the clips you need to modify for now. You've successfully assigned metadata to your clips. In Lesson 4, you will utilize that metadata to start your edit.

▶ **Even More Metadata**

What you've learned about metadata using Keywords, Ratings, and Roles is just the beginning. Final Cut Pro handles metadata behind the scenes, always awaiting your call. If you're an experienced editor, you may have noticed that info such as Reel, Scene, and Take were available in the Format rule when creating Smart Collections; but, how do you find those bits of metadata about one clip? Where is the app hiding this data? In the Inspector, specifically, the Info inspector.

The Info inspector presents a customizable list of metadata for one or more clips. The Metadata Views pop-up menu starts in Basic view with a short list of metadata. Changing the metadata view to Extended or another view serves up an inspector full of metadata.

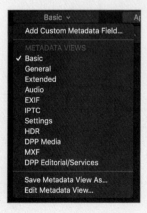

Even More Metadata *continued*

And for those fans of more metadata, the Edit Metadata View option allows you not only to customize the existing views, but also to create your own metadata views and your own metadata fields.

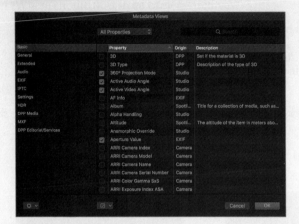

The Settings Metadata View of the Info inspector gives you access to clip interpretation metadata. Here you'll find alpha channel and log processing options, to name only two.

The Inspector may be left open throughout your edit. As you select another clip in the Browser or stop the playhead on a clip during the project edit, the Inspector automatically displays that clip's metadata.

Lesson Review

1. When applying keywords to a clip, can keywords be overlapped?
2. Which Inspector lets you add notes to a clip?
3. All clips start with which rating assigned?
4. What default filter setting prevents Rejected clip ranges from appearing in the Browser?
5. You are trying to locate a clip you imported into the library. How can you locate it?
6. What procedure is necessary to search an event using a combination of keywords?
7. How do you edit the criteria rules for an existing Smart Collection?
8. At what point in the workflow can a clip be assigned a role?

Answers

1. Yes
2. The Info inspector
3. Unrated
4. Hide Rejected
5. In the Libraries sidebar, select the Library. From the Filter pop-up menu, choose All Clips. Clear the Browser's search field.
6. Keyword combinations are searchable by clicking the magnifying glass in the search field and using the Keywords criteria rule in the Filter HUD.
7. In the Libraries sidebar, double-click the Smart Collection.
8. Clips can be assigned a role at any time in the workflow. However, roles assigned to clips shortly after import are carried with the clip throughout the editing workflow.

Lesson 4

Making the First Edit

After importing and organizing, the story elements sit as clips in the library, ready for editing. The editing phase of the post-production workflow involves crafting a story from the library clips into a project or timeline.

The first edit, or *rough cut*, of a project involves some or most of the major tasks from the remainder of the post workflow. An edit of the project is created; it's trimmed down for timing, pacing, and conciseness; additional elements, such as music, may be added; and then the project is shared out of Final Cut Pro for client or producer approval.

You are ready to embark on the post workflow with the Lifted project. In this lesson, you will assemble the interview sound bites and the helicopter B-roll to form the story. You'll trim the edits to remove any extraneous content, and then add a music clip. Lastly, you will export this first edit of the project as a file that is playable on a Mac, PC, smartphone, or tablet.

Reference 4.1
Understanding a Project

The editing phase occurs in a *project*—a timeline-based container of sequentially arranged clips that tell a story. Projects are simple or complex timelines, depending on the technical depth of the story.

GOALS

▶ Create a project

▶ Understand the attraction and repulsion behaviors of a storyline

▶ Append, insert, and rearrange clips within a storyline

▶ Batch edit a "storyboard" of clips

▶ Ripple, roll, and slip edit clips

▶ Blade, replace with gap, ripple delete, and join through edit

▶ Manipulate gap clips for pacing

▶ Perform connect edits

▶ Understand the horizontal and vertical relationships between connected clips

▶ Create and edit in a connected storyline

▶ Adjust audio levels

▶ Apply Audio Fade Handles to a clip

▶ Share the project to a media file

Finished project for Lesson 4

Projects are stored within individual events in a library: the super-container of your Final Cut Pro editing project that makes loading/unloading and transporting all your clips, events, and projects for a show, client, or movie much more convenient.

Events may contain as many projects as you need. For example, a news editor may need three projects for the VO (voiceover), the package, and the teaser. A documentary editor could easily use 10 to 30 projects when breaking down an edit by segment, creating a variety of video news releases, posting online teasers, and developing various versions of the documentary based on running time and/or content.

You already have the Lifted library with two events of clips. Let's edit.

Exercise 4.1.1
Creating a Project

To start the first edit, you must create the project. A couple of clicks and you've got yourself a starting project.

1   In the Lifted library, Control-click (or right-click) the Primary Media event, and from the shortcut menu, choose New Project.

The Project Properties dialog opens to the default automatic settings.

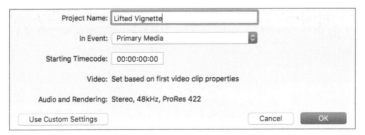

NOTE ▸ If your dialog opens to the custom settings, click the Use Automatic Settings button.

2   For the Project Name, enter *Lifted Vignette*.

3   Click the In Event pop-up menu.

In Event specifies the event in which to save the project you are creating. The pop-up menu displays the events available in the open libraries.

4   Ensure that the In Event pop-up menu is set to Primary Media, and click OK.

The project is created and saved in the Primary Media event.

5   If necessary, in the Lifted library, select the Primary Media event and switch to list view.

The project appears at the top of the Browser.

6   If necessary, double-click the project to open it in the Timeline.

The project open in the Timeline

NOTE ▸ See **Lesson 10** for more information about the automatic vs. manual project settings.

▶ **Changing Workspaces**

The Timeline, in which projects are edited, typically occupies the lower half of the interface. If the Timeline is not visible, you need to verify a couple of interface settings.

▶ Ensure that the "Show or hide the Timeline" button is activated.

▶ If you previously selected a different workspace, reset to the default workspace in the Window > Workspaces menu.

Reference 4.2
Defining the Primary Storyline

Every project in Final Cut Pro is based around the primary storyline, identified by the dark stripe across the Timeline. The primary storyline contains the clips that drive your project. For a documentary, a combination of sound bites and a narrator's VO could constitute the primary storyline. For a project that starts with a montage, you could consider placing the music intro in the storyline, followed by the on-camera host. The primary storyline is flexible content-wise.

By default, clips in the primary storyline interact with each other and incoming clips. This interaction is similar to that of two magnets: attraction or repulsion.

When you drag a new clip from the Browser to the far right of the project, that clip is attracted to the end of the primary storyline, and "magnetically" snaps to the preceding clip.

Dragging a clip to the end of a project

The storyline appends the clip to the project.

Dragging a clip between two existing clips creates a repulsion that pushes the existing clips far enough apart to insert the new clip.

Dragging a clip to a project for insertion between two storyline clips

Positioning the clip on the storyline clips reveals an insert bar, and a gap for the clip is created.

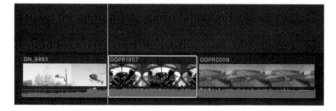

The clip is wedged between the storyline clips.

These two behaviors form the basic concepts of the magnetic storyline: As you add clips, shift clips around to change their order, or remove clips, the magnetic storyline keeps the clips snapped together, ensuring that the clips play back-to-back in a continuous stream.

Knowing the basic concepts of a primary storyline as the magnetic backbone of a project, you can start assembling your first edit.

Exercise 4.2.1
Appending the Primary Storyline

You are ready to edit your first clips into the Lifted Vignette project. Because this project is sound bite–driven, you will edit the sound bites into the primary storyline. Let's first alter the interface so you can see as many clips and notes as possible in the Browser.

1   If necessary, in the Browser, select the list view.

2   With the Interview collection selected in the Primary Media event, click the Hide Libraries sidebar button.

3   Drag the Timeline divider down to create more vertical room in the Browser.

You can drag the area dividers to vertically expand or contract the areas above and below the divider.

Mitch provided a couple of great sound bites to open with during his interview when he talked about his passion for flying. You logged those gems with a favorite rating and included the word "passion" in the notes field. Rather than opening each clip here in list view to visually scan your notes for the word "passion" and an assigned rating of favorite, you'll use the search field.

4   In the Browser, click the magnifying glass, then type *passion* in the search field that appears.

As you begin to type, the Browser updates immediately with the matching results: **MVI_1042** and **MVI_1055**.

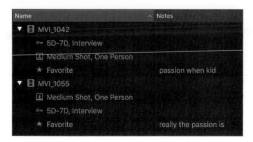

NOTE ▶   If you see only the clips' names listed, click the disclosure triangle next to each name to reveal additional metadata.

5   In the Browser select **MVI_1042**, and skim the clip to review the green, marked favorite.

As you skim the clip, notice that its audio is pitch corrected, which allows you to quickly review the clip's contents at variable speeds while maintaining the aural clarity of its contents.

NOTE ▶   You may also review the selected favorite by pressing the navigation controls: the **Spacebar**, the **J, K, L** keys, and the **/** (slash) key.

Your search results include a second clip tagged with the word "passion."

6   In the Browser, play **MVI_1055**, and review its contents.

With a little **trimming** later in the edit, both sound bites could fit back to back into your storyline. Let's edit these into the project as the first two sound bites.

7 In the Browser, select the favorite with the "passion when kid" note listed under **MVI_1042**.

8 Click the Append button, or press **E**, to add this clip selection to the project.

The clip's selection is edited into the primary storyline. The E stands for "End." No matter where the skimmer or playhead is currently located in the project, you can press E to quickly edit the active Browser selection to the end of the storyline.

Currently, the playhead is at the end of **MVI_1042**. The playhead jumps to the end of the clip you append edited to the project. This default playhead behavior in Final Cut Pro anticipates your next edit. But what happens if you move the playhead before the next append edit? Let's find out.

9 Move the playhead to the left by clicking the empty gray area above **MVI_1042**.

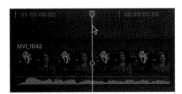

This cues the playhead over **MVI_1042**, which you can see in the Viewer. With the next clip, you will perform an append edit with the playhead placed in the middle of **MVI_1042** and observe the results.

NOTE ▶ Depending on your display's resolution, your clip may appear short and shoved to the left of the interface. After clicking to move the playhead in the previous step, press **Shift-Z** to fit the project within the Timeline. Alternatively, you could drag the Zoom slider in the Timeline's Clip Appearance pop-up to change the zoom setting.

10 Returning to the Browser, notice the Used entry under **MVI_1042**.

The Used listing identifies the clip's selection used in the open project. As that was the only favorite for that clip, you will go to the next clip for the next edit.

11 In the Browser, select the "really the passion is" favorite in the **MVI_1055** clip, and then press **E** to append this clip to the end of the storyline.

Clip selected in the Browser

Clip append edited into the primary storyline

That was quick. The clip was edited to the end of the storyline immediately following **MVI_1042**. The playhead's position had no impact on the append edit. You are two sound bites into the edit with several more to go. You could continue with this one-at-a-time approach to editing, but Final Cut Pro offers a slightly faster edit method.

NOTE ▸ If the previous edit caused the **MVI_1042** clip to not be visible in the Timeline, you need to change the zoom setting. Click once in the Timeline, and press **Shift-Z** or adjust the Zoom control in the Timeline's Clip Appearance pop-up.

4.2.1-A Appending a Batch Edit to the Primary Storyline

You can use the append function to edit more than one clip at a time into the primary storyline. As you are building your first edit, you will be looking for your next clip in the Browser. Append allows you to remain in the Browser and storyboard the next few clips with one edit. This batch editing technique is a fast and simple way to edit several clips into your project at once.

1 In the Browser, switch to filmstrip view.

Currently, you are looking at two clips that were identified in your earlier search. You'll need to clear the search field to reveal the rest of the sound bites.

2 In the Browser, click the Reset button (X) in the search field to clear the previous search.

The remaining clips in the Interview collection appear. You may select multiple sound bites to append at one time, and the order in which you select the clips is the order they will be edited into the project.

3   If desired, you may increase the size of the filmstrips by changing the Clip Appearance's Clip Height slider.

4   In the Browser's filmstrip view, click the first green range in **MVI_1043**.

The favorites you marked earlier appear as green stripes that you may use to quickly select the favorited ranges.

5   With the first favorite in **MVI_1043** selected, Command-click the previously marked favorites of the following clips in this order to add them to the selection: **MVI_1046**, **MVI_1045**, and **MVI_1044**.

6   Press **E** to perform an append edit.

The clips appear at the end of the project in the same order you selected them in the Browser.

7   To see the entire project within the Timeline, click once in the Timeline gray area and press **Shift-Z**.

▶ **How Did Final Cut Pro Know Where to Put the Clips?**

If you have prior editing experience, you may have noticed that you didn't need to assign tracks, position the playhead, or set a start point to make this edit. The append edit function efficiently takes legacy overwrite editing to the next level.

4.2.1-B Playing the Project

To play the project, you may press the Home key to cue the playhead to the beginning of the Timeline, but on Apple Wireless Keyboards and laptops, the Home key is not labeled.

1   With the Timeline active, press the Home key or **Fn-Left Arrow** to simulate pressing the Home key.

The playhead is now cued to the beginning of the project.

2   Press the **Spacebar** to start playback.

Playback will stop when the playhead reaches the end of the project.

NOTE ▶ When loop playback is enabled (by choosing View > Playback > Loop Playback), your project will not stop automatically but will repeat over and over until you manually stop playback.

Exercise 4.2.2
Rearranging Clips in the Primary Storyline

The sound bites don't quite flow yet. It's time to rearrange them into an order that more fully supports your storyline. Working in a storyline makes such changes incredibly easy. Just drag a clip to a new location in the Timeline, pause for the interface to preview the results, and then release the mouse button.

1   In the project, select the fourth clip, **MVI_1046**.

The playhead must be located over this clip to preview it. Your playhead is currently located at the end of the project. You do not need to move the playhead because the skimmer relocates the playhead if the skimmer is visible when you start playback.

2   Move the mouse pointer slightly to verify that the skimmer is active.

The skimmer extends vertically up to the timestrip across the Timeline pane, the same as the playhead; however, the skimmer does not have a marker on top as does the playhead.

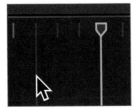

Skimmer (left) compared to playhead (right)

3   Cue the skimmer by moving the mouse toward the beginning of **MVI_1046**. Press the **Spacebar** to play the clip.

The playhead relocates to the skimmer's position and the clip plays. **MVI_1046** starts with Mitch saying, "At the end of the day." It sounds as if that phrase should be placed nearer the end of the storyline.

4   Drag **MVI_1046** toward the end of the storyline, but don't release the mouse button just yet.

5   Position the clip so that a blue clip box appears in the primary storyline after **MVI_1044**. Release the mouse button.

MVI_1046 is edited in as the last clip in your storyline.

Some extra words, phrases, and syllables remain in your clips. One clip may cut Mitch off too early. That's OK. We'll trim those troubled frames later in this lesson. For now, let's try moving another clip in the storyline.

6   Locate **MVI_1044**, which is now the second clip from the end of the project. Drag the clip between **MVI_1043** and **MVI_1045**.

As you drag **MVI_1044** between the two clips, an insert bar appears. If you continue to hold the clip in that position, **MVI_1045** will slide to the right to allow **MVI_1044** to drop into place. The magnetic storyline enables these quick reorganizing edits as you explore your story flow.

NOTE ▸ When you drag a clip, the delta, or timing change, of the clip's position in the Timeline is displayed above the clip. When you perform these exercises, your delta values may vary from those specified in the book due to slight variances in selected clip ranges.

▶ **Checkpoint 4.2.2**

Refer to Appendix C for details on reviewing a Checkpoint.

Reference 4.3
Modifying Clips in the Primary Storyline

When reviewing the storyline's flow, an additional clip or two may fill in story gaps. The flow may be disrupted by extra words or sounds at the start or end of a sound bite. Thanks to the magnetic properties of the storyline, the solutions to these problems are painless.

The append edit you performed added the selected Browser clip or clips to the end of the storyline. Sometimes a clip must be placed between those appended storyline clips. In Exercise 4.2.2, you wedged **MVI_1044** between **MVI_1043** and **MVI_1045** when rearranging the clip order in the primary storyline. This procedure is formally called an *insert edit*. Browser clips may be insert edited or wedged between two storyline clips, thereby placing additional content in the middle of an existing storyline.

After the storyline clips are in order, you may need to finesse the content to enhance your story flow. The trimming tools allow you to remove or add an extra breath, sound, word, or movement within a clip. Final Cut Pro includes several trimming tools. The basic trim tool covered in this lesson is called *ripple trim*.

The ripple trim allows you to remove media from a project clip, frame by frame if desired. The ripple trim also allows you to insert media to a project clip.

Whether you're performing an insert edit or a ripple trim in the storyline, the adjoining clips in the storyline stick together. Remove a clip and the subsequent clips move forward and hook up to the previous clip. Insert a clip between others and the subsequent clips move right to make room.

Exercise 4.3.1
Performing Insert Edits

When you dragged **MVI_1044** to its new location, you performed an insert edit. Clips to the right of the new clip slid right to make room, while clips to the left retained their positions. Previously, you marked another sound bite as a select that needs to be added to the project. In this exercise, you will insert this clip into the project, but without dragging it.

1   In the Browser, switch to filmstrip view, and then perform a search for "awe" in the Interview Keyword Collection.

The search identifies one clip, **MVI_1043**. The filmstrip displays two favorite ranges within the clip.

2   In the Browser, select (by clicking the second green stripe) then skim the second favorite of **MVI_1043**.

Depending on your display's resolution, you may have difficulty skimming the clip at a speed that makes the audio intelligible. Expanding the filmstrip by zooming in will help you skim the clip.

3   In the Clip Appearance pop-up, drag the Zoom slider to the right until the zoom scale reads 5s.

4   Skim the second favorite in **MVI_1043** again.

At this scale setting, each thumbnail in the filmstrip represents five seconds of source media. This time you can identify the sound bites by listening to the pitch-corrected audio. Notice the torn edge on the left end of the row. That indicates the clip continues from the previous line of thumbnails. The start and end of the clip are represented by a solid edge on the filmstrip.

5   In the clip's filmstrip, ensure that the second favorite range is selected.

Next, you need to choose where this clip belongs in the storyline by cueing the playhead to the desired location.

6   In the Timeline, skim between **MVI_1043** and **MVI_1044**.

MVI_1043 must be edited between those two clips with frame accuracy. To help you precisely place the playhead on the edit point between the two clips, you can turn on snapping.

At the upper right of the Timeline locate the Skimming, Audio Skimming, Audio Soloing, and Snapping buttons.

7   If necessary, click the Snapping button to turn on snapping, or press **N**.

8   Skim over several clips and edit points within the project.

Notice that the skimmer jumps to the edit points. To prepare for the insert edit, you need to cue the playhead to the desired edit point.

9   Snap the skimmer to the edit point between **MVI_1043** and **MVI_1044**, then click to cue the playhead here.

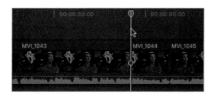

NOTE ▸   The edit point between is the start frame of the right clip (the starting clip), and not the end frame of the left clip (the ending clip). A "start bracket" is overlaid on the clip to visually identify that the playhead is on the start frame.

The "L" bracket indicates this frame is the start point.

10 In the Browser, verify that the **MVI_1043**'s second range is still selected.

11 In the Timeline toolbar, click the Insert edit button, or press **W**.

The second select of **MVI_1043** is placed into the project between the two storyline clips, and a missing sound bite becomes part of the storyline.

Exercise 4.3.2
Rippling the Primary Storyline

When you pulled your select sound bites in Lesson 3, you included some extraneous material. (The reason you left some extra material in your favorites will become apparent during this exercise.) However, everyday editing is all about trimming down to create a more concise story, or padding the story to extend its length. You will now learn how to use ripple trimming to remove that extra content, and also how to reinsert content when you trim off too much.

> **NOTE ▶** Because Final Cut Pro is context sensitive, you may not have to activate the Trim tool. The Select tool automatically switches to the Trim tool's ripple function when necessary.

1   Locate the skimmer toward the end of **MVI_1055**, the second clip in the project. Play the end of this clip to review what Mitch says.

Some extra content, where Mitch says, "Uh, so," needs to be trimmed, leaving a new end point after Mitch says, "Whole new look."

Before you perform this bit of clip trimming, zoom in on the edit so that you may operate the tools with greater precision.

2   With your skimmer or playhead cued around the end of **MVI_1055**, press **Command-=** (equals sign) to zoom in to the Timeline.

As you zoom, the thumbnails and waveforms expand to reveal where the trim should occur. The "uhh, so" phrase is displayed as the peaks of waveforms at the end of the clip. You'll remove those hesitations. In addition, Mitch takes a breath after ending the preceding sentence with the word "look." Examining the audio waveforms, you can see a drop in the waveforms after he enunciates the "k" in "look." You'll cue the playhead after the "k," and then use the ripple trim function to remove the breath and "uhh, so" material.

3   Identify the new end point by cueing the playhead after Mitch says the "k" in "look" and before Mitch breathes and says, "uhh, so" at the end of **MVI_1055**.

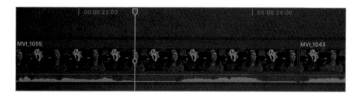

To set the playhead precisely, you can press the **J K L** keys and the **Left Arrow** and **Right Arrow** keys. Locating the playhead at the desired trim point allows you to use snapping to make an exact trim. You'll perform this ripple trim with the default Select tool. This tool automatically changes function based on its location in the Timeline.

4   In the Tools pop-up menu in the Timeline, verify that the Select tool is chosen, or press **A**.

5   In the Timeline, place the mouse pointer over the end point of the clip.

6   Without clicking, slowly move the mouse pointer back and forth across the edit point between the two clips' edit points.

Notice how the pointer icon changes as the mouse pointer moves from one side of the edit to the other. The changing icon indicates that the Select tool automatically becomes the ripple trim tool.

The ripple trim icon has a small filmstrip that always points toward the clip you will trim. Because you want to change the end point of **MVI_1055**, the filmstrip must point left toward the clip.

7   With the ripple trim's filmstrip pointing toward the left, drag the end of the clip until it snaps to the playhead.

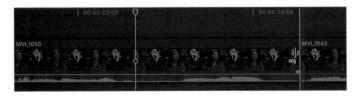

Before

After dragging the edit point to the left, it snaps to the playhead.

8   Review the edit you completed by playing this portion of the Timeline.

You easily changed the end point of the clip, thereby removing the extraneous content. The ripple trim also moved all the following clips earlier in the Timeline to fill in for the removed content. Now you'll trim off the start of the same clip.

9   To quickly scroll left in the project and jump to the start point of **MVI_1055**, press the **Up Arrow** key once, or twice if necessary. Also, you may want to zoom out a little in your Timeline view by pressing **Command--** (minus).

Pressing the **Up Arrow** key cues the playhead to the previous edit point in the project. Conversely, pressing the **Down Arrow** key cues the playhead to the next edit.

10 Play the start of **MVI_1055** to identify the new start point before Mitch says, "And really the passion."

You will cue the playhead between Mitch saying, "of film" and "And really." Ideally, you will find a frame for an edit that has the interview subject appearing with eyes open and mouth closed or nearly closed. In this clip, you'll find just such a frame as Mitch finishes the word "film."

11 With the playhead parked at the new start point's location, 00:00:05:01, place the Select tool over the clip's current start point.

This time, the filmstrip of the ripple trim pointer will point to the right toward **MVI_1055**.

12 Drag the start point of **MVI_1055** and snap it to the playhead.

When ripple trimming a start point, you may notice that the clip to the left appears to move. However, the clip did not move because it still starts at 0:00. As you trimmed content from the beginning of **MVI_1055**, the clip's duration shortened, the following clips rippled left in time, and the Timeline timecode shifted accordingly.

4.3.2-A Using the Keyboard to Ripple Trim an End Point

Sometimes the mouse or trackpad does not offer sufficiently fine control to perform a trim without setting an extreme view or altering your System Preferences. Fortunately, you can use keyboard shortcuts for greater precision.

1   Press **Command--** (minus sign) once or twice to zoom out in the Timeline view. Locate the end point of the second, shorter **MVI_1043** clip. Cue the playhead to time-code 00:00:45:16 before Mitch utters an extraneous "so."

Because you have heard this interview already, you know that Mitch runs words and sentences together, thereby making this edit more difficult. Let's turn to keyboard shortcuts to help trim this clip.

2   With the filmstrip icon pointing toward the left, select the end point of the second **MVI_1043** clip.

With the end point selected, you can use keyboard shortcuts to trim the clip one frame at a time. Note the timecode of the playhead's location. As you perform this trim edit, the playhead jumps to the point you're trimming rather than staying anchored as it did while dragging the edit point. That means you will trim the point with the keyboard while monitoring the timecode displayed beneath the Viewer to accurately trim this edit.

3   Press the **,** (comma) key multiple times to ripple trim, removing content frame by frame, until the timecode displays 00:00:45:16.

4   If necessary, press the **.** (period) key multiple times to insert content frame by frame.

5   Skim to just before the edit point, and then play back the project to check your results.

Did you remove the word "so" and not trim off the end of "experiencing"? Depending on your earlier selection of this sound bite, you may have to remove about 10 frames of material. This trim edit will take a few tries to perfect.

▶ **More Keyboard, Less Mouse**

Using the following keyboard shortcuts will have you reaching for the mouse less often:

▶ Pressing the Up Arrow or Down Arrow keys jumps the playhead to the edit point for trimming.

▶ Pressing the [(Left Bracket) key selects the end point of the clip to the left; pressing the] (Right Bracket) key selects the start point of the clip to the right.

▶ Pressing the , (comma) key nudges the selection left by 1 frame; pressing the . (period) key nudges the selection right by 1 frame.

▶ Pressing Shift-? (question mark) cues the playhead two seconds back and then plays to the edit and two seconds beyond.

6 Proceed through the project, removing extraneous clip content. You'll need to remove breaths at the start or end of clips in addition to any instances of "so" or "uhh." When you're finished, the project should resemble the following table:

Lifted Vignette Edit in Progress

Clip	Project timecode	Start dialogue	End dialogue
MVI_1042	00:00:00:00	Flying is	a little kid
MVI_1055	00:00:03:00	And really the	whole new look
MVI_1043	00:00:20:08	One thing that	what we're shooting
MVI_1043	00:00:37:15	As I'm technically	what we're experiencing
MVI_1044	00:00:44:13	You know it's	opener for me
MVI_1045	00:00:50:23	Every time we may be	see or capture
MVI_1046	00:01:00:14	At the end of the day	adventure I went on

NOTE ▶ You may hear a slight click or pop on some of your edits. You'll learn to resolve those errors later in this lesson.

Lifted Vignette in progress

▶ **Checkpoint 4.3.2**

Refer to Appendix C for details on reviewing a Checkpoint.

Reference 4.4
Timing the Primary Storyline

Every edit in a project is based upon the primary storyline. Up to this point, the concern has been to place the select sound bites into the project and organize them to reflect the story structure. Now that the structure has been established, the task switches to adjusting the timing and pacing. The sound bites should not be a hailstorm of thoughts spewed at the viewer, but should flow like everyday conversation.

The first technique to pacing the sound bites involves a gap clip, which is an empty clip container in the Timeline. Gap clips may be applied as placeholders until additional material arrives, such as more B-roll content, clips from a hard-to-schedule interview, or a late shipment of second unit content. Gap clips are also used as the spaces, pauses, and breaths that enhance your story flow.

The second technique to pacing the sound bites involves removing segments of a clip or entire clips. The Blade tool segments a clip to remove one or more clip ranges from the project. Each time you blade a clip, you create a **through edit**.

A through edit marks the clip into segments without breaking the clip into two physical clips. If you blade that clip a second time, you mark it into three segments with two through edits. You can rejoin these segments if you inadvertently blade the wrong frame. The repair is called a join through edit.

When you are ready to delete a segment, you can do so in one of two ways. Simply pressing the Delete key performs a ripple delete. The selected clip segment is removed, and the subsequent clips slide left to occupy the Timeline position of the deleted segment.

Blade to segment unwanted content.

Select segment for removal.

Press Delete to ripple delete.

The second delete method applies a replace with gap edit. This deletion, performed by pressing Shift-Delete, removes the selected segment and leaves a gap that occupies its former position in the Timeline. As a result, the following clips do not ripple, but remain in place. This edit is often referred to as a lift edit.

Blade to segment unwanted content.

Select segment for removal.

Press Shift-Delete to replace segment with a gap clip.

Exercise 4.4.1
Inserting a Gap Clip

Currently, your project sound bites are sequenced very tightly. This breathless stream of consciousness does not lend itself to clear storytelling. Let's separate some of these clips so the storytelling relaxes a bit.

1   Press the Up Arrow or Down Arrow keys to park the playhead between **MVI_1042** and **MVI_1055**.

Placing a gap clip here allows Mitch to take a breath. Don't worry about the visual break. The B-roll clips you will add later can fill in those pauses.

2   To insert a gap clip, choose Edit > Insert Generator > Gap, or press **Option-W**.

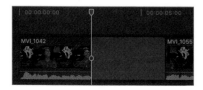

A three-second clip is inserted between the two clips at the playhead location. Those three seconds may be a little too long for this edit. As with any other clip, you may ripple trim a gap clip to adjust its duration.

3   Place the mouse pointer over the end point of the gap clip. Ensure that the ripple trim's filmstrip is pointing left, and then drag the end point to the left.

As you drag, the clip's new duration and the delta (the amount you have changed the clip's duration while dragging) appears above the edit.

4   Trim the gap clip to a new duration of one second, thereby removing two seconds from its length.

5   Skim to just before the gap clip, and play back to review the edit.

That's not bad. It allows just a moment for your audience to understand the who, what, and where of Mitch's comments. Let's repeat that for the next edit.

6   Advance the playhead to the next edit by pressing the Down Arrow key.

The playhead jumps to the edit between **MVI_1055** and **MVI_1043**.

Mitch is offering more details in **MVI_1043**, so placing a longer gap before this clip may help transition the audience into this sound bite.

7   With the playhead cued, press Option-W to insert a three-second gap clip.

8   Review the edit.

Now that you have silence between the two sound bites, you may discover the breaths that Mitch takes at the start and end of **MVI_1055**. Did you remove those already?

9   If necessary, adjust the end or start points surrounding the gap clips to tidy up the trimmed clips.

You are listening for extra syllables or breaths to remove. You are also listening for places where you may have trimmed too much. Does Mitch get a chance to enunciate the "k" in "look" before you cut him off? You may need to add back a frame or two to avoid an **upcut**.

These gap clips won't necessarily remain at the durations you just set. They may flex as you continue to build the story...or tear out parts of it.

Exercise 4.4.2
Blading and Deleting

The Blade tool allows you to quickly break a clip into smaller sections to be moved elsewhere or completely removed from your story. In the first instance of **MVI_1043**, some pauses in Mitch's interview can be removed to tighten the edit.

1   Play the project, and locate the point at which Mitch says, "And filming at the same time, (breath) uhhm," in the first **MVI_1043**. This occurs about four seconds into the clip.

2   Cue the playhead after the breath and before the "uhhm" at timecode 00:00:28:16.

You will blade the clip here to divide it into two segments. You will then blade the clip again after the "uhhm" to separate this sound from the good content that occurs before and after it.

3   From the Tools pop-up menu, choose the Blade tool, or press **B**.

4   With **snapping** turned on, move the Blade tool over the **MVI_1043** clip and toward the playhead until it snaps to the playhead.

5   With the Blade tool snapped to the playhead, click to segment the clip at this frame.

You can choose the Blade tool while still using the Select tool. Let's switch to the Select tool to blade on the other side of the "uhhm."

6   Press **A** to choose the Select tool.

A keyboard shortcut activates the Select tool's built-in blade. The blade cuts through the clip at the skimmer or playhead. For precision, you'll advance the playhead, then activate the Select tool's blade command.

7   Press the Right Arrow key—and the Left Arrow key, if necessary—to advance the playhead to after the "uhhm" and just as Mitch is starting the word "you're" at time-code 00:00:29:13.

8   Without moving the mouse, press **Command-B** to blade the clip at the playhead.

The single clip is now three segments. You need to remove the middle segment.

Remember, there are two types of clip deletion. Let's use both to see the difference between them.

9   Select the middle clip segment, and press Shift-Delete.

Before

After

The clip segment is replaced with a gap clip. The gap clip locked the storyline clips to the right in place so no clips slide in the Timeline.

10 Press **Command-Z** to undo the previous edit.

11 Reselect the "uhhm" clip segment, if necessary, and press Delete.

The segment is removed, and the following clips slide to the left to replace it.

12 Play the edit and listen to the results.

The new, second **MVI_1043** might sound like the first word is cut off a bit or still have a bit of the "uhh" remaining. In addition to that concern, does the breath at the end of the first **MVI_1043** distract and call attention to the edit? Or does the breath naturally flow into the second **MVI_1043** clip?

13 Using the ripple trim techniques you've learned, clean up the edit to smooth the audio transitions between these two new neighbors.

You may first want to remove the breath at the end of the first, or ending, clip. You may also need to insert or remove frames to the start point of the second clip, the starting clip. Refer to Using the Keyboard to Ripple Trim an End Point in this lesson to review ripple trimming.

Visually, this edit is a **jump cut**. A jump cut occurs when similar but nonsynchronized content appears to jump in space and time at an edit point. The B-roll you will add in a few minutes will hide this error.

▶ **Checkpoint 4.4.2**

Refer to Appendix C for details on reviewing a Checkpoint.

Exercise 4.4.3
Joining a Through Edit

In the previous exercise, you used the Blade and Select tools to divide a clip into segments. The resulting through edits may be easily repaired if you made them in error or change your mind about splitting up a clip.

1   In your project, locate **MVI_1044**, and then press **Command-=** (equals) to zoom in.

2   In the Tools pop-up menu, choose the Blade tool, or press **B**.

3   Skim toward the end of the clip just after Mitch says, "New" and then pauses.

The audio waveform displays a definite pause, represented as a "valley" in the waveform.

4   Click in this waveform valley to blade the clip and create a through edit.

The through edit point appears as a dashed line. Because we really did not want to split this clip, you are going to rejoin the through edit.

5   Press A to choose the Select tool.

6   With the Select tool, click the through edit point (dashed line) to select it.

Only one side of the through edit will be selected with the Select tool active. That's OK.

7   Press Delete.

The through edit point is removed and the two segments are rejoined into one clip.

Exercise 4.4.4
Refining Some Sound Bite Edits

Before progressing to the next layers of B-roll and music, let's polish the "technically flying in awe" section of the project by adjusting the sound bites' contents and pacing.

Currently, the second instance of **MVI_1043** ends with the word "shooting," which does not flow smoothly into the next clip. This occurs at roughly the 40-second mark in the Timeline.

Earlier, you trimmed off Mitch saying, "so." You could use that here to blend into the next sound bite.

1   Place the skimmer so that the ripple trim appears with the filmstrip pointing left at the end of the second instance of **MVI_1043**.

2   Ripple trim the end point of the second instance of **MVI_1043** to the right to insert roughly 11 frames of content.

3 Review the edit

That created a nice story flow.

The end of the third instance of **MVI_1043** will be a little tougher to get a clean ending—that is, a natural-sounding ending—because you are actually cutting off the sound bite in mid-sentence. The clip's current end point is at "experiencing." Let's trim that end point to a little earlier in the sentence to try a different ending.

4 Ripple trim the end point of the third instance of **MVI_1043** to the left roughly one second.

The clip should now end after Mitch says "filming," and most likely has an extra syllable or two that need to be removed.

5 With the end point still selected, press the **comma** (,) and **period** (.) keys to nudge trim frame by frame, refining the edit point.

This trim edit may take you a few moments to locate the right frame for the end point. That frame is going to be on the "g" of "filming." The repetition you must perform in fine-tuning the edit point is common in the art of editing: making frame-by-frame adjustments to remove only a few words or syllables.

NOTE ▶ Review your edit by pressing **Shift-?**. Then press **,** (comma) or **.** (period) to nudge the edit earlier or later.

As for **MVI_1044** and **MVI_1045**, these two get the axe. For timing purposes, let's leave these out of the story for now.

6   Select both clips, and press **Shift-Delete** to replace both clips with a gap clip.

7   Trim the gap clip to a duration of three seconds.

Trimming creates room for a natural sound break and music swell before Mitch segues into the next sound bite.

With these edits in place, you have built the sound bite foundation for your project. Take a moment to review your story.

Lifted Vignette's sound bite–driven primary storyline

▶ **Checkpoint 4.4.4**

Refer to Appendix C for details on reviewing a Checkpoint.

Reference 4.5
Editing Above the Primary Storyline

The primary storyline has established the content foundation, timing, and pacing for the project. It's time to see what those sound bites are discussing. At this stage, you'll edit B-roll clips into the project by placing them above the primary storyline, and connected to it.

With these B-roll edits, your editing approach changes to a "lane" above the primary story-line. Clips in a lane outside the primary storyline are vertically connected back to the primary storyline, thereby establishing a synchronized relationship in this project between the sound bite and the B-roll. When Mitch says "helicopter," your audience sees a helicopter.

These connections keep clips synchronized even when a ripple edit occurs in the primary storyline. An upstream ripple that shifts a sound bite's timing in the project will also shift the B-roll clips connected to that sound bite. The connection ensures that the sync is main-tained by shifting the connected clips the same amount. You first establish the connection and then Final Cut Pro maintains it so your focus may be on the rest of the story edit.

In the following exercises, you will connect B-roll clips to the sound bite–driven primary storyline you've already edited. Then, you will trim these connected clips and observe their unique trimming behaviors.

Exercise 4.5.1
Adding and Trimming Connected B-roll

B-roll is the editor's friend. Sometimes referred to as **cutaways**, B-roll clips allow you to smooth out discontinuity in your primary storyline, and in this project, they will help you hide the jump cuts and soften the audio edits made to the sound bites. Furthermore, good B-roll content may also include great natural sound audio, or **nats**. An editor can use the nats to cover a tight audio edit, such as the one you now have with the word "filming."

Let's start by resetting the interface and searching those keywords you applied earlier to quickly locate B-roll of a hangar door opening.

NOTE ▸ For the purpose of training, we'll start at the beginning of the project and continue forward by adding B-roll content. However, your workflow could begin by adding B-roll anywhere within your project.

1   If necessary, reset the interface by choosing the Default Workspace from the Window > Workspaces menu, or press **Command-0**.

2   In the Lifted library's Primary Media event, select the Hangar Keyword Collection.

    To ensure that you are seeing all the hangar clips, double-check the Browser's sorting and filtering options.

3   In the Browser, from the pop-up menu, choose Hide Rejected, and then ensure that the search field is clear of any criteria.

4   From the Clip Appearance pop-up menu in the Browser, set the Zoom control to All, the Group By pop-up to None, and Sort By to Name.

With the environment properly set up, you will search for the first clip of the hangar door opening.

5   In the Lifted library, verify that the four clips are displayed with the Hangar Keyword Collection selected.

The first clip you want is **DN_9390**.

6   Skim the clip to refamiliarize yourself with its contents.

This clip starts in the dark before the hangar door opens. Mitch walks in from the left, crossing to center to preflight the helicopter. The clip is currently 13 seconds long. Let's trim the clip down before connecting it to the primary storyline.

7   In **DN_9390**, mark a start point by pressing the I key after the director says, "Action." Your start point should be at 1:50:43:00.

8   Mark an end point by pressing the O key after Mitch has dropped down to inspect the camera. Your end point should be at 1:50:49:06.

The clip is ready to edit into the project.

9   In the Lifted Vignette project, cue the playhead to the beginning of the Timeline.

Cueing the playhead tells Final Cut Pro where the hangar clip belongs time-wise in the Timeline. In this case, locating that point is easy because it will be the first shot in the project.

You will edit this clip into the project so that we hear Mitch speaking while watching the hangar clip. You can do this by connecting the video clip in a higher lane.

10   In the toolbar, click the Connect button, or press **Q**.

NOTE ▶   If the Connect button is dimmed, reselect the Browser clip.

The hangar clip is stacked into a lane above the first sound bite. Let's review the edit to see the results.

11   Cue the playhead to the beginning of the project, and play the Timeline.

You see the hangar and hear the hangar motor while also hearing Mitch's sound bite. The video hierarchy rule makes the video in a higher lane visible, while mixing and playing all the audio content in the clips.

▶ **Colorful Clips**

Remember the roles you applied to the Browser clips at the end of Lesson 3? Each role and subrole is assigned a customizable color that tints the clip representations in the Timeline. As you progress through this book's exercises, the role each clip plays within your project, especially the audio role, will be visually apparent. Video clips with attached audio are tinted according to the assigned audio role. You'll learn more about the power of roles in Lesson 6.

4.5.1-A Connecting the Second B-roll Clip

As you can see, the **DN_9390** clip extends over the second sound bite. That's OK for now, so let's look at the next B-roll clip to add to the project.

1 In the Browser, skim **DN_9465**.

In this clip, Mitch enters the hangar from the right side, approaches the helicopter, and then kneels to inspect the camera. Although Mitch enters from the opposite side of the hangar, you can set a start point as he's kneeling to inspect the camera. With finessing, this clip can be made to match the previous shot of Mitch approaching the helicopter.

2 In the Browser, mark a start point at 2:37:33:17 when Mitch has started to kneel to inspect the camera.

Now you need to locate the Timeline point at which this clip can be matched to the previous edit.

3   Cue the project playhead over **DN_9390** where Mitch has started to kneel at the heli-
     copter's camera at 00:00:05:07.

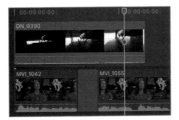

4   Click the Connect button, or press **Q**, to make a connect edit.

The second B-roll clip stacks into a higher lane above the previous edit. When two
connected clips will impact one another, Final Cut Pro automatically avoids a "clip
collision" by moving one of the clips to a different lane. The edit still cuts to the second B-roll clip at the connection point.

5   Review the edit by skimming back to the middle of **DN_9390**, and then pressing **L**.

     Does the action of Mitch kneeling flow from one clip to the other? If not, this situa-
     tion is easily corrected.

6   In the Timeline, select **DN_9465**. Press the **,** (comma) or **.** (period) key to nudge the
     clip left or right, respectively, until the action of Mitch kneeling appears to be one
     smooth movement.

     NOTE ▶ In addition to the **comma** and **period** key shortcuts used to nudge the
     selected clip, you can also try this technique: Cue your playhead to the start of
     DN_9465, nudge the clip, then press Shift-? (question mark) to review the edit using
     the Play Around command.

Once **DN_9465** is in place, you can ripple trim the end of **DN_9390** to lower **DN_9465** into the same lane. Although the video plays as expected, the overlapping audio may not be desirable.

7   Ensure that **snapping** is turned on (the Snapping button in the Timeline is blue).

NOTE ▸ Press **N** to turn snapping on and off.

8   Drag the end point of **DN_9390** to the left until **DN_9465** drops into the same lane.

With **snapping** turned on, the end point of **DN_9390** will snap to the start point of **DN_9465**.

Notice that **DN_9465** extends down the Timeline. We'll trim that clip after connecting a third B-roll clip.

4.5.1-B Connecting the Third B-roll Clip

Let's connect one more B-roll clip before analyzing what you've created.

1   In the project, cue the playhead over clip **MVI_1055** when Mitch says "nobody" at 00:00:09:02.

You're telling Final Cut Pro to make a precise start edit based upon the contents of the primary storyline. Now let's find a clip for that edit.

2   In the Browser, locate clip **DN_9470**, a close-up of Mitch inspecting the camera.

3   Mark a start point about halfway through the clip at 2:41:27:21 as Mitch turns the camera counterclockwise.

4   Set an end point as Mitch's face moves halfway behind the camera at 2:41:30:06.

5   Press **Q** to connect this clip to the primary storyline at the playhead.

Although the edit cuts nicely to the close-up, in your Timeline, **DN_9465** resumes playing after the close-up ends.

6   Trim the end point of **DN_9465** to the start of **DN_9470** so that the two B-roll clips are sequential.

Now **DN_9465** doesn't give an encore performance.

Exercise 4.5.2
Understanding Connected Clip Sync and Trimming Behaviors

Each of the three B-roll clips has a vertical connection point that synchronizes it to the primary storyline. These vertical relationships remain intact even when you alter the primary storyline. Let's see how this works.

In the project, notice the connection points that anchor the B-roll clips to the sound bites in the primary storyline. Those are the connections you established by making a connect edit.

If a sound bite moves within the Timeline, that movement will also be applied to any connected clips.

1   Drag the middle of **MVI_1042** to the right until the clip is located after **MVI_1055**.

Notice that **DN_9390** was relocated with the sound bite, and the other two B-roll clips also slid to the left to remain synchronized with their connected sound bite.

2   Press **Command-Z** to undo the previous edit.

Connected clips are still independent clips that can be moved away from their synchronized, primary storyline clip.

3   Drag the middle of **DN_9465** to the right until it connects after **DN_9470**.

DN_9465 establishes a new connection with the primary storyline.

NOTE ▶ Every clip outside the primary storyline must connect to the primary storyline.

4   Press **Command-Z** to undo the edit.

Final Cut Pro will maintain the synchronization of connected clips until you change the connection point or tell Final Cut Pro to ignore the connection.

4.5.2-A Overriding the Connection

After connecting your B-roll clips, you may realize that you need to move a sound bite elsewhere in the primary storyline, but also need to leave the connected B-roll clips in place. The B-roll story you've created works great, but you've discovered your project is running too long. Or you may want to experiment with a different arrangement of the sound bites without disturbing the B-roll order. You can temporarily suspend a connected clip's sync point while adjusting the primary storyline clip.

1   In the project, position the mouse pointer over **MVI_1055**.

2   Hold down the ` (grave accent) key, and drag **MVI_1055** after the second gap clip.

When you press the grave accent key, the pointer becomes a crossed-out connection symbol. Dragging a clip while holding down the grave accent key tells Final Cut Pro to ignore any connected clips during that edit.

The **DN_9465** and the **DN_9470** B-roll clips remain in place while the sound bite is moved later in the primary storyline. When the move is completed, the **MVI_1055** sound bite slides to the right leaving behind one connected B-roll clip while reattaching to the other at a new connection point.

3   Press **Command-Z** to undo the edit.

Connected clips help your editing by maintaining the sync between clips you established when initially making the edit. Final Cut Pro lets you change your mind while maintaining that sync, or will sync to a different clip if you desire.

4.5.2-B Trimming Connected Clips

Unlike the sound bites in the primary storyline, connected clips are independent of other connected clips and do not have a horizontal relationship with them. As a result, performing a trim edit on a connected clip produces results different from applying a trim edit to a clip in the primary storyline.

1   Place the Select tool over the end point of **DN_9390**.

Notice that a filmstrip does not appear on the trim icon as it would when trimming a clip in the primary storyline. You cannot ripple trim connected clips because no horizontal relationship exists between them.

2   Drag the end point to the left to trim the clip.

Only **DN_9390** was affected by this trim edit.

3   Press **Command-Z** to undo the edit.

This default behavior gives connected clips horizontal independence. So trimming one of two adjacent connected clips will not affect the timing of the second adjacent connected clip. However, you can establish a horizontal relationship between connected clips when necessary.

Reference 4.6
Creating a Connected Storyline

When B-roll clips are connected to the primary storyline, the B-roll takes over the video storytelling of the project. When reviewing the project, you may want to shift the B-roll timing to better align the visuals with the audio-driven storyline. Because each connected clip is independent, trimming one B-roll clip does not ripple trim to affect the others. The vertical relationships of each connected clip isolates it from adjacent clips.

However, an editor may establish relationships between connected clips by placing them within a **connected storyline**. Doing so creates a horizontal relationship between the grouped connected clips, and reduces their individual vertical relationships to a single connection between the connected and primary storylines. Furthermore, by creating a connected storyline, you gain access to several trimming options, such as ripple trim.

A connected storyline is a container that is identified by a gray bar across the top of the grouped clips. This bar is the selection point when you want to apply an edit to a connected storyline rather than apply the edit to the primary storyline.

Creating a connected storyline is as simple as selecting connected clips and instructing Final Cut Pro to group them as a storyline. However, not all connected clips may be added to a group. Only connected clips that can exist in the same lane without overlapping may be converted into a connected storyline.

Exercise 4.6.1
Converting Connected Clips into a Connected Storyline

You can create a connected storyline comprising the first three B-roll clips in two easy steps.

1   Select the three connected B-roll clips at the start of the project.

2   Control-click any one of the three, and from the shortcut menu, choose Create Story-line, or press **Command-G**.

Notice the gray bar above the clips that becomes the outline of a container surrounding the clips. Now that the clips are contained in a storyline, you can ripple trim them.

3   Place the Select tool over the end point of **DN_9390**.

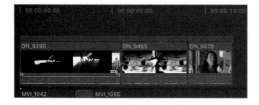

The ripple trim icon appears with the filmstrip.

4 Drag the end point to the left to shorten the clip, but do not release the mouse button yet.

A few things for you to notice. First, the two following B-roll clips ripple along with the trim. The storyline established a horizontal, magnetic relationship similar to the primary storyline clips.

Second, as you ripple trim the edit point, a *two-up display* appears in the Viewer. The area to the left shows the new end point of the hangar door opening clip while the right shows the existing start point of **DN_9465** recorded from under the helicopter. The two-up display allows you to see both sides of the edit so you may match the action between the two clips.

5 Referencing the two-up display, ripple trim the end point of **DN_9390** appearing on the left to match the action appearing on the right in the Viewer's two-up display. You should drag left and right to locate the best match.

Enclosing connected clips in a storyline gives you the advantages of a storyline's magnetic properties when trimming and rearranging the B-roll clips.

Another trim tool similar to ripple trim is roll trim. Whereas ripple trim modifies the duration of one clip (and potentially the project's duration), the roll trim modifies the adjoining points of two clips, not affecting other clips or the total project duration. The roll trim achieves this net-zero duration change by trimming the opposing edit points in opposite directions: inserting frames at one edit point while removing the same number of frames from the adjoining edit point.

In the edit you just completed, the roll trim is handy for fine-tuning the cut's trigger. With the ripple trim, your focus was on continuity of action at the edit. Now that the continuity is in place, you may need to adjust when the cut happens. Should the cut to the shot underneath the helicopter occur as Mitch reaches for the camera, while Mitch is dropping down, or even after Mitch has stopped moving? The roll trim allows you to explore all of those options.

6   From the Tools pop-up menu, choose the Trim tool.

The roll trim function requires that the Trim tool be selected.

7   Place the Trim tool over the edit point between **DN_9390** and **DN_9465**.

With the Trim tool on the edit point, the tool becomes the roll trim, with filmstrips pointing at both clips to indicate that the end point of **DN_9390** and the start of **DN_9465** are about to be changed.

8   Drag to the right until Mitch has squatted down, which you can see in the Viewer two-up.

9   Drag back to the left and decide where within the action to cut between the two clips.

The roll trim allowed you to move the edit to find the best cut point between the two clips. This roll trim and the earlier ripple trim worked because the clips are enclosed in a storyline. Grouping clips together in a connected storyline brings the trimming and magnetic properties of the primary storyline to these clips.

Exercise 4.6.2
Appending Clips to a Connected Storyline

In this exercise, you will create a connected storyline, and append additional B-roll clips to it. This editing method offers the speed and convenience of the batch and ripple trim techniques you previously performed on the primary storyline.

1   Press **A** to return to the Select tool, and in the Libraries sidebar, select the Preflight Keyword Collection.

2   In the Preflight collection, find **DN_9455**.

This clip shows Mitch getting into his helicopter, and is the first of a series of clips depicting the preflight and startup.

3   In **DN_9455**, mark a start point just before Mitch appears in the frame at 02:27:27:11. Set an end point after Mitch is in the helicopter at 02:27:35:20.

Next you need to define where this clip goes timing-wise within the Timeline.

4   In the project, cue the playhead to 00:00:15:17 after Mitch says, "has been shot on the ground."

You'll connect the first clip of this series of B-roll clips at this point.

5   Click the Connect button, or press **Q** to make the edit.

NOTE ▶   To enable the Connect button when it is dimmed, move the mouse pointer back into the Browser to activate the Browser pane.

To quickly set up an append edit for the following B-roll clips, you will convert this one clip into a storyline.

6   Control-click **DN_9455**, and from the shortcut menu, choose Create Storyline, or press **Command-G**.

The clip is now contained in a storyline. To make additional edits to this storyline, you must select the storyline's bar rather than the clip inside.

7   Click the storyline's bar to select it.

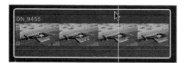

When you select its gray bar, the storyline is outlined in yellow. The goal is to efficiently add the subsequent B-roll clips to the selected storyline.

8   In the Browser, locate **DN_9446**.

9   Mark a start point on the jib's first take of Mitch's feet on the pedals at 02:19:23:06. Set an end point after Mitch has reached for the instrument panel at 02:19:30:12, leaving the clip duration at approximately seven seconds.

10 Press **E** to append this clip to the end of the selected storyline.

You also can batch edit clips into this storyline.

11 Mark the following ranges for each listed clip:

Clip	Start	End	Result
DN_9453	Start of third take tilt/pan on Mitch (2:26:30:00)	End of tilt/pan move to panel (2:26:34:19)	
DN_9454	Two seconds before flips switch and the displays change (2:27:06:18)	Releases switch and hand leaves frame (2:27:10:16)	
DN_9452	Before rotors start turning (2:24:21:00)	End of clip	

After marking these three clips, you can select all three for the append edit into the **DN_9455** and **DN_9446** storyline, which we'll call the preflight storyline.

12 With **DN_9452** still selected, Command-click the ranges you marked for **DN_9454** and **DN_9453** to select the three clip ranges.

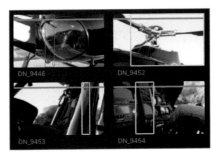

13 In the project, ensure the gray bar of the preflight storyline is still selected.

Make sure you select the gray bar and not **DN_9455** or **DN_9446**.

14 Click the Append button, or press **E**, to append the three clips to the selected, preflight storyline.

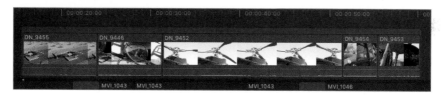

The clips are added to the preflight storyline in the order you selected them.

NOTE ▶ With the Timeline pane active (move the skimmer into the Timeline to make it active), press **Command--** (minus sign) to zoom out the Timeline view.

4.6.2-A Editing Within a Connected Storyline

Because these clips are now inside a storyline, rearranging and ripple trimming them is a breeze.

1 Drag **DN_9452** to the end of the preflight storyline after **DN_9453**.

NOTE ▶ Ensure that you keep **DN_9452** inside the preflight storyline.

Soon, you'll ripple trim each of these storyline clips to reduce their durations. The goal is to finish playing the first four clips in the preflight storyline by the end of the **MVI_1055** sound bite. There's a lot of content to remove!

No joke. **DN_9453** should end a few moments before the end of **MVI_1055**. This is a common editing scenario and the reason why you batch edited the clips into the storyline. The durations you marked earlier in the Browser were set to narrow down the clips to the needed content. But the timing of these clips with the sound bite and to each other is what determines their final durations and positions.

The art of editing is the art of compromise. You need to present just enough information for the viewers to understand the actions they are seeing and tell the story. You want to present these four preflight actions while Mitch is talking about the whole new look of shooting something from the air. When he finishes that statement, the rotors start turning and the helicopter takes off. The compromise to make that edit happen is to adjust the timing of not only these preflight clips to Mitch's sound bites, but also adjust the earlier hangar storyline clips' timing to the sound bites. Don't be afraid to look at previous edits when trying to make up time in a project.

Let's first gain a few seconds by trimming clips in the project's first storyline, the hangar storyline.

2   In the hangar storyline, ripple trim the start point of **DN_9390** so the clip begins with just a sliver of light visible through the hangar door.

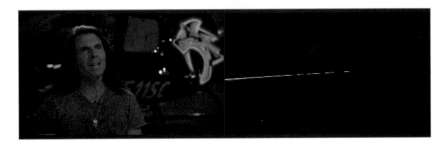

Reference the start frame of **DN_9390** in the Viewer's two-up display.

NOTE ▶ You may need to disable snapping (**N**) to ripple trim to the specific desired frame. Enable snapping after completing the trim.

After trimming the start of **DN_9390**, the start of **MVI_1042** is now visible. You can drag the hangar storyline to realign it with the beginning of the project.

3   Drag the hangar storyline to the beginning of the project.

Remember the gap clip you previously added between the two sound bites at the beginning of the primary storyline? You can gain some additional time by lengthening that gap clip. Increasing its duration allows you to shift the start of the preflight storyline earlier in relation to the sound bite **MVI_1055**.

4   In the primary storyline, drag the end point of the first gap clip to the right to a duration of about 2:15.

NOTE ▶ You may need to disable snapping (**N**) to create the precise desired duration. Then, enable snapping to perform the next step.

The hangar storyline now ends and Mitch's interview video becomes visible as he says, "really ever seen." Mitch needs to be on camera for a short time to accommodate a graphic that you will add in a later lesson, so you'll leave a few seconds of him visible. The preflight storyline can now start a little earlier.

5   Drag the preflight storyline so that its first clip starts at the "standpoint" audio cue (00:00:14:16).

NOTE ► Remember, a quick way to perform this type of edit is to enable snapping, cue the playhead to the audio cue or timecode point, and then drag the storyline until it snaps to the playhead.

That edit gained you another two seconds, more or less. But more trimming is still needed.

DN_9455 is much too long. When you review the clip's content, you see that the real action occurs at the end of the clip when Mitch gets in the helicopter. Cutting the clip duration to that last action will make the shot more interesting and gain you time.

When you trimmed the start of **DN_9390**, you did so using the Select tool and moving the entire storyline to the beginning of the project after the trim. This time, you'll save a step by performing a ripple trim using the Trim tool.

6   From the Tools pop-up menu, choose the Trim tool, or press **T**.

7   Drag the start of **DN_9455** to the right, but don't release the mouse button yet.

As you drag with the Trim tool, the two-up display appears in the Viewer. The area on the right shows the new start point you are setting for **DN_9455** with the Trim tool.

8   While watching the right frame of the Viewer's two-up, drag the start point until you see Mitch stepping on the skid to get in the helicopter. The delta or change length for the trim should be about +5:10. Release the mouse button.

Now you'll trim the end point of **DN_9455** to further tighten the shot.

NOTE ▶   Ensure that the mouse pointer displays the ripple edit, single filmstrip icon to perform this edit. If the ripple edit filmstrip is not visible, click in the empty, gray area of the Timeline to deselect the storyline.

9   Drag the end point of **DN_9455** to the left until the two-up display shows that Mitch just got into the helicopter and lowered his right arm.

NOTE ▶   Don't forget, when you are adding to or removing from a clip, position the Trim tool to see a single filmstrip pointing at the receiving clip.

The end result is a clip just over two seconds long. That's quite a bit of tightening for that clip. Let's shorten **DN_9446** too.

10 Using the Trim tool, drag the start point of **DN_9446** to the right until the two-up display in the Viewer shows the bottom tip of the door at the bottom of the frame.

11 Now trim the end point of **DN_9446** to realize an overall clip duration of two seconds.

NOTE ▶ Don't forget to disable or enable snapping using the **N** key, when necessary.

The next clip should be **DN_9453** followed by **DN_9454**. Because these two clips are inside a storyline, this involves only a simple rearrangement of the two clips.

12 Switch to the Select tool, and then drag **DN_9453** left to insert the clip before **DN_9454**.

13 Staying on **DN_9453**, trim the start point to where Mitch is centered in the image and starts to reach forward.

14 Trim the end point to a clip duration of around 1:18, the point at which Mitch's fingers have landed on a switch.

To create the pacing and the feel that Mitch is starting the engine, you will cut from this movement to a closer "throwing the switch" shot.

15 In **DN_9454**, trim the start point to where Mitch's hand is still open before pointing and throwing the switch.

NOTE ► This may require dragging to the left to add frames.

16 Trim the end point to realize about a 1:10 clip duration ending while Mitch is holding the switch.

Finally, you'll trim the clip of the helicopter rotors starting to move.

17 Trim **DN_9452**'s start point so the rotors have already started to turn. Trim the end point to a clip duration of about two seconds. Review the edit.

You've completed your assembly of the preflight storyline. Now, you'll make an edit pass to check for mistimed clips and to ensure that the storyline fits the timing of the sound bite. Here are just a few items to check:

▶   **DN_9454** should end align to the end of **MVI_1055**. Some additional frames may be added to the end of this clip to emphasize the switch activation.

▶   A continuity issue exists in the edit between **DN_9446** and **DN_9453**. Mitch reaches for the instrument panel with his right arm and then his left arm. You can remove frames from the end of **DN_9446** to avoid seeing his arm or add frames to show Mitch lowering his right arm.

18 Continue to adjust your edits as necessary to achieve this alignment while tweaking the other edits.

You have just one more B-roll storyline to go!

4.6.2-B Creating and Editing the Third Connected Storyline

Use the following table to select and trim clips for the third storyline, takeoff. You will use the rating system to gather the clips.

> **NOTE ►** Don't forget that you have two events in the Lifted library that contain clips for this project. Also remember that dragging a range point displays the range's duration.

1 Mark each clip as detailed in the following table, and apply the favorite rating (**F**) to each:

Clip	Keyword	Start	End	Result
DN_9463	Takeoff	As forward movement begins (02:36:05:16)	Exits frame (02:36:08:11)	
DN_9415	In Flight	A second before the mountain is behind the helicopter (01:58:30:17)	Duration of five seconds	
GOPR1857	In Flight	Two seconds before Mitch stretches his arm out behind the seat (24:05) (An existing favorite overlaps this range and is discussed in step 3.)	Duration of five seconds	
IMG_6493	Flight Controls	Before 1st long, lensflare ends (20:23)	Before tilt up to follow hand (25:14)	

Clip	Keyword	Start	End	Result
GOPR3310	In Flight	Last third of clip; before Mitch leans forward into sunlight (32:00)	Duration of five seconds	
DN_9503	In Flight	Helicopter behind tree (03:22:36:18)	Helicopter exits frame (03:22:42:07)	
DN_9420	In Flight	Helicopter is just off screen (02:02:04:00)	Helicopter exits frame (02:02:10:00)	

Now that you've marked the clips, you'll batch connect them to the project. However, when you are in the Primary Media event, the GoPro event clips are not visible. Selecting the Lifted library reveals all the clips from all events in the library.

2   In the Libraries sidebar, select the Lifted library.

Now you see all of the clip, but you still need to cull down that display a little bit, which you already did somewhat by favoriting the clips you marked. The library has a prebuilt Smart Collection to help cull the library.

3   Inside the Lifted library's Smart Collections folder, click the Favorites Smart Collection.

The sound bites you previously marked as favorites are displayed along with the B-roll clips you need. Only the favorited range of each clip is displayed, which includes **GOPR1857** that appears with a rather long favorite and a small marked range. The marked range shown is what you favorited just moments ago. That range lives inside a pre-existing favorite range for the clip. Ratings do not overlap. The favorite you marked for this storyline edit will be absorbed into the existing favorite if you click outside that range.

With the favorites visible, you'll batch edit these to the Lifted Vignette project.

4   Click to select **DN_9463**, the first clip in the previous table.

5   Command-click the additional B-roll clips in the order that they are listed in the table.

6   In the project, press the Up Arrow and Down Arrow keys to cue the playhead immediately after **DN_9452**, if necessary.

You will perform a connect edit first to place these clips in the project, and then group these clips into a connected storyline.

7   Click the Connect button, or press **Q**, to connect edit the selected clips into the project. Press **Shift-Z** to fit the project within the Timeline.

Now that the clips are part of the project, you can group them into a connected storyline.

8 In the project, select the connected clips you just added. Control-click any one of the selected clips, and from the shortcut menu, choose Create Storyline, or press **Command-G**.

The clips are grouped into a connected storyline, the third such storyline in your project, which we'll refer to as the Takeoff storyline.

You have two more B-roll clips to add. You also have some very loud nats on a couple of B-roll clips, but let's take a break from B-roll to add a music clip, and align some edits to it.

Reference 4.7
Editing Below the Primary Storyline

Audio clips are typically edited "below the line," meaning physically beneath the video clips. In Final Cut Pro, you may place audio clips below or above the primary storyline. The vertical positioning of audio clips is not as critical as when prioritizing video clips because Final Cut Pro mixes together all audio clips—such as sound effects and music— and plays them simultaneously.

Exercise 4.7.1
Connecting a Music Clip

For this first rough cut, you will include a music clip that plays in the background during the entire edit. The music contains an apex moment towards the end that you will synchronize with a specific clip.

1 In the Lifted library's Audio Only Smart Collection, select the **Tears of Joy-Short** clip.

2   With the playhead cued to the beginning of the project, click the Connect button, or
    press **Q**.

    The music clip is added to the beginning of the project. The music will be a little too
    loud, or *hot*. You can adjust its volume level in the Timeline. Every audio clip has a
    volume control: a black horizontal line that overlays the clip's audio waveforms.

3   Move the Select tool over the volume control in the **Tears of Joy-Short** music clip.

    The current volume level setting appears as 0 dB (decibels), which means that Final
    Cut Pro currently plays the clip at its original volume level.

4   Drag the Volume control down to around –15 dB to play the music clip at 15 dB
    below its original recorded level.

    NOTE ▸ Hold down the Command key while dragging the Volume control for
    greater precision.

    As with all the other clips, this is not the final volume setting for the music. This was
    simply a "sanity" adjustment so the rest of the audio clips are audible while editing.
    There is more audio work to be done.

Reference 4.8
Finessing the Rough Cut

Your project is racing to the end of this phase of the workflow. The details and adjustments you need to perform become more granular as you finish addressing the major editorial issues. You may still perform some major changes, but you should now see the light
shining at the end of this editorial tunnel. At this stage, a project generally needs audio

adjustments and a bit more trimming. By now, your project is definitely ready for a run-through with the slip trim.

The slip trim changes the content within the clip container. You change the start and end points of the content simultaneously, revealing earlier or later source materials without changing the clip's duration or position in the project. Think of the clip as your iPhone and the clip content as the photos on your iPhone. When you want to see earlier photos, you swipe with your finger from left to right to pull the earlier photos into view. The reverse to see later content is to swipe right to left to pull that content into view.

Dragging right to slip earlier content into view

While performing a slip trim, the two-up display of the new start and end points appears in the Viewer. The two-up display shows your changes in real time as you drag the slip trim across the clip. When you release the mouse button, the clip is already updated in the project.

You may also slip trim audio-only clips. However, for smoothing out audio edits at this stage of the workflow, adding some transitions and audio fade handles will do the job. Every clip that contains audio content has fade handles to create audio envelopes for ramping. You can create ramps to soften the audio edits and avoid calling attention to the edit with an abrupt audio change.

Your project has a basic music bed, the B-roll edits, and even the sound bites generally positioned and somewhat trimmed. For this first rough cut, you will adjust some clip positions and timings to coincide with the music clip's major moments.

Exercise 4.8.1
Adjusting the Edits

In **DN_9420**, the sunset shines dramatically through the helicopter's windows, and during the clip, the music **swells** to a climax. But you can do better. In this exercise, you will align those audiovisual moments for maximum effect.

1　In the project, select **DN_9420**, and skim to the first frame of the sun coming through the helicopter windows.

You'll set a **marker** to identify the visual cue of the sunlight through the windows that you want to align to the music swell.

2   Press **M** to set a **marker** at that dramatic visual moment.

A marker appears along the clip's upper edge.

Now you need to set a **marker** on the music swell. Unfortunately, it's a little hard to hear while the sound bite is playing.

3   Select the music clip, and then click the **Solo** button, or press **Option-S**.

Only the selected audio clip is audible and in full color, while the nonselected clips' audio is muted and desaturated in the interface.

Now that you can hear the music clearly, you'll place a marker on the music swell.

4   Using the Select tool, click the music clip, skim to the music swell at 00:00:54:21, and press **M** to set a marker.

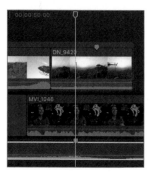

5   With the marker set, click the Solo button again, or press **Option-S**, to disable the Solo function.

Now the task is to align those two markers. You'll perform two edits with the ripple trim: shortening the B-roll and extending the last gap clip to align the music swell with the sunset.

6   Ripple trim to remove a few frames from each clip of the takeoff storyline. Your goal is to move the sunset marker closer to the music swell.

Here are some trim points to consider:

▶   Start of **DN_9463**: Could the helicopter be farther along the ramp? Use the Trim tool or you'll need to reposition the storyline after any adjustment to this point.

▶   **DN_9415**: Don't trim too much here. This is a "landscape" shot that needs time for the viewer to gain perspective, but you could tighten the shot a bit.

▶   Start of **GOPR1857**: Trim to just before Mitch turns his head and stretches his arm out.

These edits should get you very close to aligning the markers.

7   Also using the ripple trim, push the last sound bite farther out by lengthening the gap clip. Insert enough frames so that the last sound bite starts at 00:00:59:00, after the music restarts.

You can finish aligning the two markers using one or both of the following methods: ripple trim more of the earlier B-roll clips, or slip edit the content of **DN_9420**.

4.8.1-A Using the Slip Edit

The slip edit is a safe edit for setting the B-roll clips to their best content without disturbing other edits.

1   From the Tools pop-up menu, choose the Trim tool, or press **T**.

2 Move the Trim tool over the middle of **DN_9420**.

The Slip tool appears.

3 With snapping (**N**) enabled, drag inside **DN_9420** until the marker aligns to the music marker.

While dragging with the slip trim, a two-up display of **DN_9420** appears in the Viewer.

The image on the left shows the start point of the clip, while the right image shows the end point. The start and end points are updating in real time as you drag the slip trim. Although not particularly needed for this edit, the two-up display is great for ensuring that the best content is included between the displayed start and end points.

4 With the two markers aligned, play the entire project, slip trim at the ready, evaluating whether the B-roll clips are displaying their best content within their current durations. You may want to do so with your speaker/headphone volume lowered.

While you review the project, ask questions about the effectiveness of your results. Can you avoid the lens flare in the instrument/GPS panel shot? Should there be more lens flare content? Should the project show less of Mitch leaning back and pointing out the side window, or should you slip the clip to include Mitch pointing out the front?

▶ **Checkpoint 4.8.1**

Refer to Appendix C for details on reviewing a Checkpoint.

Exercise 4.8.2
Adjusting Clip Volume Levels

The two basic rules of mixing audio are: Don't **peak** the **meters**, and if it doesn't sound good, change it. That change should not be a knee-jerk reaction. Don't get in the trap of continuing to boost the volume of a clip to make it louder than the other clips. If the sound bites are too quiet, you don't necessarily crank up the sound bites. Maybe you need to turn down the volume of the music or B-roll **nats**.

In this exercise, you will perform some simple volume level adjustments to ensure that the sound bites are clearly audible, and that the overall audio mix does not reach up to 0 dB on the Audio meters. A safe target is to not allow any of your loudest audio to go above –6 dB on the meters.

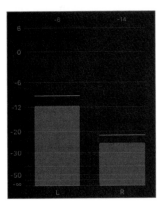

The Audio meters in Final Cut Pro
averaging a good, safe -12 dB playback level

1   In the Dashboard, click the Audio Meter button.

The larger Audio meters open to the right of the Timeline. Although you'll delve deeper into audio mixing in Lesson 6, right now you just want to ensure that during playback your audio levels don't peak at or beyond the 0 dB level on the meters.

A few minutes ago, you changed the volume of a single music clip. When you want to change the volume levels of multiple clips at once, you can use a keyboard shortcut.

2   In the takeoff storyline, select all the B-roll clips.

NOTE ▶   Remember, you may click **DN_9463** and then Shift-click **DN_9420** to make the selection.

3   While watching the clips' volume controls, press **Control--** (minus sign) and **Control-=** (equals sign) to lower and raise the volumes of the selected clips.

Each shortcut key press lowers or raises the playback volume level of the selected clips by 1 dB. As these clips have wildly different audio content, you should adjust only one or a few at a time.

4   Play through the entire project, listening to the mix while watching the Audio meters. Select a clip or multiple clips, and drag the volume control or press the shortcut keys so you can clearly hear Mitch talking, and also to keep the Audio meters below –6 dB.

The peak indicators, the thin lines left over from the highest meter reading, should not go much over –6 dB.

NOTE ▶   You'll modify the sound bites in Lesson 6 so Mitch can be heard in both the Left and Right outputs.

▶ **Know Your Volume Controls**

When dealing with audio, always remember that you have access to at least two volume controls. The volume level controls internal to Final Cut Pro are the only ones that affect your audience. Turning down your Mac computer's volume or external speaker volume control does not affect the audio volume in Final Cut Pro.

The built-in Mac speakers are good quality for a computer, but they won't do the job for professional editing. At the very least, you'll want to have good over-the-ear studio headphones, and at best, powered near-field loudspeakers. Audio monitoring equipment is a key investment that will add immeasurably to your final output's quality. Just because you're not listening on good equipment doesn't mean others won't either; viewers with high-quality equipment will probably notice audio issues you couldn't even hear.

Exercise 4.8.3
Connecting Two Additional B-Roll Clips

To complete this rough cut's B-roll edits, you've got two concluding B-roll clips to add. Currently, the sunset shines through the helicopter's windows at the **music swell** and **grand pause**. Then the music starts again, and Mitch begins his last sound bite. Time to land the helicopter "at the end of the day," and to fly off into the sunset when remembering the day's adventures.

1   In the GoPro event, locate a clip assigned the Landing keyword.

Looking in the Landing Keyword Collection of the GoPro event, you find **GOPR0009**.

2   In the Browser, skim to where the helicopter is completely visible in the frame, and
mark a start point (00:00:07:24).

Although you just trimmed this clip, its duration is still almost 30 seconds. You might
need only 10 of those seconds.

3   Skim **GOPR0009** and set an end point as the helicopter touches down (00:00:17:28).

The duration should now be roughly 10 seconds.

4   Using the connect edit method of your choice, connect edit the landing clip to the
primary storyline about where the music restarts at 00:00:58:16. This will also be just
as or slightly before Mitch starts talking. Play the results.

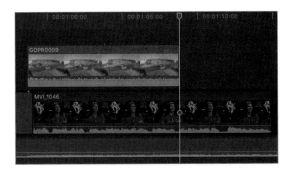

This edit feels choppy because the sunset clip cuts to black followed by another clip cutting in from black. Before fixing that, you have one more clip to edit into the project.

5   In the Browser, search for an In Flight B-roll clip that shows the helicopter flying off
into the sunset. You should find **DN_9424**.

6 You will later trim this clip in the Timeline to get it just right, but for now, set a start point before the helicopter enters the frame (02:05:51:06). You want that action to happen just as Mitch is finishing his last sound bite.

7 Connect edit **DN_9424**, "flying into the sunset," just as Mitch is saying at 00:01:14:13, "Adventure I went on." Trim the clip to end with the music.

That works. To finish with this clip, give its content some breathing room by adding several seconds to the clip's start.

8 Drag the start point of **DN_9424**, and extend the start point to the left to when Mitch says, "Wow."

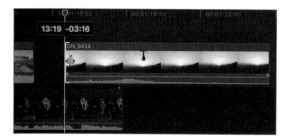

9 Since you just added these two clips, take a moment to adjust their audio levels to more closely match the previous adjustments you made to the other clips.

Great! All the clips for your first edit are in your project. A final refinement pass will soften some not-so-clean edits.

► **Checkpoint 4.8.3**

Refer to Appendix C for details on reviewing a Checkpoint.

Exercise 4.8.4
Refining Edits Using Cross Dissolves and Fade Handles

Some of your audio edits may contain a click or pop at their start or end points. Every clip that has audio has the potential to "catch a click." A quick solution is to rapidly fade the audio in or out using a technique called **ramping**.

► **Catch a Click**

Pleasant-sounding audio travels in a sine wave with a peak and a trough per cycle.

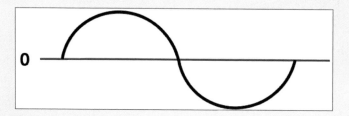

Each cycle of the waveform traverses the zero crossing point two times as the soundwave peaks and then goes down to the trough and then repeats. When an audio clip has a start point that catches the audio soundwave anywhere other than at zero, you may hear a click as the playhead grabs on to the soundwave in progress.

1   At the end of the first sound bite, move your pointer over the audio waveform of **MVI_1042**.

Two fade handles, or "birds-eyes," appear at the ends of the clip. These envelope handles allow you to quickly or gradually ramp the audio into or out of the edit.

2   Move your pointer over the ending fade handle.

When positioned over the handle, the pointer changes to a pair of arrowheads pointing left and right.

NOTE ▶ If you have difficulty seeing the fade handles, use the Clip Appearance button at right to increase the clip height. Also, you may select a larger waveform presentation.

3   Drag the fade handle to the left about five frames.

The number of frames to move is dependent upon how tight the edit is against "kid." You do not want to cut off the last word Mitch says.

4   Position the pointer over the beginning of the next sound bite.

5   Drag the fade handle right from the start point to add a small ramp into the clip's audio.

The clicks and pops are fading away. These audio ramps also soften the clip's entry and exit. When an audio clip was recorded in a noisy environment, a cut into or out of the clip will make the edit undesirably obvious as the noise pops into or out of the mix. In addition to audio edits, let's soften some video edits. A fade-in is not necessarily required if your edit starts with black. But the sunset clip definitely needs an easy, blending transition in and out.

For now, you will use a keyboard shortcut to apply the default transition: cross dissolve. When placed between two clips, a cross dissolve transition blends two images together by varying their levels of transparency. One appears to fade away while the other appears to fade into view. When applied to a single edge of a clip that does not adjoin another clip, the **Command-T** cross dissolve will either fade the clip in from black or fade out to black. A few cross dissolves placed into your project will smooth the clips' entries and exits.

6　Using the Select tool, click the start point of **DN_9420**, and press **Command-T** to add a cross dissolve.

A cross dissolve with a one-second duration blends the previous shot into the sunset shot. This sets up the shot and begins to slow down the pacing for the ending segment.

While you may apply many transition types and customizations here, let's add a few more cross dissolves to your project.

7　Select the end point of **DN_9420**, and press **Command-T**.

8　Select the start point of the **GOPR0009** clip, and press **Command-T**.

NOTE ► Connected clips are automatically placed within a connected storyline when a transition is applied.

9   Review this transition by playing the project.

Notice that while the video is fading in from black, a momentary cut to Mitch on-camera appears as the helicopter landing clip continues to fade in. This occurs because the Mitch clip starts while the transition from black is still in progress.

10 Lengthen the gap clip to push Mitch's sound bite, **MVI_1046**, to start after the transition is completed.

Now Mitch doesn't make a surprise appearance during the landing. So far, you've applied one transition at a time. As easy as it is, selecting single points is tedious. Fortunately, you can apply a transition to both points of the same clip at once.

11 In the project, select the **DN_9424** clip, and press **Command-T**.

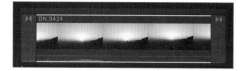

A cross dissolve is applied to both edit points, but the ending dissolve should be a little longer than the default duration of one second.

12 Place your pointer over the left edge of the transition in the project.

The pointer becomes a resize icon without a filmstrip. This allows you to set the transition's duration.

13 Drag the transition's start edge to the left away from the transition's center until the duration info indicates two seconds.

Now you have a slower fade to black at the end of the project.

14 Review your project, looking and listening for edits that could be softened with a cross dissolve or audio ramp. A quick tip while you are reviewing: When it comes to video transitions, less is more.

NOTE ▶ You'll learn more about mixing audio and working with transitions in later lessons.

With a few audio ramps and a couple of video cross dissolves, your rough cut is ready to show to the client.

Reference 4.9
Sharing Your Progress

When a project is ready to be shared, the project is exported from Final Cut Pro. The Share pop-up menu includes several preset **destinations** for many popular delivery platforms.

The preset destinations include desktop formats such as Apple ProRes and H.264 as well as iOS devices; DVD/Blu-ray; and online services such as YouTube, Vimeo, and Facebook. These presets may be customized and additional presets added to this list within preferences. The destinations are even more customizable through the use of Compressor, the Apple batch transcoding application available in the App Store.

> **NOTE ▶** Due to copyright restrictions, you cannot use the supplied media materials for any purpose other than performing the exercises in this book.

Exercise 4.9.1
Sharing an iOS-Compatible File

You've done a lot in this first edit of Lifted Vignette. In this and the previous lessons, you've gone through a typical post-production workflow using Final Cut Pro. Although it's not perfect, this rough cut must be shown to the client, the producer, or your colleagues attending an upcoming lunch meeting. The following exercise briefly describes exporting your project to a media file that is playable on a Mac, PC, smartphone, or tablet. Such media files are also acceptable for upload to most popular online video-hosting services.

1   With the Lifted Vignette project open, ensure that no clip or range is selected in the project by pressing **Command-Shift-A**.

This keyboard shortcut deselects any selected items and clears any marked ranges, which is important because Final Cut Pro will share a range if one is selected instead of the entire Timeline.

2   In the toolbar, click the Share button.

The Share Project pop-up menu appears with a list of preset destinations. Most of these presets focus on delivering high-definition content to online hosting sites or to desktop, portable, and handheld devices. For this exercise, let's create a file that we can AirPlay to the conference room's projector by way of an Apple TV.

3   From the list of destinations, choose Apple Devices 720p.

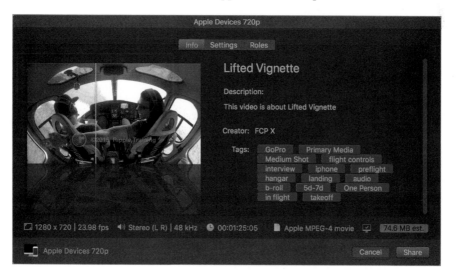

The Share dialog that appears contains five main elements: a skimmable preview area to verify the content for export; Info, Settings, and Roles panes; and a File inspector that summarizes the exporting file's settings.

The Info pane displays the metadata that will be embedded into the file. This metadata will be visible in the exported media file's Info inspector when it is opened in QuickTime Player.

4   Set the following metadata information:

▶   Title: *Lifted-Rough Cut*

▶   Description: *A helicopter pilot and cinematographer describes his passion for sharing aerial cinematography.*

▶   Creator: [insert your name]

▶   Tags: *aerial cinematography, helicopters, aviation*

NOTE ▶ To enter the tag "tokens," type the tag's text followed by a comma, or press Return to close each tag.

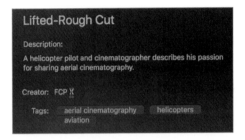

5   After entering the metadata, click the Settings tab to modify the file's delivery options.

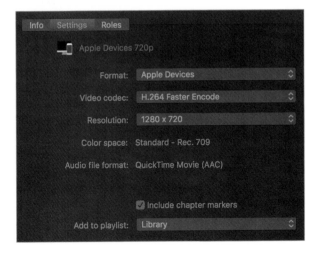

By default, the selected destination preset automatically saves the file to your iTunes Library. You may alter this behavior in the "Add to playlist" pop-up menu.

6   From the "Add to playlist" pop-up menu, choose "Open with QuickTime Player."

NOTE ▶   If the Open With option lists another application, choose Other from the Open With list, select QuickTime Player from the Applications folder, and then click Open.

7   In the Settings pane, verify the "Add to playlist" line has converted to "Open with QuickTime Player."

8   Click Next.

9   In the Save As dialog, enter *Lifted-Rough Cut*, if necessary, and from the Where pop-up menu, choose Desktop. Click Save.

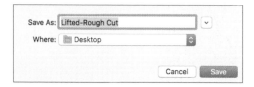

The Background Tasks button displays the progress of the share.

When the file has been shared, the file automatically opens into QuickTime Player and a macOS notification appears.

NOTE ▶ The QuickTime Inspector window is available by pressing Command-I in the QuickTime Player application.

10 Play the movie file in QuickTime Player.

If the file looks and sounds as expected, you're ready to AirPlay to an Apple TV.

11 To the right of the QuickTime Player transport controls, click the AirPlay pop-up menu.

12 From the list that appears, select the networked Apple TV to begin broadcasting the shared file to the Apple TV–connected display/projector.

In addition to streaming to an Apple TV, a shared file may be uploaded to cloud-based services such as iCloud, Dropbox, Frame.io, or YouTube. Many distribution options are available within Final Cut Pro and even more are available in Compressor and macOS.

Congratulations on completing the first edit of the Lifted Vignette project. You have gone from nothing to a rough edit in a brief period of time. You created a project and learned the various edit commands of append, insert, and connect to get clips into a project. Rearranging clips in the primary storyline introduced you to the magnetic properties of a storyline. For the B-roll, you created connected storylines and then used a variety of tools for trimming clips, softening the edits, and adjusting the audio levels. Finally, you discovered some ways to share the project out of Final Cut Pro. No matter which projects you will edit in the future, you will edit every one of them using this same import, edit, and share workflow.

Lesson Review

1. What do Automatic Settings do when creating a new project?

2. Where are projects stored?

3. Which edit command is depicted in the following figure?

4. Which edit command is depicted in the following figure?

5. Which toolbar button performs an append edit?

6. What do the green-, blue-, and purple-colored stripes overlaying a Browser clip identify?

7. When in filmstrip view, which modifier key do you hold down to edit clips into the project in the order that you selected the clips in the Browser?

8. When performing an insert edit, what marks the Timeline location for the edit: the playhead or the skimmer?

9. Identify the edit type used in the following figure.

10. Which two interface items provide additional skimming precision in the Browser?

11. In the following figure, what does the Viewer overlay indicate?

12. With the primary storyline determining a project's timing, what generic clip can be inserted to "create" time between storyline clips?

13. In the scenario shown below, what type of edit was performed in one command?

Before

After

14. In the following figures, identify the edit functions indicated by the mouse pointer.

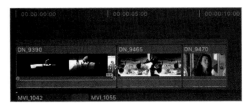

A

B

C

15. To append edit a clip into a connected storyline, what must you select and not select before pressing E?

16. In the following figure, what does the –15 dB indicate?

17. Which interface element displays the Audio meters?

18. Describe what will occur during playback of the following transition.

19. Which interface element lets you export an iOS-compatible file of your project?

Answers

1. They conform the project's resolution and frame rate to the first video clip added to the project.

2. Projects are stored within a designated event.

3. Append edit

4. Insert edit

5. The Append edit button

6. Favorite, user-applied keyword, and analysis keyword

7. Command

8. The skimmer, if active; otherwise, the playhead

9. Ripple edit

10. The Clip Appearance options for clip height and zoom, which allow you to see more clip content vertically and horizontally, respectively.

11. The playhead or skimmer is cued to the start frame of a clip.

12. A gap clip

13. Replace with gap edit (keyboard shortcut: Shift-Delete)

14. A: Ripple; B: Roll; and C: Slip

15. The connected storyline's gray bar must be selected, but any clip inside the connected storyline must not be selected.

16. The audio volume control has been lowered to play the audio clip –15 dB quieter than the audio clip's recorded level.

17. The Audio Meter button in the Dashboard

18. The **GOPR0009** clip will fade in from black, but halfway through the transition, Mitch's interview will suddenly cut in and be visible until the GoPro clip becomes fully opaque.

19. The Share pop-up menu

Lesson 5
Revising the Edit

GOALS

- ▶ Define and distinguish the two types of project duplication
- ▶ Utilize the "Lift from Storyline" command
- ▶ Harness Finder tags as Keyword Collections
- ▶ Understand the replace edit options
- ▶ Use markers for clip synchronization and task notes
- ▶ Perform non-magnetic editing with the Overwrite command and Position tool
- ▶ Create and edit with an audition clip
- ▶ Understand the similarities and differences between skimming and clip skimming
- ▶ Define and distinguish the status of solo'd clips and clips assigned a deactivated role
- ▶ Refine clip duration using trim to playhead and trim to selection
- ▶ Expand experience with the edit options available using the Select and Trim tools

The second editing pass is all about implementing changes: the notes from the producer, comments from the client, issues you notice after getting some sleep and taking a fresh look. One or all of these feedback channels will influence the choices you make during this second pass. Editing is all about resolving creative differences, making compromises, and balancing art and reality. Speaking of reality, you also have a schedule and a budget to meet. How creative can you be in X number of days with only Y dollars?

Since our sample client is imaginary, let's be optimistic. Happily, the notes you've received commend you for a "nice job" on the first edit of Lifted Vignette. The client likes the edit; so much so, they have ideas—one of which is excellent. The client located some aerial clips that weren't submitted. He would like you to work in some of those aerial shots and make the project a little longer.

In this lesson, you'll explore a different workflow for the primary storyline. Although you could leave the primary storyline as-is for this revision, let's explore the tools and features that allow you to change, shift, and regroup your previous edits. You will change the driving content of the primary storyline to a longer cut of the music while creating a relationship between the music and sound bites. You'll incorporate some gyro-stabilized aerial footage to visually support the sound bites. Adding more good music and B-roll will allow you to spread out the sound bite sections a little and open up some breathing room.

While performing this second pass, you will learn about replace edits, auditions, and trimming to the playhead or a range. It sounds like a lot to explore, but these tools are easy to learn and a snap to use. All the metadata organization you did earlier will pay off. In addition, the Magnetic Timeline, connected clips, and storylines allow you to experiment with story flow and make big structural changes easily and painlessly. Once again, Final Cut Pro lets you focus on the artistic aspect of storytelling by helping you execute the technical aspects.

Reference 5.1
Versioning a Project

Before you begin a rework of the rough cut, we need to discuss versioning, which is simply copying or duplicating a backup version of your project. You could do this regularly at editing milestones (rough draft, musical edit, color grading) to create a just-in-case backup copy, or when you wish to experiment and want to preserve a "safe" version of the previous edit. Final Cut Pro allows you to make as many versions as you need to complete your project, creating either a snapshot or a duplicate.

5.1-A Duplicate Project as Snapshot

The favored method for its speed and simplicity, creating a snapshot is like taking a digital picture of your project. A snapshot is a unique "freeze" of the project at the time the snapshot was made. That freeze may represent a milestone moment you want to save. Or a snapshot may be used as a creative or experimentation edit, leaving the original project safe and sound. The contents of the snapshot are independent of changes made to the project and any duplicate versions of the project.

The text "Snapshot" is auto-appended to the project name.

5.1-B Duplicate Project

A duplicate is a little more robust and lively. When a project is duplicated, there are special situations where a change to a specific clip type (compound clips, for example) affects the same clip in the other versions, but not the snapshots.

Exercise 5.1.1
Snapshotting a Project

Your project has reached the first edit milestone. You are ready to dissect it in some areas and build the next version. But first, you will make a snapshot to back up this version of the project for later reference.

1   In the Lifted library's Projects Smart Collection, locate the Lifted Vignette project.

2   Control-click (or right-click) the Lifted Vignette project. From the shortcut menu, choose "Duplicate Project as Snapshot" to create a current snapshot of your project.

3   Click the name of the snapshot, and rename the snapshot *Lifted Vignette - Rough Cut,* then press Return.

You can continue editing with the Lifted Vignette project with the knowledge that you have this and future snapshots as points of return in case the client changes his mind or an editorial "inspiration" hits a dead end.

Reference 5.2
Lifting from a Storyline

In a second pass edit, the editing needs can vary widely. The first edit may have nailed what the client wanted, so you can jump right to cleaning up the edit and exporting for distribution. More commonly, you'll embark on a second pass edit that may require some editorial changes, possibly major, which reroute the flow of the piece. Whichever editing strategy you must accept during the second edit, Final Cut Pro will keep everything in sync. The Magnetic Timeline, connected clips, and storylines you created during the first pass will pay off when you're moving and refining elements in this second pass.

Sound bites replaced with music in primary storyline

The music and sound bites will drive this second edit. Because you are going to explore a variation of the workflow, you will lift the sound bites out of the primary storyline, and replace them with a longer version of Tears of Joy. Even this somewhat radical change will be surprisingly easy because Final Cut Pro will maintain the sync of all the connected clips and storylines.

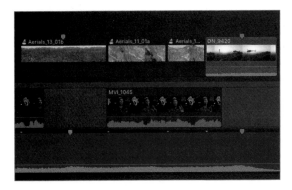

Additional B-roll in the form of connected audition clips

You will add the aerial media depicting expansive landscapes: shots that scream out for the **crescendo** of a musical score. You'll see how weaving sound and image together in Final Cut Pro can be a joy for the editor.

Exercise 5.2.1
Lifting Clips Out of a Storyline

Replacing primary storyline sound bites with music sounds like a daunting task, but have no worries. Final Cut Pro will do the hard work for you.

1   In the primary storyline, select **MVI_1042**, the first sound bite, and then Shift-click the last sound bite, **MVI_1046**, to select all the sound bites and gap clips.

2   Control-click any one of the selected sound bites, and from the shortcut menu, choose Lift from Storyline.

The sound bites and gap clips move out of the primary storyline, and into a new connected storyline that we'll call the "sound bite storyline." In their places, one big gap clip is placed inside the primary storyline. As you learned earlier, Final Cut Pro avoids clip collisions by pushing the existing second lane clips and storylines up to the third lane. The project plays back in the Viewer exactly as it did before the lift edit. Now your project is ready to receive the new music into the primary storyline.

Reference 5.3
Replacing a Clip

Sometimes a clip doesn't work out, and must be replaced with another clip. Or perhaps a structural change requires exchanging one clip for another. Final Cut Pro includes five versions of the replace edit. Right now, we'll discuss the top three: Replace, Replace from Start, and Replace from End. All three commands become choices when you drag a replacement clip to a project clip.

The Replace command places the marked duration of the Browser clip into the storyline. If the Browser clip is longer than the project clip it's replacing, the project clip expands to receive the longer clip. If the Browser clip is shorter, the project clip's duration decreases.

Replace Edit

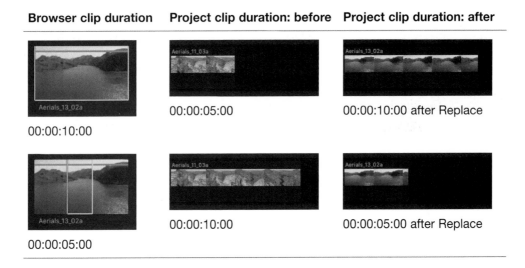

Browser clip duration	Project clip duration: before	Project clip duration: after
00:00:10:00	00:00:05:00	00:00:10:00 after Replace
00:00:05:00	00:00:10:00	00:00:05:00 after Replace

"Replace from Start" and "Replace from End" place the Browser clip within the duration of the current project clip. If the Browser clip is longer than the project clip, the Browser clip is truncated. "Replace from Start" aligns the start points of the two clips, and then truncates the end of the Browser clip. "Replace from End" aligns the end points and then truncates the start of the clip.

Replace from Start and Replace from End

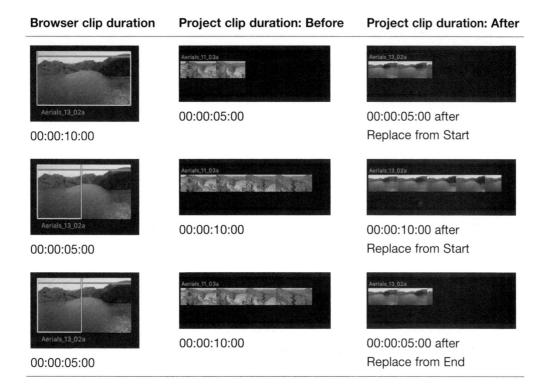

Browser clip duration	Project clip duration: Before	Project clip duration: After
00:00:10:00	00:00:05:00	00:00:05:00 after Replace from Start
00:00:05:00	00:00:10:00	00:00:10:00 after Replace from Start
00:00:05:00	00:00:10:00	00:00:05:00 after Replace from End

If the Browser clip has insufficient content to fill out any of the replace edits, Final Cut Pro performs a ripple trim, shortening the clip. If source media is available in the clip beyond the selected range, that extra media is used to avoid shortening the clip.

Exercise 5.3.1
Replacing the Primary Storyline

You've already lifted the sound bites out of the primary storyline. Let's first delete the old music, and get ready to add the longer version.

1 In the Lifted Vignette project, select the existing music clip, and then press **Delete**.

The shorter music clip is now gone. The project is ready for the new, longer music clip, which will replace the primary storyline's gap clip.

2 In the Lifted library, select the Audio Only Smart Collection and locate **Tears Of Joy-Long**.

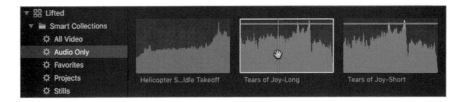

3 Drag the **Tears of Joy-Long** music clip from the Browser to the gap clip in the primary storyline. When the gap clip is highlighted in white, release the mouse button.

4   A shortcut menu appears. Because you want the entire music clip used for this replace edit, choose Replace from the shortcut menu. Play the project to hear the results.

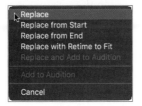

The gap clip is replaced. You now have a new score for your project, and a loud score it is. You can fix that quickly.

5   Lower the volume level of the new music clip by approximately –12 dB by placing the Select tool over the volume control (the horizontal line) in the audio waveform, and dragging down.

NOTE ▸   Press **Shift-Z** to fit the entire project in the Timeline pane.

▶ **Do I Have to Lift and Replace?**

Lift from Storyline is a great example of the power and flexibility of Final Cut Pro. You could accomplish this second version edit without performing the lift edit and leaving the sound bites in the primary storyline. In a later lesson, you'll return the sound bites to the primary storyline after your edits have been synchronized to the music. The workflows explored here demonstrate just a few of the many editing methods available in Final Cut Pro.

Exercise 5.3.2
Creating Time at 0:00

With a new project duration of almost two minutes, you have quite a bit of time to fill. Before you import the new aerial footage, you'll explore some edits you can make while preparing for the additional footage.

The intro is a great place to add a few seconds of filler. The first shot in the project is already a little long and contains a complete action that should not be lengthened. What you need is another clip of the hangar door opening to insert at the beginning.

1   In the Primary Media event, select the Hangar Keyword Collection, and skim **DN_9488**.

This clip shows the hangar door closing, but don't reject the clip just yet because of that small technicality. You can reverse playback of the clip to make it an opening shot.

NOTE ▶   If necessary, enable skimming in the upper right of the Timeline area, or by pressing **S**.

2   In **DN_9488**, click to position the playhead where the hangar door has just closed (03:12:29:05), and mark an end point.

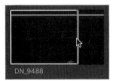

Guessing, you think the clip should be about three seconds long. So you need to set the start point three seconds from the current playhead position. You may enter a numerical value to move the playhead to the left by three seconds.

3   Press **Control-P** to invoke a move command for the playhead. The timecode display at the bottom of the Viewer clears, awaiting the value.

When typing a time value, you may choose to enter an absolute timecode to move the playhead to an exact location, or type the duration you want to add or subtract from the current playhead position.

4   On the keyboard, press the – (minus sign) key followed by the number 3 and a period (.).

The timecode display indicates that the playhead will move three seconds to the left.

5   Press Return, and press **I** to mark a start point.

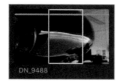

To get a feel for the timing of cutting from this new hangar clip to the previous hangar clip, let's first perform a connect edit.

6   With the playhead at the beginning of the project, press **Q** to connect edit the Browser clip into the project.

The new clip is in the right place, but playing in the wrong direction. Let's play the clip in reverse so the door appears to open rather than close.

7   In the project, select **DN_9488**, and at the lower left of the Viewer, click the Retime button.

We'll explore retiming clips in Lesson 6, but for now, you'll just perform a simple reverse effect.

8   From the Retime pop-up menu, choose Reverse Clip.

A small stripe appears above the clip to indicate that the clip plays at normal speed but in reverse, which makes the hangar door seem to be opening. The stripe represents the clip's Retime Editor, which you'll hide for now.

9   From the Retime pop-up menu, choose Hide Retime Editor, or press **Command-R**.

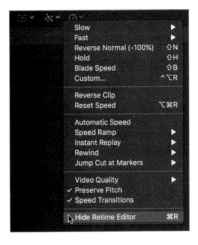

That reverse speed change effect looks good, and the two hangar opening shots break up the action. But, you need this new hangar clip to play before rather than simultaneously with the old hangar clip to fill some time. Also, you do not need to hear Mitch speaking right away. As you did previously, you will insert a gap clip to adjust the timing and pacing. However, this time you'll place the gap clip into the sound bite storyline.

10 Select the gray bar of the sound bite storyline, and cue the playhead to the beginning of the storyline.

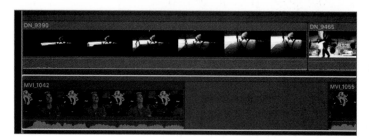

11 Press **Option-W** to insert the default, three-second gap clip.

The sound bites shift three seconds down the Timeline. The B-roll clips did not move as they did previously. The B-roll storylines are now connected to the music in the primary storyline. Because the hangar clip is connected to the music as well, it is not affected by the ripple edit in the sound bite storyline. Let's get **DN_9488** into the hangar storyline.

12 Drag **DN_9488** to **DN_9390** and wait until an insert bar and subsequent blue box appear at the beginning of the hangar storyline.

13 When the gap opens up, release the mouse button.

Getting clips into a storyline creates the horizontal, magnetic relationships between clips. Now you can interactively use the Trim tool between the two clips.

Skimming over the edit, the end of the first clip now cuts to the hangar door when it is just barely open.

NOTE ▶ Click and hold either side of the edit point as if you were going to trim a clip to invoke the two-up display in the Viewer. You'll clearly see the continuity mismatch.

14 Place the pointer over the start of **DN_9390**.

15 With the ripple edit filmstrip pointing to the right, drag right while watching the Viewer.

Trim both hangar door clips until the movement feels natural. You're trying to achieve smooth continuity between the movement of the hangar door, Mitch walking toward the helicopter, and the pacing of the edit.

In the first two clips, the sound effect of a motor opening the door is really needed. You'll add that sound effect in Lesson 6, but for now, let's create space for that sound effect by delaying the start of the music.

16 Move the playhead to the beginning of the project, and press **Option-W** to insert a gap clip.

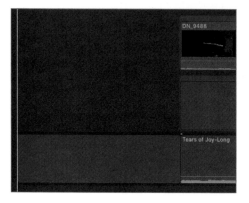

The gap clip appears in the primary storyline. You will cover that gap with the hangar storyline.

17 Drag the gray bar of the hangar storyline to the left to cover the gap.

18 To address pacing, lengthen the primary storyline gap clip at the beginning to start the music at about three and a half seconds from the beginning of the project.

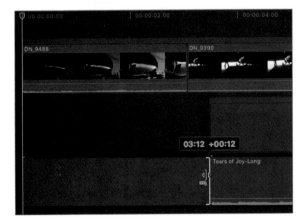

This delay will allow a sound effect (that you'll add later) to immerse the viewer in the hangar environment. And as the shot changes with the movement of the door, the music will seem to move Mitch forward. At this point, you can make one more tweak to increase your storytelling momentum: adjusting the timing of Mitch's first sound bite to fit with the music.

NOTE ▸ The project is formatted to 23.98 frames per second, hence the 3:12 duration for the gap clip.

19 Adjust the sound bite storyline's gap clip so that Mitch starts speaking after the downbeat in **bar** two of the music (at 00:00:05:21 in the project).

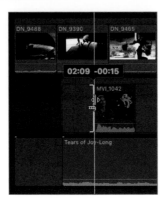

Depending on your earlier choices for clip content and timing, you may need/want additional B-roll to cover the second gap in the sound bite storyline. You could adjust the durations of **DN_9465** and **DN_9470**, but you have something else to consider: What's happening with the music? And the first two clips in the project will later need a motor/winding sound. Time to create some "notes to self."

▶ **Checkpoint 5.3.2**

Refer to Appendix C for details on reviewing a Checkpoint.

Reference 5.4
Working with Markers

Admit it. You have little notes all over your editing desk. The marker system in Final Cut Pro can keep those notes for you and make them searchable. Furthermore, notes attached to clips and markers travel with the library, so your comments can carry on to the next collaborator.

Final Cut Pro has four types of markers:

▶ Standard: Default, simplest marker type

▶ To-do: A checkbox marker type

▶ Completed: A selected checkbox marker only accessible when the original marker is a to-do marker

▶ Chapter: A marker with a user-defined thumbnail optionally included with some Share formats

The marker name of each type may be customized and that custom name is searchable. For Browser clips, you use the search field to locate named markers. For Timeline clips, marker names appear and are searchable in the Timeline Index.

5.4-A Using the Timeline Index

The Timeline Index presents three indices: Clips, Tags, and Roles. The Clips Index presents a chronological list of every clip, title, generator, and transition in a project. It also indicates the selected clip and playhead position. Clicking a listed item both selects the item and cues the playhead to the start of that item. The Clips Index is searchable and allows for multiple selection.

The Tags Index lists all markers, keywords, analysis keywords, to-do markers, completed markers, and chapter markers in a project. These may be filtered using the sub-panel controls at the bottom of the Index.

The Roles Index allows you to disable, select, and arrange audio clips into audio lanes according to assigned audio roles and subroles. Clips in selected roles may be minimized or brought into focus as your workflow goes from identifying a single mic issue to final mixdown.

Using any one of these three indices, you can find any clip used in the project not just by its clip name but also by the metadata you added earlier in the Browser.

Exercise 5.4.1
Creating Markers

Since you've now identified a few places that will need attention, adding a few markers to track those tasks for the revision edit would be worthwhile. In this exercise, you will create standard and to-do markers in the project.

1   Cue the skimmer over the first clip, the close-up of the helicopter while the hangar
door is opening.

Before you press **M** to place a marker, you should know which clip under the skimmer
will receive that marker.

2   Click in the empty area above the clips to cue the playhead to the skimmer.

The "ball" on the playhead indicates which clip will receive an edit command. The
ball is on the hangar clip, so the hangar clip, and not the gap clip, will receive the
marker. Barring a selected clip, the highest clip "has got the ball" and receives the edit
commands.

3   Press **M** twice to set a standard marker and also access the marker's information.

The marker is pre-named Marker 3 because this is the third marker you've created in
this project.

NOTE ▶   If you added additional markers, the marker's name will differ from the one here.

4 Change the marker type to a to-do marker. The marker turns red and a Completed checkbox appears.

5 Rename the marker *Add SFX*. Click Done.

You can locate markers in the Timeline when you are working near a marker, but the Timeline Index allows you to browse all of a project's markers in an easy-to-read list.

6 Access the Timeline Index by clicking the index button at left in the Timeline area.

7 With the Timeline Index set to display All Tags, the marker should be toward the top of the list.

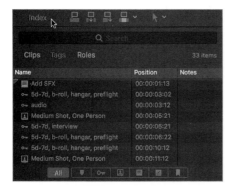

You may restrict the list by using the buttons below the list to select criteria such as marker or keyword type. The All setting will suffice for now, however, so let's return to setting markers as editorial notes. In this second round of editing, you will use the music to pace the edit. You'll craft the edit around "visual" moments in the music. Two of these moments are a **swell** and the **grand pause** toward the end. Other examples include strong **crescendos**, or changes to or accents within the **rhythmic cadence**. Let's mark two of these musical events now for later use. To do so without distraction from Mitch or the B-roll, you will solo the music clip.

8   In the project, select the music clip. Press **Option-S** to solo the clip, and then play back a short section of the project.

The nonselected clips are dimmed in the Timeline. When you play the project, you will still see the video in the Viewer, but the music will be the only audible clip.

To both see and hear the music, let's make the audio waveforms bigger and hide the video thumbnails.

9   In the Timeline's Clip Appearance window, select the first clip display option. Adjust the Clip Height slider as desired, and click in the Timeline to close the window.

Now you can also see what you are hearing.

10 Listen to the music between timecodes 00:00:24:00 and 00:00:34:00, especially around the 28-second mark.

Prior to this point, the piano carries more of the melody in the verse. Just before 28 seconds, the strings take over and soar above the piano. That flight of melody in the chorus calls out for the flight of the helicopter.

11 As the chorus takes off at 00:00:27:22, select the music clip, press the **M** key twice to place a standard marker, and rename the marker *takeoff*.

NOTE ► Remember, "who's got the ball?" You'll need to select the music clip to intercept the clip in the preflight storyline from receiving the marker. Once you have the playhead cued, press Command-Up Arrow to select the music.

12 Continue listening to the music while setting the following markers:

Music-Based Markers

Timecode	Marker Name	Marker Type
00:01:16:13	Swell	Standard
00:01:31:01	Sunset through windows	Standard

13 Click the Solo button to return to monitoring all audio.

14 Also before continuing, reset Clip Appearance to the third display option.

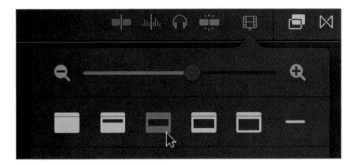

15 Set these additional markers:

NOTE ▶ An alternative method to customize a marker's name and type is to create a marker by pressing M, then double-click or Control-click the marker.

Content-Based Markers

Timecode	On Clip	Marker Name	Marker Type
00:00:15:00	MVI_1055	Add a Title	To-do
00:00:27:00	DN_9452	Speed and SFX	To-do

Take a moment to look at the various views of the Tags Index while changing the filter controls. You will find the various markers you've created listed in the indices.

Reference 5.5
Using the Position Tool

The Position tool overrides a storyline's magnetic properties and allows a clip to be moved horizontally much like a connected clip, but with slightly destructive properties. A storyline clip, dragged with the Position tool, erases any existing clips and gaps that it contacts, leaving a new gap clip. The Position tool is in a constant overwrite state. **Overwrite** editing allows one clip to erase the contents of another clip by dragging.

The Position tool is very handy when you are locked-to-time, as in a commercial spot, and need to edit within a storyline without rippling the adjoining edits.

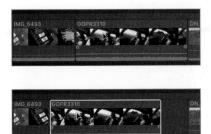

The Position tool leaves a gap behind while removing earlier content.

Exercise 5.5.1
Realigning Sound Bites and B-roll to Music

Before returning to the editing tasks, let's get a feel for the difference between the Select and Position tools. Select is magnetic while Position is not. Dragging a clip with the Select tool uses magnetic attraction or repulsion to keep clips attached to each other horizontally within a storyline. Dragging a clip with the Position tool "bulldozes" over adjoining clips, leaving a gap clip in place of the existing content.

1 With the Select tool active, in the Timeline, drag the middle (not the edges) of the **MVI_1055** sound bite to the left.

The sound bite swaps position with the gap clip before it. That's the expected magnetic behavior.

2 Press **Command-Z** to undo the edit.

Repeat the same edit, but this time using the Position tool.

3 From the Tools pop-up menu, choose the Position tool, or press **P**.

4 Once again, drag the **MVI_1055** sound bite slightly to the left in the storyline.

The gap before the sound bite becomes shorter.

5 If you don't see the difference between this behavior and the behavior when using the Select tool, press **Command-Z** to undo the edit, and try again while carefully watching the back end of **MVI_1055**.

When you drag a clip with the Position tool, a new gap clip or growing gap clip is left behind. Let's use the Position tool to adjust the timing between the second sound bite and the start of the music chorus. You want the sound bite to finish close to the take-off marker you added earlier.

6 Using the Position tool, realign **MVI_1055** to end just to the left of the takeoff marker (00:00:27:17).

NOTE ► Depending on your earlier edits, this may entail dragging **MVI_1055** right to end closer to the marker.

7 Choose the Select tool, or press **A**.

You will use the Select tool after your takeoff marker to make room for the takeoff and new aerial B-roll. To fit with the music and open that room, the second set of sound bites will start after the eighth **bar** of the chorus (44 seconds into the Timeline).

8 Park your playhead on the music downbeat after Mitch says, "sure that," at 00:00:44:04.

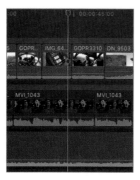

This is after the eighth **bar** of the chorus, just where you want to begin the next set of sound bites.

9   Using the Select tool, ripple trim the gap before the first **MVI_1043** clip to push the start of it to the playhead.

Don't worry about the B-roll. Just as you did during the first pass edit, your task is to interweave the new sound bite audio story with the music story. When that's done, the B-roll will flow together smoothly.

5.5.1-A Breaking Up and Adding New Sound Bites

With more time available in the project, you can slow Mitch down a bit by breaking apart existing sound bites and adding more gap clips. You will also add some additional sound bites. Let's start by using roles to focus on the sound bite audio.

1   In the Roles Index, deselect the Video, Music, and Natural Sound roles.

The video clips, the music clip, and the natural sound clips are disabled in the project, which lessens the distraction of the video and other audio edits and allows you to concentrate on the sound bites.

NOTE ▶   If you find some clips are still audible when you expected them to be muted, check the clip's assigned roles in the Info inspector. Reassign the role, if necessary.

2   In the second instance of **MVI_1043**, cue the playhead after Mitch says, "Imagery of what you're shooting." at 00:00:50:19.

3   Select the sound bite beneath the playhead by either clicking the clip or by pressing Command-Up Arrow twice.

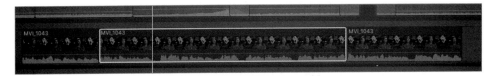

4   Press **Command-B** to blade the sound bite at the playhead.

> **NOTE ▸**   If the skimmer is active, you may place a cut where you didn't intend it. If so, press **Command-Z** to undo the edit, press **S** to disable the skimmer, and repeat the edit.

To create a pause, you'll use the Position tool.

5   Select both sound bites after the cut you just made.

6   Press **P** to choose the Position tool, and then drag the two sound bites to the right about 12 frames.

The existing **MVI_1046** is the sound bite that goes after the big musical crescendo as the sunlight shines into the helicopter. Let's push that clip into position to make room for the new sound bites.

7   Using the Select tool, ripple trim the gap clip before **MVI_1046** to push it to the last section of the music. The ripple edit adds 17:01 to the gap clip length, resulting in a 27:22 duration.

You've created a large gap that is ready to receive the two additional sound bites. You'll place the first in the project roughly three seconds after the end of **MVI_1043**.

8   Cue the playhead three seconds after **MVI_1043**.

You have already identified the sound bite that goes here as a favorite, so you can search for it in the Browser.

9   With the Interview Keyword Collection selected, from the filter pop-up menu, choose Favorites, and in the Browser's search field, type *new*.

MVI_1044 appears in the Browser.

10   Press **/** (slash) to preview the clip.

11   Set a start point before Mitch says "virtually," and an end point after he says, "for me."

This additional sound bite requires an edit that:

▶   Retains the clip's duration, similar to a replace edit

▶   Doesn't affect the location of nearby clips inside or outside a storyline, similar to a connect edit

▶   Erases existing project clips at the destination storyline location

That edit is an **overwrite** edit. It stamps the selected Browser item into the primary or selected storyline at the skimmer or playhead, and it erases whatever content exists at that location. Nearby clips do not ripple, shift, or move. You already cued the playhead, so now you need to select the destination storyline.

12 With the playhead cued, select the sound bite storyline's gray bar. Then click the Overwrite button, or press **D**.

Overwrite button

The sound bite is placed on top of the gap clip in the sound bite storyline. The edit does not ripple any other clip.

One more sound bite to go. Again, you'll place the new clip about three seconds after the sound bite you just added.

13 With the playhead at the end of MVI_1044, deselect the sound bite storyline by pressing **Command-Shift-A**, and then press **Control-P**.

The timecode display clears, awaiting your time entry for moving the playhead. You want to move the playhead three seconds down the Timeline. You can do so using the + (plus sign) key.

14 Press the + (plus sign) key, type *3.* (3 period), and press Return.

The playhead advances three seconds and is ready for the sound bite.

15 With the Interview Keyword Collection still selected, change the search text to *capture*.

MVI_1045 appears in the Browser because you previously assigned the word "capture" to the clip's notes.

16 Select the Browser clip, and then press / (slash) to preview it.

17 Overwrite edit this clip into the sound bite storyline by selecting the storyline's bar, and pressing **D**.

18 In the Roles Index, re-enable the Video, Music, and Natural Sound roles. Review the last edit you performed, making sure that all audio and video clips are enabled.

Let's move this last edited sound bite closer to the big musical **crescendo** at the **grand pause**.

19 Using the method you prefer, move **MVI_1045** so that the clip ends just before the "Sunset through windows" marker you set earlier. Ensure that this move does not affect other project clips.

Before you take a break, you should snapshot your project because you will be making large additional changes in upcoming exercises.

20 In the Projects Smart Collection, Control-click the Lifted Vignette project, and from the shortcut menu, choose Duplicate Project as Snapshot. Rename the snapshot *Lifted Vignette - Before Aerials*.

You performed quite a few edits already in this lesson. And not only edits. You added some markers to serve as editing notes. You also began exploring the Timeline Index and roles. Don't forget, this lesson started with moving the sound bites out of the primary storyline to be replaced by a new music clip. With the connected clips, story-lines, and magnetic timelines that Final Cut Pro watches over, you should feel enabled in your projects to push and pull things around throughout the Timeline.

▶ **Checkpoint 5.5.1**

Refer to Appendix C for details on reviewing a Checkpoint.

Reference 5.6
Working with Auditions

When your editing project involves on-camera talent, that talent may be directed to per-form the same dialogue multiple times, each time with a different interpretation. When it comes time to edit those takes, many editors cut the performer's first take into the project and review it. Then they replace edit the second take into the project—which requires finding the second take, dragging it to the first take, and selecting Replace—and review it. The editor tediously has to repeat this process to evaluate every additional take.

Final Cut Pro auditions allow you to bundle multiple takes into a single clip that you can cut into your project. They allow you to switch between takes within the clip to compare them without performing multiple edits. Audition clips are not limited to containing takes of the same performance, however. You can use an audition to try out a clip in combination with various visual and/or audio effects. You can also use auditions to quickly apply different clips to a specific section of your project.

To select a take, the Audition window presents all the takes in a simple carousel display. Clicking a take thumbnail or pressing a keyboard shortcut performs the replace edit. And using a preview mode, you may cycle through every take during a playback loop.

Exercise 5.6.1
Repositioning Storylines and Deleting Within

Before you create and start editing with auditions, you'll need to make some Timeline changes to prepare for the audition clip. Final Cut Pro makes this easy; just remember to zoom in so you can see everything that is happening. Starting from the beginning, make these changes in anticipation of new aerial clips.

> **NOTE ▸** Don't forget to toggle snapping on or off with the **N** key as needed while editing, and remember to zoom in to the edits for a detailed view. You may zoom by dragging the Zoom slider in Clip Appearance or by pressing **Command-=** (equals sign).

1   Trim two seconds from the first gap clip in the primary storyline.

This shifts the music and all items connected to the music, keeping them in sync.

The start of the takeoff storyline is **DN_9463**. This clip should start on the takeoff marker you set previously. Although the preflight storyline and its last clip, **DN_9452**, are above that marker, the preflight storyline will get out of the way so you may achieve the desired edit.

2   Dragging the takeoff storyline's gray bar, align the storyline with the major musical downbeat that occurs around the 26-second point (00:00:25:22) in the Timeline. That point should be at the takeoff marker.

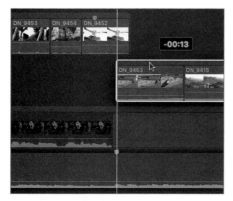

The second B-roll storyline, preflight, shifted above **DN_9463** to overlap the takeoff storyline. In a later lesson, you will apply a speed change to accelerate the rotor turning and decrease the clip's duration. For now, you'll slide the preflight storyline left to reveal **DN_9463** at the takeoff marker.

3   Drag the preflight storyline's gray bar to the left until it drops down because it no longer overlaps the takeoff storyline. With snapping turned on, ensure that the two storylines abut each other.

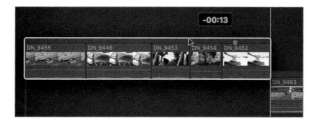

After the takeoff occurs in **DN_9463**, you'll want to see some of the new aerial shots. Let's remove one of the next B-roll clips to create space for the new clips.

Clip **DN_9415** will be removed from this storyline. Performing a replace with gap deletion leaves a gap clip in the storyline for the next series of edits.

4   Select **DN_9415**, and press **Shift-Delete**.

A gap clip replaces the deleted clip. You will use this gap as a reference point for the next edit series. This series requires you to import the new aerial clips.

Exercise 5.6.2
Importing the Aerial Clips Using Finder Tags

For the Lifted Vignette project, you will create an audition clip to edit all the new aerial clips into the project as a single clip. You will then cycle through those aerial clips within the audition clip to find the desired shot.

To prepare for this exercise, you must import the aerial media source files, and organize them as library clips. These new clips were cataloged and organized using macOS Finder tags you will import as keywords for each clip. Let's begin by viewing the tags in the Finder.

1   Hide Final Cut Pro by pressing **Command-H**.

2   In the Dock, click the Finder icon to open a Finder window.

3   Navigate to your downloaded FCP X Media > LV2 > LV Aerials folder.

The tags assigned to the aerial clips are hidden by default in list view.

4   If necessary, switch the window to list view, Control-click the Name column header, and from the shortcut menu, choose Tags.

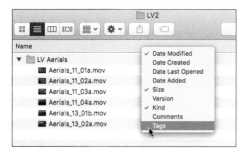

The tags are revealed for each of the aerial clips. While importing these clips, you'll take advantage of these tags to create Keyword Collections.

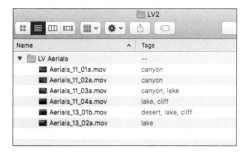

5   Return to Final Cut Pro by clicking the application's icon in the Dock.

6   Back in Final Cut Pro, click the Media Import button in the toolbar.

The Media Import window opens. In the left sidebar, you will locate the aerial clips for import.

7   Navigate to your downloaded FCP X Media > LV2 > LV Aerials folder.

8   Select the LV Aerials folder.

9 In the Import Options sidebar, set the following:

▶ Add to the existing Primary Media.

▶ Select to leave files in place.

▶ Select "From Finder tags" and "From folders."

▶ Deselect all other analysis and transcoding options.

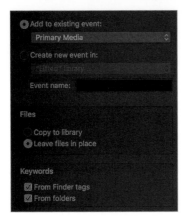

10 Click Import Selected.

All six aerial clips are placed in an LV Aerials Keyword Collection within the Primary Media event. The six clips are also spread amongst four additional Keyword Collections according to the tags assigned in the Finder: canyon, cliff, desert, and lake.

You should assign an additional metadata value, roles, before proceeding.

11 In the Browser, in the LV Aerials Keyword Collection, select all six aerial clips.

12 Control-click any one of the selected clips, and from the shortcut menu, choose Assign Video Roles > B-roll.

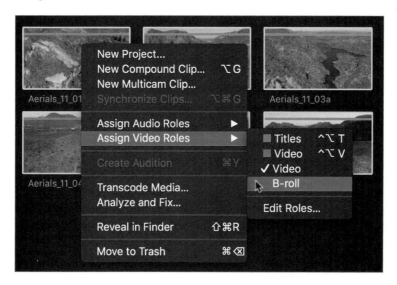

The aerial clips contain no source audio, so no audio role is applicable.

Exercise 5.6.3
Working with an Audition Clip

The Audition feature is a great way to review multiple takes, and even completely different clips. You will use it in this exercise as one approach to adding clips to a project. You'll start by building an audition clip in the Browser.

1 Verify that the six aerial clips in the LV Aerials Keyword Collection are selected.

2 Control-click any one of the selected clips, and from the shortcut menu, choose Create Audition to create an audition clip.

The audition clip appears in the Browser. The audition clip is identified by the "spot-light" icon in the upper-left of its thumbnail. This audition clip will serve as an in-line browser of the aerial clips.

5.6.3-A Experiencing the Audition Window

Let's take the audition clip for a spin by inserting it into the various B-roll storylines.

> **NOTE ▶** The steps in this part of the exercise and in following exercises may feel as if you've lost control of the edit. However, Final Cut Pro will keep everything in sync.

1   In the Browser, click the audition clip's spotlight badge to open the Audition window.

The Audition window appears, showing the current pick. The pick is the currently active clip within the audition clip.

2   Press the Left or Right Arrow keys to cycle through the clips within the audition clip.

NOTE ▶ Alternatively, you may click the next thumbnail to select a different clip.

Notice that the selected clip's name and duration appears in the window. The audition clip works by performing a replace edit for you.

3   Using the Audition window, select **Aerials_11_02a** as the pick, and click Done.

The Audition window closes, leaving the new pick in the audition clip. This canyon clip is currently 39 seconds in length. Let's cut that down to about six seconds.

4   With the audition clip (with the spotlight badge) selected in the Browser, create an approximately six-second clip starting around timecode 00:00:54:00. Here are a few tips to accomplish the task:

▶   Press the **J K L** and the **Left Arrow** and **Right Arrow** keys to cue the playhead.

▶   The clip's timecode is visible in the timecode display while you skim/play the clip.

> ▶ 00:00:54:00

▶   When the timecode display indicates 00:00:54:00, press **I**.

▶   Set the duration by pressing **Control-D**, typing *6 0 0*, and then pressing Return.

5   From the Browser, insert edit the audition clip after **DN_9463**. Remember, you must select the storyline's gray bar before clicking the Insert button or pressing **W**.

NOTE ▶ With no source audio to receive the Natural Sound audio role, the aerial clips are tinted according to their assigned video roles.

An audition clip performs a replace edit using the duration of each clip at the time you created the audition clip. Because you marked a duration of only one clip in the audition clip, the other aerial clips will ripple the B-roll storyline when they are selected as the pick.

6 Open the Audition window in the Timeline by clicking the spotlight icon next to the clip's name.

As you cycle the window between the alternate takes, the clip's duration is rippling the storyline.

7 Cycle the audition clip back to **Aerials_11_02a**, and click Done.

This operation may seem a little hazardous to perform within a Timeline in which you've spent some time to "lock" sync specific clips to other clips. The subsequent storyline clips will realign after you trim the pick to the needed replacement duration.

▶ **Avoiding an Audition-Induced Ripple**

You may use a storylined audition clip without causing a ripple edit sync panic. The "Lift from Storyline" command gets the clip out of the storyline as a connected clip, leaving a gap. Now, as a connected clip, the audition's duration change is independent. After selecting the pick, and trimming the audition to the gap clip's duration, you have the option of returning the clip to the storyline or leaving it as a connected clip.

▶ **Relocating a Connection Point**

A connected clip or storyline defaults to a connection point at the start point of the clip/storyline. You may reset this connection to anywhere within the clip/storyline. The new connection point is defined by **Command-Option-clicking** the bottom of the clip (or top of a clip if below the primary storyline).

Connecting storylines at different points is slightly different in that you **Command-Option-click** the storyline's gray bar to set a new connection point.

Reference 5.7
Trimming the Tops and Tails

Whether you are working with a connected clip or a clip in a storyline, you may also use the "top and tail" trimming tools that support three trim methods.

The first two methods are "top the head" and "trim the tail." If you have extraneous material to remove from the start of the clip, park the playhead on the first frame you want to keep, and then use the Trim Start command. To trim material at the end of the clip, place the playhead after the last frame you want to keep, and use the Trim End command.

A connected clip before the trim command

After performing a Trim Start to playhead
command. From the Before image,
clip material from the playhead to the end is kept.

A connected clip before the trim command

After performing a Trim End to playhead
command. From the Before image,
clip material from the start to the playhead is kept.

The third method trims "top and tail" simultaneously using "Trim to Selection." You use the Range Selection tool, or mark start and end points with the help of clip skimming, to select the material you want to keep, and then "Trim to Selection" to delete the extraneous content outside that selection.

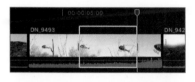

Trim to the selected range

Trim Start, Trim End, and "Trim to Selection" may be used during playback. This gives you real-time editing in context.

Exercise 5.7.1
Trimming the Aerials

You will continue using the audition clip to add the aerial B-roll clips. You'll trim those clips using the "top and tail" commands: Trim Start, Trim End, and "Trim to Selection."

1   From the Browser, select the audition clip, and drag it to the gap between your first audition edit with **Aerials_11_02a** and **GOPR1857**. Perform a replace edit.

2   Open the Audition window by clicking the spotlight on the second instance of the audition clip, **Aerials_11_02a**.

3   Press the Left or Right Arrow keys to select **Aerials_13_02a**. Click Done.

For the moment, you will trim the end of **Aerials_13_02a** to the start of the sound bite.

4   Cue the playhead to the start of the sound bite.

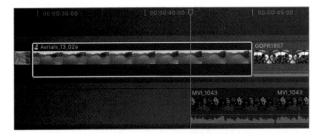

5   Select **Aerials_13_02a**, and press **Option-]** (right bracket).

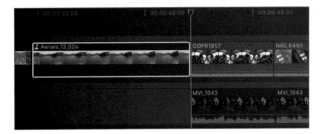

The end of the clip is trimmed to the playhead, and the rest of the storyline ripples.

Let's add another clip here. You'll set up a pattern where the helicopter performs a low pass to "buzz the camera" before returning to Mitch's sound bites.

6   In the In Flight Keyword Collection, locate clip **DN_9493**. Mark an end point for the clip when all that's visible in the Viewer is the helicopter's tail (03:16:37:11).

7   Back up the playhead about three seconds, and set a start point.

> **NOTE ▶**   After marking the end point with the O key, pressing Control-P, – (minus), 3, . (period), Return, and the I key achieves the task in step 7.

8   Insert the trimmed **DN_9493** between **Aerials_13_02a** and **GOPR1857**.

The helicopter should buzz the camera before the sound bite plays. You can quickly trim the prior two aerials to place the loudest waveform of **DN_9493** before Mitch starts talking.

9   Start playback at the beginning of **Aerials_11_02a**. Look for a visual cue or listen for a musical hit that would make a suitable end point.

This point could be visually where the dry stream bed is about to reach the bottom of the screen. Musically, the edit could be at the start of a **bar**.

10   Deselect the storyline and clips, if necessary. Park the playhead at the end point you've identified, and press **Option-]** (right bracket).

That point could be at 00:00:34:02 on the beat and where the dry bed is at the Viewer's lower edge.

11 Trim the end of **Aerials_13_02a** by once again listening and watching for an appropriate end point. Ending the clip at 00:00:40:03 works.

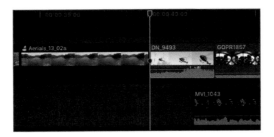

The loudest waveforms in **DN_9493** probably occur just before the sound bite, or just as it starts. You should attempt to edit the clip so the Doppler shift occurs at the start of the sound bite.

12 If necessary, trim some additional frames from (or to) **Aerials_11_02a**, **Aerials_13_02a**, and/or **DN_9493** to position the "buzzing" waveform before the sound bite. Alternatively, you could try a slip edit with the Trim tool by –14 frames.

13 Lower the volume of **DN_9493** to –15 dB.

This is not the final mix level, but merely an adjustment to tame this audio content and avoid sonic aggravation until you remix the audio in **Lesson 7**. Also, the end of this clip is abrupt and overlapping the sound bite. In Lesson 6, you'll add a transition and split the audio to blend this clip into the next clip. You'll also adjust the clip so it carries the viewer into the sound bite.

5.7.1-A Continuing to Add B-roll

Still more to go in this second edit pass. You've explored the theory and the tools. Now it's down to the physical work of assembling the edit.

1 Cue the playhead between **GOPR1857** and **IMG_6493**, and select the storyline's gray bar.

2 In the Browser, select the iPhone Keyword Collection, and locate the B-roll clip
IMG_6486. From the beginning of the clip, mark a 2:10 duration.

3 Press **W** to insert the clip into the takeoff storyline, and then lower the clip's volume level.

4 For **IMG_6493**, ripple edit the clip, if necessary, so that the clip ends with Mitch's hand
and arm at the top of the frame, but before the camera starts to pan.

The "bracket" at right in the Viewer indicates this is the last frame for IMG_6493.

In Lesson 6, you will create a composite "split screen" of the next clip, **GOPR3310**, and
an aerial clip. In anticipation of that composite, let's trim **GOPR3310**.

5 With **GOPR3310** selected in the project, press **Control-D**, and set a duration of 08:10.

The duration of a project selection appears to the right of the
current project's name at the center of the Timeline area.

There's more to add to the project. But, like a typical house remodel, there are some
more old things that have to be removed to make room for the new.

5.7.1-B Removing a Transition and Moving Clips

In the first edit pass, you applied some transitions to quickly smooth out some start and end points. One of those is now in the way and must be removed.

1 Use the Select tool to select the transition between **DN_9503** and **DN_9420**.

2 Press Delete.

NOTE ▶ Press the "Big Delete" or Backspace key. Do not press the small Forward Delete key found on full-size keyboards.

A couple of B-roll clips toward the end need some attention. Both of these clips, **GOPR0009** and **DN_9424**, should be moved to the Timeline's final sound bite.

3 Using the storyline's gray bar, drag **GOPR0009**, the helicopter landing, above **MVI_1046**. Continue dragging to align the start transition with the music as it restarts after the big musical hit and the moment of silence.

NOTE ▶ You may notice the not-so-clean transition introduced by the overlap with **MVI_1046**. You'll clean that up during another pass at the end of this lesson.

4 Using the storyline's gray bar, drag **DN_9424**, the flying-into-the-sunset clip, over **MVI_1046**. Continue dragging to align the start of the storyline to Mitch saying,

"Wow!" which aligns the peak of the B-roll's audio waveform to occur just after the sound bite ends.

DN_9420 is the sunlight-through-the-windows clip. You may recall the great music hit at the **grand pause** that would sync well with this clip. That hit is the apex of the music.

Not only can you see the highest peak in the music waveform, you also placed **MVI_1045** so it ends slightly before the musical hit. The sound bite has Mitch stating that you never know what you are going to see or capture.

5   From the takeoff storyline, drag **DN_9420** toward the end of **MVI_1045**. Because you want **DN_9420** to reposition, drag the clip, and not the handle, so that you pull the clip out of the storyline. Use the markers you set earlier to align the visual effect to the musical hit.

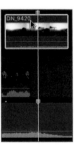

NOTE ▶ To snap the markers, first move the clip out of the storyline, and then drag the clip with snapping enabled to align the markers.

5.7.1-C Aligning the Bites and Bits

There are several edits to go in this pass; however, you've learned the necessary tools and workflow to tell your story. Storytelling is not only about describing actions in a linear format, but video storytelling looks for ways to enhance the story with both video and audio accents.

To start this series of edits, you want to establish a pattern, as mentioned earlier. Previously, you edited **DN_9493** to low-pass over the camera before Mitch started talking again. You are going to perform the same edit again with **DN_9503** and **MVI_1044**. However, this edit currently has little useable clip content with which to make the edit. For the transition to correctly take the viewer from the helicopter to Mitch, you need overlapping media. The sound bite must start, at minimum, when the transition above starts the dissolve to the sound bite. You'll create more useable content with which to achieve this overlap by trimming the start of **DN_9503** and adjusting the gap's duration.

NOTE ▶ Don't forget to zoom in on the edits. Position the skimmer over what you need to zoom in on in the Timeline and then use the keyboard shortcut **Command-=** (equals sign) to zoom in for a detailed view of the edit.

1   Ripple edit the end point of the gap preceding **MVI_1044** so that the start of **MVI_1044** is aligned to the start of the transition.

Depending on your earlier edits, you may have not been able to complete the previous step, or aligning the start points of the clip and transition resulted in a very short gap.

2   If you completed step 1 successfully, skip to step 5.

3   If you need to lengthen **DN_9503** to increase the gap and ensure that the transition is over **MVI_1044**, ripple edit frames to the start of **DN_9503** by dragging left.

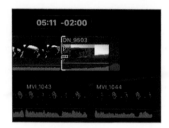

Dragging left with the Ripple tool on the start of **DN_9503** will supply the additional media, if needed.

4   If necessary, adjust the gap clip's duration under **DN_9503** to align the start of **MVI_1044** to the start of the transition in **DN_9503**.

You have three more B-roll clips to edit from the aerials audition clip. The three start during the **MVI_1044** sound bite.

5   From the Browser, connect edit the aerials audition clip to **MVI_1044** when Mitch says "new" a second time.

Remember, the audition clip has the spotlight icon.

6   Within the audition clip, select **Aerials_13_01b** as the pick.

As it is, this clip is rather dull and too long. But you haven't yet seen the reveal to the lake that occurs later in the clip. Right now, you can just place the clip for timing. In Lesson 6, you'll apply a speed change on the clip that will rush to that reveal. You'll create a reminder to do this.

7   With the clip still selected, skim toward the start of **Aerials_13_01b**, the run-over-the-desert audition clip, and press **M** twice.

A standard marker is set, and the Marker window appears.

8   Name the marker *speed to reveal*, change the marker type to to-do, and then click Done.

A new to-do reminder is created (and one less sticky note is tagging your display). Let's get back to chopping the desert run audition clip down to size.

9   Cue the playhead to the start point of **MVI_1045**.

10 With the clip selected, press **Command-B** to blade the **Aerials_13_01b** audition clip, but don't delete the second half.

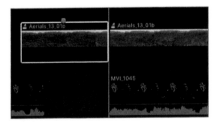

You can use this second half of the audition clip to select the second B-roll clip.

11 Switch the second audition clip you just created to **Aerials_11_01a**.

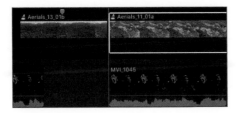

The clip is much too long, but you can take advantage of that to find the range you need.

12 If necessary, from the View menu, enable clip skimming.

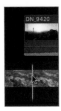

With clip skimming turned on, you can solo the audio and video of a clip. The skimmer is contained to the clip you are skimming, providing a skimmer solo option. No matter where the clip is in vertical relationship to other clips, the clip skimmer solos that clip's contents.

13 Clip skim **Aerials_11_01a** to a timecode of 00:00:37:00. This is the source timecode of the clip. Press **I** to mark a start point.

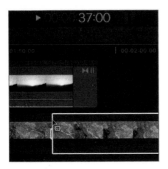

14 Continue clip skimming to the right until the timecode display reads 00:00:42:00. Mark this as the end point by pressing **O**.

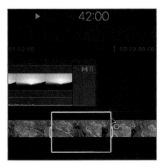

Now you will perform a "Trim to Selection" to remove the extraneous material outside that range.

15 Press **Option-** (backslash).

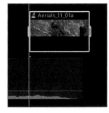

Because this is only a connected clip, it comes to rest at the range's location rather than sliding left to the head of a storyline.

16 Using the Select tool, snap the clip to the end of **Aerials_13_01b**, which is toward the left.

Now you need one more copy of the audition clip for the third aerial clip in this series. You can make that copy from the existing audition clips in the Timeline.

17 Option-drag a copy of the Aerials audition clip from itself, and snap the copied clip to the end of the audition clip from which you copied. Release the mouse button before releasing the Option key.

This technique duplicates the clip, creating a copy you can place elsewhere in the Timeline.

18 Change the pick of this third audition clip to **Aerials_11_03a**.

19 Clip skim this audition clip and then set a start point at 1:42:00 and an end point at 1:46:00. Press **Option-** (backslash) to "top and tail" the clip to the marked range.

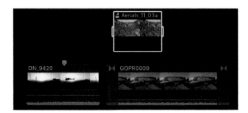

20 Snap this trimmed clip to the end of the **Aerials_11_01a** clip.

21 Trim the end of **Aerials_11_03a** to create a clean snap to **DN_9420**.

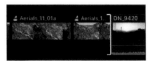

Although these four clips could be wraped into their own connected storyline, leave these clips as connected for now. Only one more quick tweak to the last sound bite in the project is needed.

22 Ripple edit the end point of the gap before **MVI_1046** to push the sound bite's start point after **GOPR0009** has fully transitioned onscreen. Play the project.

As you watch your project, you'll notice a few things that aren't fully realized. You still have to add sound effects, apply some speed changes, place some transitions, mix the audio, and create that split-screen clip. These will be enjoyable edits you'll experience in the following lessons.

But look at what you've accomplished on this second pass. To experience a different workflow approach, you lifted the sound bites out of the primary storyline to be replaced by a longer music clip. You shifted and created some additional connected storylines for grouping the B-roll. You created an audition clip to house the similar aerial clips. That audition allowed you to stay in the Timeline when working with the aerial B-roll rather than digging back into the Browser to get the clip you need. You made some big changes, but Final Cut Pro has made those changes easy.

Your current Timeline

▶ **Checkpoint 5.7.1**

Refer to Appendix C for details on reviewing a Checkpoint.

Lesson Review

1. Describe the results of using the following commands: Duplicate Project as Snapshot, and Duplicate Project.

2. Which replace edit command replaces the project clip using the duration of the browser clip: Replace, Replace from Start, or Replace from End?

3. Identify and define (from left to right) the four buttons in the following figure.

4. What action results from the displayed indication in the Dashboard?

5. Where do you find a list of all markers used in a project?

6. What command was invoked on the clip in this figure?

   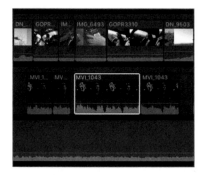

7. Which tool repositions storyline clips relative to time, allowing a clip to overwrite other clips?

8. Where may you assign a role to a clip?

9. What types of clips may go into an audition?

10. What icon badge identifies an audition clip?

11. What command was used in the scenario shown below?

Before

After

Answers

1. Duplicate Project creates a "live" version that updates its compound and multicam clips used in other projects. Duplicate Project as Snapshot produces a complete freeze of the project at the time of the duplication.

2. The Replace edit command

3. Skimming (**S**): Enable/disable the video skimmer. Audio Skimming (**Shift-S**): Enable/disable audio skimming (skimming must be enabled). Solo (**Option-S**): Monitor the audio playback of the selected clip(s). Snapping (**N**): Magnetically align the skimmer/playhead while dragging to the start of clips, keyframes, and markers.

4. The playhead will move three seconds to the left. This adjustment was performed by pressing **Control-P**.

5. The Tags Index found in the Timeline Index

6. The Solo command, **Option-S**

7. Position tool

8. Roles may be assigned in the Info inspector, Timeline, Timeline Index, Browser, or Modify menu.

9. Commonly used for multiple takes of an on-camera performance or of an audio-only VO, the audition clip collects whatever clip types you add to the audition.

10. A spotlight badge identifies and is an access point to an audition clip.

11. Trim to Selection, **Option-** (backward slash)

Lesson 6
Enhancing the Edit

The second pass at revising your project has led to this enhancement pass. Not every project will need the techniques presented here, while other projects may require all of them. Regardless of how much work remains to be done, a third enhancement pass is when your creativity may flourish—not just while polishing your edit, but also when covering a production or post-production error.

The Lifted Vignette project received some significant revisions in second pass. Now you will insert the necessary speed effects, apply visual effects to enhance an image or two, and further unify your story elements by adding more transitions. You'll learn how to composite two clips, and then collapse that composite into a manageable compound clip.

GOALS

▶ Vary the playback speed of clips

▶ Modify the look of clips with effects

▶ Utilize transitions

▶ Adjust transform and compositing controls

▶ Create compound clips

Reference 6.1
Retiming Clips

Speed effects can serve many purposes in a project. For instance, you might want to suggest the compression of time in a training video to more quickly demonstrate the entire action of a time-consuming process. The slightly faster playback speed can demonstrate that process without boring your viewers. Speed effects can also exert an emotional impact. In a narrative piece with a character or narrator reflecting on past events, slowing the playback speed may visually heighten the emotion expressed in the voiceover.

Regardless of your reason for applying a retiming effect, always make sure that you do have that reason. Using speed effects merely for the sake of adding an effect will distract viewers, and distance them from your storytelling.

You already applied a constant speed change to a clip when you previously reversed playback of the first clip, the reflection of the hangar door opening. That speed change was very easy to apply by choosing Reverse Clip from the Retiming pop-up menu. The Retime Editor set the clip to play at normal speed, but backward.

However, Final Cut Pro includes many more retiming options than simply playing a clip in reverse. The Retiming pop-up menu and the Retime Editor feature several retiming presets we'll explore in this lesson.

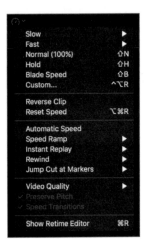

Exercise 6.1.1
Setting a Constant Speed Change

In your Lifted Vignette project, several clips require a speed change effect. You placed to-do markers on them as a reminder that they needed later attention. Let's review that to-do list in the Timeline Index; but before you make any more changes to this project, take a snapshot for later reference and to save as a backup.

1 With the project active in the Timeline, choose Edit > Duplicate Project as Snapshot, or press **Command-Shift-D**.

2 In the Browser, rename the snapshot *Lifted Vignette - Before Speed Changes*.

3 Staying in the Lifted Vignette project, click the Timeline Index button, or press **Command-Shift-2**, to open the Timeline Index.

You may need to reset the Index to view the Tags pane that filters the to-do markers.

4 In the upper section of the Timeline Index, click the Tags button.

5 In the lower section, click the Incomplete To-Do Items button (the third button from the right).

The index now lists the to-do markers you created during your previous edit passes.

6 In the Timeline Index, select the to-do marker titled "Speed and SFX."

The marker on **DN_9452** is selected, and the playhead is cued to the clip.

7 Play the clip to recall that it shows the helicopter starting up.

What if this clip started a little bit faster? Inherently, the clip's content is accelerating. You could give it a little boost to get the rotors up to speed faster for the next clip where the helicopter is taking off.

8   Select the clip, and then press **Command-R** to display the clip's Retime Editor.

Every clip has an associated Retime Editor you may view to see if any adjustments have been made. As indicated, the clip currently plays at normal, 100-percent speed.

NOTE ▶ **Command-Down Arrow** may be used to select the clip in the highest lane under the playhead when no prior selection exists.

6.1.1-A Setting Playback Speed Manually

A retiming effect can realize more emotion from a clip's contents; make a shot usable within continuity, or create a noticeable visual effect. The Retiming pop-up menu and a clip's Retime Editor, "the stripe," include several presets to get you started creating the effect you need. To understand the power of the Retime Editor, you'll try the manual adjustments.

1   At the right end of the Retime Editor for **DN_9452**, drag the retiming handle right and left while watching the stripe's speed indicator.

The clip's duration changes as the speed value changes. When you drag the retiming handle to the right, the Retime Editor indicates that the clip will play slower than normal speed and the clip's duration lengthens. When you drag the handle to the left, the clip will play faster than normal and the clip's duration shortens.

Be aware that this is not a trim edit. Despite the speed change, the clip's end point remains the same. The frame cadence is altered to implement the new speed settings. In a nutshell, a clip at 100-percent speed plays frames 1, 2, 3, 4, and so on, just as the clip was recorded. When you play the clip at 200-percent speed, the clip skips alternate frames and plays frames 1, 3, 5, and so on. The side effect of skipping frames is that the clip's duration is shortened; however, the start and end points don't change.

Before you continue, you should reset the clip to normal, 100-percent forward speed.

2   With **DN_9452** selected, from the Retiming pop-up menu at the lower-left of the Viewer, choose Reset Speed.

By dragging the retiming handle, you may alter the duration or the playback speed of a clip. But you may also change speed using another manual method that utilizes a numeric entry.

3   In the Retime Editor, click the Speed pop-up menu located to the right of the percentage display.

The Speed pop-up menu contains some of the same options as the Retiming pop-up menu, including the Custom speed option.

4   From the Speed pop-up menu, choose Custom.

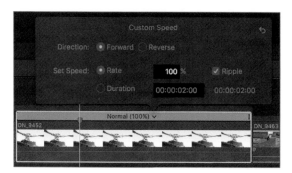

The Custom Speed window opens.

Here you may numerically enter a playback rate for a clip or the desired duration, and allow Final Cut Pro to calculate the necessary speed change. For **DN_9452**, you want to play the clip faster. Because the clip duration is already set as needed, you'll adjust the rate.

5   In the Rate percentage field, type *200*, but don't press Return yet.

When you increase the playback rate of a clip you also shorten its duration, which can create gaps in your timeline. Selecting the Ripple checkbox addresses the shortened length by rippling the following clips to avoid such gaps. Let's test that in action.

6   Verify that Ripple is selected, and then press Return.

The clip plays at 2x (200 percent of) its original speed, but also shortens to half its original length. Unfortunately, you want the shot to play at the faster rate while continuing until the beginning of **DN_9463**. Let's try another technique to fix the problem.

7   Undo the rate change by pressing **Command-Z**.

Clip **DN_9452** resets to its normal 100 percent rate and returns to its original length. The Custom Speed window is still open, so let's redo that speed change but without the ripple setting.

8   Deselect the Ripple checkbox. In the Rate percentage field, type *200* and press Return.

The clip plays back at the faster rate, but **DN_9452**'s duration remains consistent before and after the retiming. As long as media is available beyond the clip's end point, deselecting Ripple will lock that clip's duration during the custom speed change by utilizing that extra available media.

NOTE ▶   Click outside the Custom Speed window to close it.

The results still aren't dramatic enough to convey the power of a turbine-powered helicopter. Let's redo the Speed change to 600 percent. That should get those rotors turning.

9   In the Custom Speed window, verify that the Ripple checkbox is deselected. Change the Rate to *600*, and press Return.

NOTE ▶ Click the Retime Editor's Speed button to reopen the Custom Speed window.

That's more like it. The helicopter is about to take flight, and the rotor blades visually convey that speed. Now you've applied two constant speed effects to your project. With the helicopter starting clip, you may notice the "sound effect" provided by the crew. It's not quite the real, mechanical sound, so you'll later insert a different sound effect.

Exercise 6.1.2
Editing with Blade Speed

Another retiming effect, the variable speed change, applies at least two different playback rates within a single clip. This effect requires dividing the clip into segments, one for each speed rate. Aerials_13_01b is the perfect clip for this effect. It shows the helicopter racing above the desert and then flying over the cliff, revealing the lake.

Right now, this clip is trimmed to the necessary story duration, but would be better if it included the cliff and lake views. To perform this edit and apply the effect, you need to see the entire clip to identify the speed segments. Although you could temporarily ripple edit the clip to extend it to its full length, here's another method.

1   Using the Timeline Index, locate **Aerials_13_01b**, which has the "speed to reveal" to-do marker.

   You could drag to extend the **Aerials_13_01b** end point to view the entire clip; or you could change the clip's duration numerically, as you will do here.

2   With **Aerials_13_01b** selected in the Timeline, press **Control-D**.

   The clip's current duration appears in the timecode display. You may recall that the source clip is rather long, so entering a new, longer duration will include the "reveal" of the lake.

3   Without clicking (because the timecode display is already prepared to receive a new value), enter *45.* (four five period), and press Return.

   Aerials_13_01b lengthens to 45 seconds. Skimming the clip shows the reveal to the lake. You will use the Blade Speed option to "break" the clip into speed segments.

   You will tie together two elements with these speed segments: the music and the visual reveal. The first speed segment will play the clip at normal speed, which is the clip's current status. So what you are first looking and listening for is where to start the speed change and place the second speed segment.

   Close to the end of the **MVI_1044** sound bite, Mitch says, "eye opener." Let's use that as the kickstart for the speed change.

4   Cue the playhead where Mitch says, "eye opener."

5   Select **Aerials_13_01b**, and from the Retiming pop-up menu, choose Blade Speed, or
press **Shift-B**.

The clip's Retime Editor opens, indicating the two speed segments you created. The
start of the second speed segment identifies where in the shot (flying over the desert)
and when in the sound bite's audio ("eye opener") the speed change will occur. Starting at this segment, you will accelerate the playback to the point in the clip where the
helicopter reaches the edge of the cliff and the lake is revealed. That's where you'll
start a third speed segment.

6   In the View menu, activate Clip Skimming, and skim to when the helicopter has gone
halfway over the cliff.

7   Option-click **Aerials_13_01b** to move the playhead to the skimmer's location, and then
press **Shift-B**.

You've established what you want to see at the start of the third segment. Now you're
ready to set the speed change relative to the music. Earlier, you created a marker
named Swell. You may locate that musical swell using the Timeline Index, set to All
tags; or you may reference the nearby marker in the Timeline.

8   Cue the playhead to the musical swell at roughly 00:01:14:14 in the project.

Setting the playhead at this musical point identifies a reference point for the end of the second speed segment.

9   At the end of that second speed segment, drag the retiming handle to the left until it aligns to the playhead.

Review the entire clip. Watch and listen as the helicopter races across the desert floor and the lake is revealed with the musical swell.

6.1.2-A Working with Speed Transitions

While reviewing the overall effect of these changes, you may notice an acceleration into and deceleration out of the second speed segment. Although the acceleration is effective at the start of the segment, you would like a more abrupt speed change to coincide with the lake reveal.

The speed segments include speed transitions that control the speed change between segments. Of course, they are adjustable.

1   Locate the mouse pointer over the left edge of the second speed transition.

2   Drag the left edge of the transition toward the center of the transition until its left half is removed.

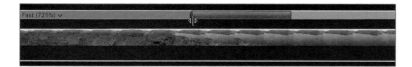

When you examine the edit, you'll see that a deceleration transition is still present, but it does not occur until the point at which you speed-bladed the clip.

3   Vary the duration of the speed transition's right half to alter the deceleration and observe how it impacts the dramatic relationship between image and music. Is the abrupt drop from jet speed to walking speed a good thing?

After reviewing an edit, if you decide that you speed-bladed at the wrong frame, you can still adjust where the transition occurs relative to the content.

4   With the retiming icon visible, double-click the retiming handle at the end of speed segment 2.

The Speed Transition HUD opens.

NOTE ▶ If the HUD does not open, press **Command-Z** until at least one of the speed transitions reappears, and then double-click the transition.

In the Speed Transition HUD, you can enable or disable both sides of the speed transition. You'll also find the Source Frame Editor here, which allows you to roll edit the clip within the speed change without changing the speed segment.

5   Deselect the Speed Transition checkbox, and then click the Source Frame Edit button.

The Source Frame Editor appears as a film-frame icon. The editor roll edits the content between the two speed segments, changing the end frame of the left speed segment while changing the start frame of the right speed segment.

6   Drag the source frame's film-frame icon left and right until the Viewer displays the cliff frame at which you want the speed change to occur.

7   Double-click the source frame icon to close the editor.

Now, you'll perform a cleanup edit to trim the end point of Aerials_13_01b to the correct duration.

8   Select **Aerials_13_01b** and cue the playhead to the start point of the next clip, **Aerials_11_01a**.

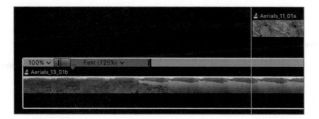

9   With the playhead and skimmer cued, press **Option-]** (right bracket).

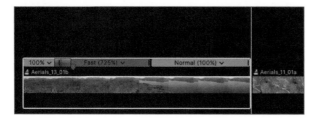

The four adjacent, connected clips here in the project may be enclosed within a connected storyline; however, that's not required. You'll see later in this lesson where a storyline is required.

▶ **Checkpoint 6.1.2**

Refer to **Appendix C** for details on reviewing a Checkpoint.

Reference 6.2
Working with Video Effects

Sometimes a clip needs the extra visual punch of a video effect or a color grade. A video effect could be a vignette to direct the viewer's attention to the center of the image. A color grade could increase (or decrease) the contrast to look as if the clip came from an old movie.

Final Cut Pro includes over 200 video and audio effects. Plus, the number of available third-party effects is growing every day. You may even create original effects and share them with fellow Final Cut Pro users.

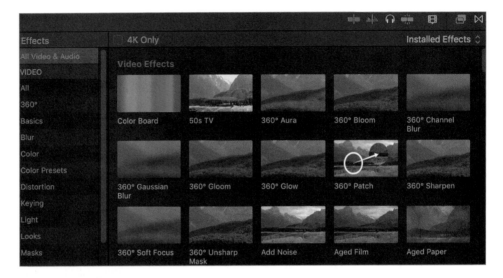

All video and audio effects are displayed in the Effects Browser. In its left sidebar, effects are organized into video and audio subcategories. A search field at the lower end of the browser supports text-based searching for effects.

After applying a video effect to a clip, you'll find settings for adjusting that effect in the clip's Video inspector.

Each effect appears within the Effects section in the order it was applied. The number of available settings varies by effect.

By default, a video effect will alter pixels within the entire visual, but sometimes you may wish to limit an effect to pixels of a single hue, or to a specific area, or to single pixel colors in a specific area. For example, you may want to enrich the blue of the sky without changing other blue objects within a clip. Most effects allow you to apply these types of limiters using **masks** built into each effect.

You can create complex visual effects by combining the masks of a single effect with multiple effects applied to a single clip.

Exercise 6.2.1
Experimenting with Video Effects

Applying an effect is simple. First, select one or more destination project clips. In the Effects Browser, double-click the desired effect to apply the effect, which is now ready for additional customization.

In Lifted Vignette, let's apply a vignette effect to the last shot of the helicopter flying into the sunset.

1   Cue the playhead to the last B-roll clip, **DN_9424**, and select the clip.

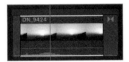

This clip may be enhanced by applying a vignette that darkens the corners of the image.

2   In the Effects Browser to the upper right of the Timeline, ensure that "All Video & Audio" is selected in the sidebar, and search for *vignette*.

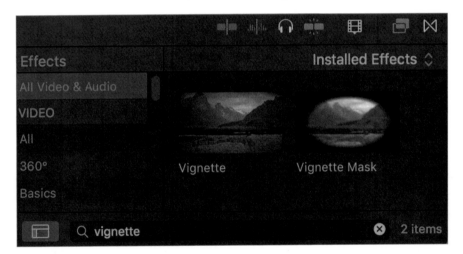

Two effects appear. You may preview each effect by skimming its thumbnail in the Browser.

3   Skim the Vignette and Vignette Mask effects.

You do not need a mask version of this effect, so the regular Vignette effect will do.

4   Skim over the Vignette effect again, and then press the Spacebar to start playback.

You see a live preview of the Vignette effect applied to **DN_9424**. Some settings specific to this Vignette effect may be modified. To do so, you must first apply the effect to a project clip.

5 Ensure that **DN_9424** is selected, and then double-click the Vignette effect.

> **NOTE ▶** Alternatively, you may drag an effect to a Timeline clip.

With the playhead cued over the clip, the results are visible in the Viewer. A key thing to remember when working with effects is to cue the playhead over the clip you are altering. You will then immediately see the results when you modify the effect.

6.2.1-A Modifying an Effect

With the effect applied, you may adjust its settings in the Video inspector. Remember that the settings for effects, transitions, and titles are available only after the effect is applied to a Timeline clip.

The available adjustments will vary depending on the effect. Some effects have only two or three parameters, while others have dozens. You may change these parameters to customize the effect for a specific clip, as you've started to do with the Vignette applied to the last clip. Because exploring and experimenting is so easy and reversible, you're missing an opportunity to discover the possibilities if you don't tweak a parameter or two.

1 Open the Video inspector by clicking the Inspector button, or pressing **Command-4**, if necessary.

2 In the Video inspector, accessed by selecting the Video button at the top of the Inspector pane, Vignette is listed in the first category, Effects.

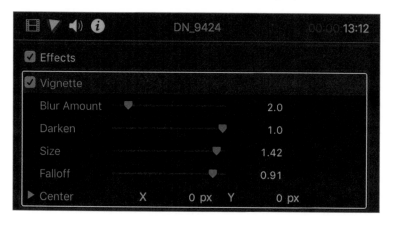

The Vignette parameters appear in the Video inspector because you selected the clip with that effect at the end of the previous exercise.

NOTE ▶ If Vignette is not listed, ensure that the playhead is over **DN_9424** and that no other clip is selected.

3   Drag the fourth slider, Falloff, left to a value of 0.57.

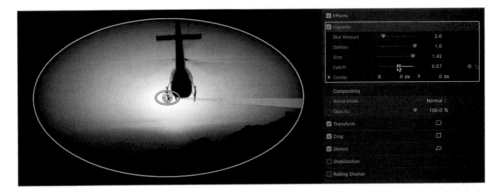

The Vignette collapses, shrinking the viewable portion of the clip. That may be too much falloff. But before addressing that, let's tweak some other parameters. Some of those parameters are adjustable in the Viewer and Inspector, while others are adjustable only in the Inspector.

4   In the Viewer, adjust the inner concentric oval.

The image updates in the Viewer as the Size and Falloff parameters update in the Video inspector.

After you've experimented with an effect, you may want to reset the effect and start over. Reset buttons are available in the Inspector to the right of the effect.

At right of the Vignette effect is a pop-up menu, which you can use to reset all the parameters of the effect.

5   In the Video inspector, click the Vignette's pop-up menu and choose Reset Parameter.

The Vignette effect returns to its default settings. Since trying one effect is so easy, let's now see how easy it is to try a couple of effects at once.

6.2.1-B Stacking Effects

You can apply more than one effect to a clip. You should not go overboard by applying 20 to 30 effects to a clip without reason, but two or three may be called for in your project. Some effects are corrective effects. Depending on a clip's content, it may need a few corrective filters. Other effects function as decorative filters that add a visual style to an image.

One technique when using multiple effects is to change their stacking order in the Inspector. When you apply an effect to a clip, the effect is added to the bottom of the Effects category in the Video inspector. The order in which the effects appear in the Video inspector may affect their impact on the final image.

1   With **DN_9424** selected, ensure that the Video inspector is still visible.

2   In the Effects Browser, clear the previous search text, then locate and double-click the Aged Paper effect.

The sunset image appears to be part of the texture from the Aged Paper effect.

In the Inspector, notice the layering order of the effects. Vignette is applied to the image first, and then Aged Paper is applied to the composite of the clip and the previously applied vignette. To better understand what's happening, let's add a blur effect.

3   In the Effects Browser, locate and apply the Focus effect to **DN_9424**.

Because Focus was the last effect applied to this clip, Focus is the last effect listed. The Focus effect blurred the mountains and sky in the clip, and also blurred the texture added by the Aged Paper effect. Let's make another change to test the impact of the effect layering order.

NOTE ▶ With the pointer located over an effect's title bar, you can click the Hide button at right of the effect's name to collapse its parameters, if desired.

Depending on your display's resolution, the Inspector may not display all the effects without scrolling. You may expand the Inspector vertically to increase the number of visible details.

4   Choose View > Toggle Inspector Height to expand the Inspector area.

5   In the Inspector, drag Focus on top of Aged Paper. The Aged Paper effect automatically drops down to place Focus after Vignette.

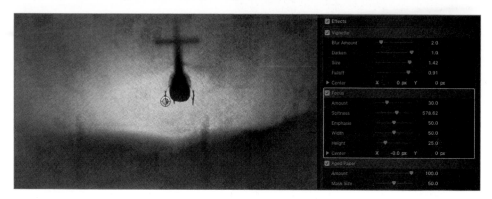

Notice the difference in the clip appearance as Aged Paper is composited onto the Focus effect. The paper texture is processed after the Focus-applied blur because effects processing starts with the topmost effect, and then proceeds down through the stack. As a result, the bottom effect can dramatically alter every previously applied effect.

6.2.1-C Saving Effects as a Preset

After ordering and adjusting effects to achieve a desired look, you can save a single effect or a combination of effects (along with their settings) as a preset for later use. Saved effects are global in Final Cut Pro, so they become available for reuse in any project in any library.

> **NOTE** ▶ Effect presets are saved locally on your computer in your Library/Application Support/ProApps/Effects Presets folder.

1   In the Video inspector, click the Save Effects Preset button.

Save Effects Preset

The Save Video Effects Preset dialog appears, allowing you to cherry-pick from the applied effects and additional video settings. These additional settings include the Transform and Crop parameters, which you'll learn about later in this lesson.

2   In the Name field, type *My Vignette*, but don't press Enter yet.

In addition to saving the preset under a custom name, you can assign the preset to an existing or custom category.

3   From the Category pop-up menu, choose New Category.

4   In the "Name of new category" field that appears, type *Vignettes*, and then click Create.

5   Deselect the Aged Paper effect, and click Save.

The Effects Browser updates with the Video Effect category you created, Vignettes, and the newly saved preset, My Vignette.

As with other video effects, you may preview this effect's look with any project clip.

6   In the Timeline, cue the playhead over **DN_9420** where the sunlight shines through the windows.

7   Preview the My Vignette effect on **DN_9420** by skimming the effect in the Effects browser. Apply the effect to the clip.

The preview appears within the effect's thumbnail and in the Viewer. If a project calls for you to use this or another effect frequently, you may designate it as the default effect.

8   In the Effects browser, Control-click the effect thumbnail to view the Make Default Video Effect option in the shortcut menu.

Designating default status to a video effect assigns it to the keyboard shortcut **Option-E**.

After previewing, you'll see that this effect is a little too much for this clip and for **DN_9424**. So let's learn how to remove an applied effect.

6.2.1-D Deleting Effects and Removing Attributes
Any effect may be disabled or deleted in the Inspector. If you think you may later need a particular effect, you can disable it. But if the results of that effect don't suit your project at all, and you're sure you won't use it later, feel free to delete it. In the current project, the

Aged Paper and Focus effects are highly deletable. You'll utilize two methods for deleting or removing an effect from a clip.

1   In the Timeline, cue the playhead over and select **DN_9424**, the last video clip.

2   In the Video inspector, select Aged Paper, and press Delete to remove the effect.

NOTE ▶   Be sure that you press the Delete (Backspace) key, not the Forward Delete key (which would delete the entire clip).

The effect is removed permanently from the clip. If you wanted to disable this effect, you could have deselected the checkbox to the left of the effect's name.

The Focus effect must also be removed for both **DN_9420** and **DN_9424**. Rather than deleting the effect from both clips simultaneously using the Inspector, there is another option.

3   Select both **DN_9420** and **DN_9424**.

4   Choose Edit > Remove Attributes.

The Remove Attributes window lists the selected clips' applied and built-in effects. One advantage of using the Remove Attributes command instead of the Inspector: This command lists all the effects applied to the selection even when an effect is not applied to both clips. In the command's window, you'll remove the Aged Paper effect that remains on one clip while also removing the Focus effect applied to both clips.

5   Deselect the Vignette effect and the Volume setting, leaving the Aged Paper and Focus effects selected. Click Remove.

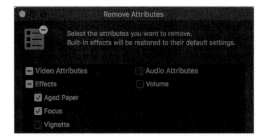

You're left with the Vignette effect applied to both clips. Although Vignette dramatically alters the edges of the image, the effect manipulates the entire image. Let's work with a different effect to alter only a portion of an image.

Exercise 6.2.2
Creating a Depth of Field Effect

GOPR0009 has a couple of distracting natural elements in the foreground. A simple solution would be to use the Transform controls to enlarge the image and crop out those distractions. But let's try using a blur effect to create a filter that will make those elements less distracting: a far-focused, shallow depth of field. You will blur the parapet wall to remove focus from those foreground elements.

1   In the Lifted Vignette project, go to **GOPR0009** where the helicopter is landing at the end of the day. Cue the playhead to and select the **GOPR0009** clip.

To blur the foreground slightly, you'll need to add a blur effect, such as the Gaussian effect, to defocus the parapet wall.

2   In the Effects Browser, locate and apply the Gaussian effect to **GOPR0009**.

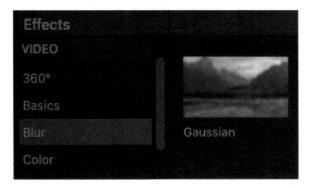

As you might have expected after you applied the Gaussian effect, the entire visual of **GOPR0009** was blurred in the Viewer. You can limit the area the effect changes by creating and applying a mask.

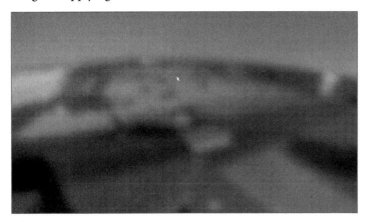

6.2.2-A Creating a Mask

To get the results you want from the Gaussian effect, you need to limit its blur to the parapet wall. You can achieve the needed partial blur by adding a **mask** that identifies the parapet to be blurred while leaving the rest of the image in focus. The effects in Final Cut Pro include built-in masks to limit the effect based on two controls: shape and color. In this exercise, you will use a shape mask to restrict the blur to the wall. You will find this easier to do if you first reduce the Viewer zoom level.

1   In the Viewer, from the Zoom pop-up menu, choose a value less than the currently displayed zoom level.

For example, if the zoom currently reads 60%, choose 50%. Doing so will open up some space around the Viewer's image in which you can adjust the mask.

2   In the Video inspector, place your mouse pointer over the Gaussian effect's title. Click the Apply Effect Masks button that appears, and choose Add Shape Mask.

The mask's onscreen controls appear as two concentric borders. The inner border includes control handles to define the scale, position, and rotation of the mask. The outer border's distance from the inner sets the mask's edge feathering. The closer the two borders are, the sharper the mask's edge. The roundness of the mask's corners is controlled by the Border Radius handle located on the inner border. Let's start by transforming the mask into a square.

3   Drag the Corner Radius handle away from the the border's center until the circle becomes a square.

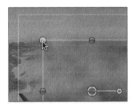

Using the onscreen controls, you will further transform the mask into a rectangle to encompass the longer, horizontal wall edge. Let's start by changing the shape to a rectangle.

4   Drag the control handle on the right edge to elongate the mask into a rectangle.

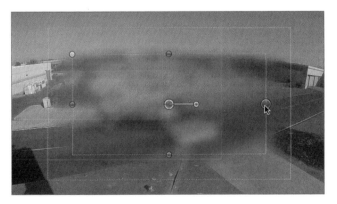

5   Drag the center handle and the attached rotation handle to align the mask to the wall's upper edge. Decrease the edge feathering by narrowing the gap between the outer and inner rectangles.

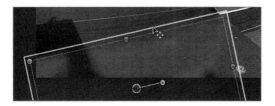

NOTE ▶ Although the wall is not quite square, the edge feathering should cover any difference.

To verify the alignment of the mask and the wall's edge, you may want to hide the onscreen controls.

6   In the Inspector, cycle the mask's onscreen controls off and on by clicking the button to the right of Shape Mask 1. Adjust the mask as necessary after re-enabling the onscreen controls.

7   When you're finished setting the mask, drag the Gaussian Amount slider to around 15 to make the effect a little more subtle.

NOTE ▶ Alternatively, you could click the text field at right to enter a numerical value and press Return.

As you've noticed, the mask does not cover the vertical edge of the wall. An additional shape mask on the Gaussian effect will expand the mask to complete the desired blur effect.

8   As you did in step 2, add a second shape mask.

9   Position, scale, and rotate the mask as shown in the following figure to align the mask with the vertical edge. Also, adjust the edge feathering and Corner Radius to match Shape Mask 1.

10   To see the image before and after the effect is applied, deselect the checkbox next to the Gaussian effect. Make sure you re-enable the effect when you're done examining the results.

The viewer's eyes are now more likely to go to the helicopter than the wall.

▶ Effect Mask Blend Mode

The mask blend modes control the ways multiple masks within an effect can interact with each other. Activating the View Masks button in the effect's title bar displays the masks' alpha channels created by one of the three blend modes: Add, Subtract, and Intersect.

▶   Add: Sums the masks together and expands the effect's alpha channel

▶   Subtract: Subtracts the selected mask from the previous mask to create a cutout in the effect's alpha channel

▶   Intersect: Confines the effect's alpha channel to the area where the masks overlap

NOTE ▶   A color mask may be limited to a region of an image by blending a color mask with one or more shape masks.

▶ **Checkpoint 6.2.2**

Refer to **Appendix C** for details on reviewing a Checkpoint.

Reference 6.3
Working with Video Transitions

In the syntax of video, transitions can help indicate a change in time and/or place: A slow dissolve sustains the emotional impact of the tragedy-just-happened into a scene a year later as the character returns to the tragedy site to find closure. Or a soft-edge wipe carries the viewer across the galaxy from C3PO and R2D2 on the Millennium Falcon to Darth Vader overseeing construction of the Death Star. As effective and versatile as transitions are, you do have to be careful when adding them. While these visual devices can link storytelling elements across time and space, they can easily become disruptive and confusing when overused.

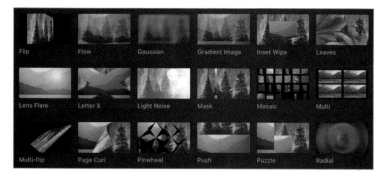

Just a small sample of the built-in transitions

With so many transitions available in Final Cut Pro, you may be tempted to use too many transition types within a single project. You should resist the temptation, and use transitions consistently within a project. Too much variation in transition types may lower a project's perceived production values.

You don't know what to avoid until you've at least seen or experienced other transitions. Let's look beyond the cut and cross dissolve transitions to see the other possibilities. You'll start by learning the three ways a clip or an edit point may receive a transition.

Exercise 6.3.1
Experimenting with Transitions

You'll find that applying and modifying transitions is similar to applying and modifying effects, although there is a difference when selecting clips versus edits points.

A transition between two clips involves two edit points: the end of the previous clip and the start of the next clip. Here's how Final Cut Pro sees and applies the transition to the edit points:

As you've already learned, selecting an edit point applied a transition between the selected and adjacent points.

A selected edit point...

...applies the transition to that point

Selecting a clip applies the transition to both ends of the clip, which is faster than applying the transition to one edit point at a time.

When you are creating a montage or collage edit, selecting all your Timeline clips and then pressing **Command-T** places the default transition, Cross Dissolve, on every edit point.

6.3.1-A Applying Cross Dissolves

Let's see a few cross dissolves in action in your project.

1 Select the start point of **Aerials_11_02a**, at around 29 seconds in the project.

A dissolve applied to this first aerials clip will transition the viewer from the take-off B-roll to the "landscape" clips. It's a nice setup that glides the audience into the aerial clips.

2 Press **Command-T** to apply the default cross dissolve transition.

The cross dissolve appears with a one-second duration and gently invites the viewer to fly along. To return to the interview, you'll apply a cross dissolve to the end of the clip with the helicopter buzzing the camera, at about 0:42 in the project.

3 Select the end point of **DN_9493**, and press **Command-T**.

These transitions soften the visual edits. The audience is encouraged to glide in and out of the interviews, the associated B-roll, and the music with connected aerials.

6.3.1-B Defining Media Handles for Transitions

So far, your transitions were easily applied due to the existence of media handles. When you trimmed down the clips, you told Final Cut Pro to ignore the rest of the clip's source media. That remaining content is referred to as the clip's media *handles*, the source media that exists beyond a clip's start and end points.

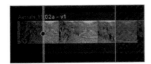

The left and right hashed sections represent the media handles.

When an edit point is set to the beginning or end of the clip's source media, no media handle is available to use with a transition, but that doesn't mean a transition cannot be applied. A transition may be applied when no media handle exists. Final Cut Pro will do it, but your content may suffer.

Final Cut Pro visually indicates whether a selected clip or edit point does or does not have a media handle. The clip's edit points are bracketed in yellow or red brackets. A yellow bracket indicates at least a two-frame media handle for a transition. A red bracket indicates the absence of a media handle.

Let's get back to the project to see these red and yellow brackets and learn how Final Cut Pro addresses a red-bracket, no-media-handle situation.

1   Activate the Trim tool, then select both the end point of **Aerials_11_02a** and the start point of **Aerials_13_02a** when the pointer changes to the Roll icon.

Something looks a little different here. The end point displays a yellow bracket, indicating the presence of a source media handle after the end point. The start point, however, displays a red bracket, indicating that no media handle is available prior to the clip's start point.

2   Press **Command-T** to apply the default cross dissolve.

A warning dialog points out that the clip lacks adequate media handles for this transition. Final Cut Pro can complete the transition request only by performing a ripple trim.

3   Click the Create Transition button while watching the end of the storyline.

Before the transition

After the transition

Note the rippling shift to the left in the storyline. To permit the transition, you agreed to ripple trim the clip to create a media handle. In response, Final Cut Pro created the transition by eating away some of the selected content.

The application moved the clip to fall under the transition, but that also affected the positioning of later clips. In some cases, that's not a bad thing. In this project, the ripple trim results in a potentially undesirable edit, which is why the warning dialog appeared. That undesirable edit is the cross dissolve at the end of the storyline back to Mitch on camera.

NOTE ▶ This change also affects the cross dissolve that occurs during the audio segue and extends from the helicopter low-pass to the sound bite. However, depending upon your earlier trimming, this edit may flow more smoothly.

6.3.1-C Slipping to Create Media Handles

When no media handle exists at one edit point for a transition, and you do not want Final Cut Pro to ripple trim the clip with the potential to affect subsequent clips, you have another solution: a slip edit. A slip edit allows you to change the visible (and audible) portion of content within a clip container. The clip container's duration and position within the Timeline stays the same, but the start and end points of the content change.

1   Press **Command-Z** to undo the previous transition that ripple trimmed the project.

2   From the Tools pop-up menu, choose the Trim tool, or press **T**, if necessary.

3   Place the Trim tool in the middle of **Aerials_13_02a**. The slip edit enables.

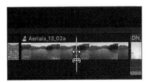

4   Drag the clip's contents to the left to move content before the start point, thereby creating a media handle.

NOTE ▶ The media handle should be at least half the duration of the transition you want to apply.

5 Press **A** to choose the Select tool.

6 With only the start point of **Aerials_13_02a** selected, press **Command-T** to apply the default cross dissolve.

A one-second cross dissolve is applied, but it does not ripple subsequent clips.

When a red bracket encloses an edit point that needs a transition, a transition may be applied at the expense of losing content under the transition. A slip edit allows you to create a media handle while still exercising some content control.

6.3.1-D Using the Transitions Browser

The Transitions Browser gives you easy access to organize your transitions, whether they are installed with Final Cut Pro, added from a third-party provider, or saved as one of your customized transitions. In addition to organizing your transitions, the browser also allows you to preview each transition before applying it to a project.

1 At the upper right of the Timeline area, click the Transitions Browser button.

Similar to some of the other browsers, a sidebar to the left displays subcategories of transitions. A search field is present for manually locating transitions.

2 In the Timeline, select the edit point between **Aerials_13_02a** and **DN_9493**. This edit point requires a cross dissolve, but let's first explore some other transitions.

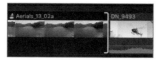

3 In the Transitions Browser, skim over several of the transition thumbnails.

The Viewer and the browser thumbnail demonstrate the effect of each transition by using two template images.

4 While skimming a transition's thumbnail, press the Spacebar to preview the transition in real time.

When you find a transition you will use over and over again in your project, you can set it as the default transition, applied when you press **Command-T**.

5 Find the Page Curl transition. Control-click it, and from the shortcut menu, choose Make Default.

Page Curl jumps to the top of the Transitions Browser and becomes the default transition. It may now be applied to an edit by pressing **Command-T**.

6 With the Timeline window active and the edit still selected, press **Command-T**.

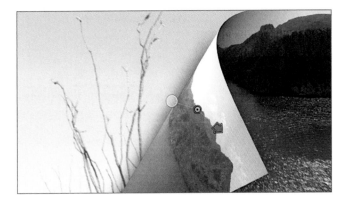

The new default, Page Curl, is applied to the selected edit point.

6.3.1-E Customizing Transitions

As with clips and effects, when a transition is edited into a project, you gain access to transition parameters you may customize in the Inspector pane.

1   Select the Page Curl transition you just applied in the Timeline, and cue the playhead over the transition.

The Transition inspector appears in the Inspector pane. Any parameters attached to the transition can be modified here. Also, the Page Curl transition has an onscreen control to adjust in the Viewer.

NOTE ▸   Option-clicking a transition or clip both selects the transition and cues the playhead to the selection.

In addition to parameters available in the Transition inspector, in the Timeline, the transition itself has adjustable controls for duration, ripple trim, and roll edit.

A transition has control points as shown in the following table.

Transition Adjustment Options in the Timeline

Ripple trim the start of incoming clip	
Ripple trim the end of outgoing clip	
Roll the underlying edit	
Change a transition's duration	

2   Place the mouse pointer over the left or right edge of the transition.

3   Slowly move the pointer toward the top of the transition and back down.

   Two different edit tools appear: Ripple Trim and Resize (duration).

4   Position the mouse pointer to enable the Resize tool (no filmstrip), and then drag away from the center of the transition.

The transition increases in duration, which slows the rate of transition between the two clips. Because transitions require media handles, the transition may be lengthened only to the duration of the shortest media handle.

Alternatively, you may adjust a selected transition's duration using the Dashboard.

5   With the transition selected, press **Control-D** to reveal the duration in the timecode display.

> **NOTE** ▸ The transition, and not its edges, must be selected.

6   With the timecode display indicating the transition's duration, type *1.* (one period), and press Return.

The transition returns to a one-second duration.

Before applying more cross dissolves to your project, you should reset the default transition to Cross Dissolve.

7   In the Transitions Browser, Control-click the Cross Dissolve transition, and from the shortcut menu, choose Make Default.

8   To replace the Page Curl with a Cross Dissolve transition (the new default), select the Page Curl transition in the project, and then double-click the Cross Dissolve in the Transitions Browser.

Cross Dissolve replaces Page Curl in the Timeline.

> **NOTE** ▸ To delete a selected transition, press Delete.

6.3.1-F Adding More Cross Dissolves

After learning more about using transitions, you're ready to resume your Lifted Vignette edit. Using the following list, verify and add a cross dissolve at the following edit points, if necessary. The location is given by the starting clips' start point unless otherwise noted.

For example, the second clip listed indicates that a cross dissolve should be applied at the start of **Aerials_11_02a**.

▸ Start of project

▸ **Aerials_11_02a**

▸ **Aerials_13_02a**

▸ **DN_9493**

▸ **GOPR1857**

▸ **Aerials_11_01a**

▸ **Aerials_11_03a**

▸ End of **DN_9420**

▸ Start and end of **DN_9424**

The majority of the required transitions are now applied to Lifted Vignette. There may be a few, very minor tweaks necessary as you get closer to sharing the project, but overall, the transitions are a great addition to the edit.

▶ **Checkpoint 6.3.1**

Refer to Appendix C for details on reviewing a Checkpoint.

Reference 6.4
Compositing Using Spatial Parameters

Final Cut Pro allows you to position an image from any visual clip—video, still, title, or animation—anywhere within the Viewer, and then rotate, scale, crop, and trim that image. This allows you to scale down an image, reframe an image, or place two images side by side to create a split-screen effect. Combined with the "top-down" compositing behavior, you can create simple to complex composited images within the Timeline.

Here's a quick rundown of the clip parameters you'll encounter when compositing multiple lanes of vertically stacked clips.

▶ Transform, Crop, and Distort: You'll find these parameters in two places for easy adjustment: the Video inspector and the lower-left of the Viewer. A combination of these parameters allows you to place visual images anywhere within the Viewer.

Inspector

Viewer

▶ Opacity: A spatial parameter that may be adjusted in the Video inspector and the Video Animation Editor.

Inspector

Video Animation Editor

Exercise 6.4.1
Creating a Two-Up Split Screen

In Lifted Vignette, you made an edit, GOPR3310, that shows Mitch flying the helicopter. He leans forward to get a better view. Let's composite two images on the screen at once so the viewer can see what Mitch was looking at.

6.4.1-A Using a Timeline-Based Range for a Backtimed Edit

Although the following technique seems complex for creating a single edit, after you've learned the edit you'll be able to perform it without hesitation.

1   In the project, locate GOPR3310.

    You're about to connect a B-roll clip, Aerials_11_04a, to the same Timeline point as GOPR3310, and match its duration. To do so, you will mark a range in the Timeline.

2   Select the GOPR3310 clip, and with the mouse pointer over the clip, press **X** to mark a range around it.

    Selecting the Timeline clip alone does not set the duration for this edit. Pressing **X** sets start and end points around the duration of the Timeline clip. The visible difference between a selected and marked clip is represented by handles at the edges of the marked clip.

3   In the Browser, find Aerials_11_04a.

4   In Aerials_11_04a, cue the playhead or skimmer to around a clip time of 2:33:15 as the helicopter has rounded the cliff. Set an end point by pressing **O**.

In addition to editing the aerial clip into the project to match the duration of the GoPro clip, you want to ensure that the end of the aerial clip is included in the final edit. The technique for doing this is referred to as a **backtimed** edit. A backtimed edit synchronizes the end point of the source Browser clip with the marked range end in the Timeline. Final Cut Pro then backfills the Timeline range with the source Browser clip until the Timeline range is filled back to the range start. Here you are backtiming to ensure that the helicopter has rounded the corner of the cliff, which ensures that the viewer will understand what Mitch is leaning forward to see.

You've already set up the edit, so you need only press the key command to perform the backtimed edit: **Shift-Q**, which is the Connect Edit key command (**Q**) in combination with Shift.

5   Press **Shift-Q** to perform the backtimed connect edit.

You can't see the desired result just yet. The aerial clip, layered above the GoPro clip in the project, is blocking the view. The images from the clips may be repositioned to create a composite.

NOTE ▸ If you received a warning (as shown in the following figure), your selection in **Aerials_11_04a** was too short. Click Cancel, adjust the end point of **Aerials_11_04a** to the right a few frames, and then perform step 5 again.

6.4.1-B Positioning the Images in the Viewer

Your two B-roll clips are stacked one above the other. Now you will separate them in the Viewer so that both are simultaneously visible in the Viewer.

1   In the Timeline, Option-click **Aerials_11_04a** to select and cue the playhead over the clip.

2   In the Viewer, select the Transform tool.

A wireframe appears around the aerials clip's image, along with control handles indicating that the onscreen Transform controls are active. You can scale and rotate the image using the wireframe, and move the image by dragging the center handle. Let's offset the image to make room for the clip of Mitch.

3   In the Viewer, drag the center handle of the cliff/lake clip to the left.

4   Watch the guides to keep the image vertically centered, and continue dragging until Position X value indicates –240px in the upper area of the Viewer.

The image must be scaled down so that it fits in the Viewer. You can drag a corner control point to do so.

5   Drag the lower-right corner point of the wireframe toward the center of the wireframe until the Scale value is 58%.

You've roughly positioned and scaled the aerial clip. Now let's bring in Mitch's clip.

6   In the project, select **GOPR3310**.

The clip's wireframe appears in the Viewer. Because the aerials clip is active and on a higher lane than the Mitch clip, the aerials clip is composited as the uppermost level.

7   In the Viewer, drag the lower-left wireframe corner toward the center of the wireframe. Stop dragging when the vertical size of the wireframe matches the vertical size of the aerials clip at the same scale of 58%.

Mitch's clip becomes smaller as you drag. Both clips will not fit side by side without dramatically shrinking the images. To retain some image size, you will trim the edges of the Mitch clip to scale up both images on the screen.

8   Place the mouse pointer over the image within the wireframe and drag the Mitch clip to the right, finally aligning Mitch's face with the right third of the Viewer at a Position X value of 390px.

A bigger interview clip image of Mitch is visible in the background. But let's wait to address that. First, to fit a larger image of Mitch in the helicopter to the right and an even larger aerial shot on the left side of the Viewer, you will crop the Mitch clip.

9   At the lower-left of the Viewer, from the pop-up menu, choose the Crop tool.

The Crop tool has three modes—Trim, Crop, and Ken Burns—you choose using buttons in the Viewer. Trim allows you to cut off parts of the image. Crop also trims off parts of the image, but then scales up the result to fill the current frame size of the clip. Finally, Ken Burns allows you to animate the visual image using zooms and pans.

10   With the Crop tool's Trim effect chosen, Option-drag the left edge of the image toward the center to more tightly frame Mitch.

Option-dragging an edge with the Crop tool's Trim effect crops the opposite edge simultaneously.

11 Remember that Mitch is going to lean forward, so leave some room for him to do so. Also, trim the top in tighter as well.

With more space available in the Viewer for the split screen, you may scale up both images to reveal more details.

12 Return to the Transform tool and adjust the split-screen effect to suit yourself. In the Viewer, click Done, and review the edit.

In the clip, Mitch leans forward several times while looking for traffic or hazards. It would be an appropriate moment for Mitch to lean forward when the helicopter comes around the cliff. If necessary, you will slip edit an instance of that action toward the middle of the clip to coincide with the flight around the cliff.

NOTE ▶ If Mitch's action and the aerial clip's contents already are aligned in your split screen, you can skip to the next exercise.

13 In the Timeline, activate the Trim tool by pressing **T**.

14 With the Trim tool placed in the middle of **GOPR3310**, drag left and then right to align the clip.

As you drag, the two-up appears in the Viewer showing the clip's start and end points.

15 Continue dragging until you see Mitch sitting back in the chair in the start frame (left) and slightly leaning forward before he reaches for the sunshade at the end (right). Release the mouse button.

NOTE ▶ You can watch the mountains in the background of the previous image for additional guidance when locating the edit points.

When you release the mouse button, the Timeline clip is already updated with the new points.

16 Review the edit and repeat steps 14 and 15 as necessary to align the aerial view and Mitch's movements.

Exercise 6.4.2
Exploring the Video Animation Editor

In addition to manipulating parameters in the Inspector and with onscreen controls, you have a third way to access and edit parameters in the Video Animation Editor, and compare those settings with the parameters and settings of the same or other Timeline clips. To learn about this, you'll use the Opacity control to remove Mitch's interview behind the split screen.

1   Control-click the first **MVI_1043** located beneath the **GOPR3310** clip, and choose Show Video Animation.

The Video Animation Editor displays the spatial parameters, along with additional controls for some applied effects. As you can see, the Compositing Opacity parameter is available along the lower edge of the editor.

When a parameter is accessible, a Maximize button is visible.

2   To view the opacity controls, click the Maximize button.

Three types of controls are available to alter opacity. The first are fade handles such as those you used with audio clips when softening the edits in Lesson 4. Here, the handles can be used to create a video fade-in or fade-out.

3   Drag the fade-out handle toward the center and review the edit.

The clip's video fades out to black as if you had applied a transition from a gap clip.

4   Press **Command-Z** to return the handle to the start point.

The second control type for adjusting opacity is similar to adjusting the audio level.

5   Place the mouse pointer over the opacity control line, and drag the line down to 0%.

The interview of Mitch disappears behind the split screen.

Displayed as a percentage of total opacity, any value less than 100% is translucent until the value reaches 0%, which produces total transparency.

NOTE ▶ The third control type utilizes keyframes, but we'll save that for Lesson 7.

6   Close the Video Animation Editor by clicking the close button.

One down, and one more interview clip to remove visually from the split-screen composite.

6.4.2-A Copying and Pasting Attributes

For the second **MVI_1043** under the split screen, you may use a specialized copy and paste feature called Paste Attributes. You will notice during this exercise that the Paste Attributes feature may be used to speed up the sharing of specific parameter settings amongst many clips.

1   Select the **MVI_1043** clip in which you adjusted the opacity, and then press **Command-C** to copy it.

2   Select the next **MVI_1043** to the right, and choose Edit > Paste Attributes, or press **Command-Shift-V**, to determine which of the copied clip's parameters will be pasted to this clip.

The dialog lists the video and audio attributes available from the copied clip. You can cherry-pick the parameters you wish to copy to the second clip. You may have noticed that opacity is not listed. If you'll recall, in the Video Animation Editor, opacity was listed as Compositing: Opacity. Similarly, in the Inspector, Opacity is listed in the Compositing category.

3 Verify that the checkbox next to Compositing is selected. Deselect Volume, and click Paste.

You can verify that the opacity was changed to 0% by reviewing the edit in the project. The full transparency means that you can no longer see the interview with Mitch behind the split screen.

Reference 6.5
Compounding Clips

Everything in Final Cut Pro is a container: clips, the project, events, the library—all containers. Another container in Final Cut Pro, the compound clip, is really the container framework used to create the project and clip media containers. Compound clips, like storylines, are a way to contain media files with similar attributes or purpose within a project.

> **NOTE** ▶ In the Browser, a compound clip is identified by the special icon in the upper left of a clip's thumbnail. The same icon (minus the surrounding square) appears to the left of a compound clip's name in the Timeline.

Compound clips can be placed inside projects and inside other compound clips. A common industry term for this attribute is **nesting**. However, nesting falls short when describing the power of compound clips.

A compound clip can contain one or more clips, storylines, stills, animations, music, sfx, and so on. If something can go into a project, it can go into a compound clip.

Respect the power of compound clips. Compounds are "live" or "hot" clips with contents that remain in sync regardless of where they are used. For example, if Compound A is edited into both Project 1 and Project 2, a change to Compound A in Project 1 is also implemented (hot changes) in the Project 2 Compound A instance. Although you can isolate a compound from its clones, it is not the default behavior. You can find more information about making compound clips into independent clips in the Final Cut Pro X User Guide by searching for the "Reference New Parent Clip" command.

Exercise 6.5.1
Collapsing a Composite into a Compound

One of the best reasons to use a compound clip is to collapse a composite of multiple clips into one easily manageable clip. Collapsing multiple lanes into a single clip tidies up the

Timeline, and also allows you to apply an effect to the compound clip, thereby modifying all of its contained clips.

In the Lifted Vignette project, compounding the split-screen composite enables you to simultaneously apply an effect to both clips, move both clips as one, and prevent any accidental movement of a single clip that might throw off the timing between the two clips in the composite. The compound of those two clips also allows you to modify their audio channels with a single volume control, which makes for easier mixing.

1   In the project, locate the split-screen composite clips, and select both of the clips you previously composited.

2   With both clips selected, Control-click either one, and from the shortcut menu, choose New Compound Clip, or press **Option-G**.

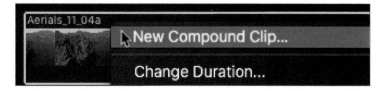

A dialog appears requesting a name for the compound clip and an event in which to store it. Similar to a newly created project, a compound is stored within an event.

3   In the Name field of the dialog, enter *Split-Screen Composite*. Set the Event to Primary Media. Click OK.

The two clips collapse into one compound clip that is stored in the Primary Media event. The **Split-Screen Composite** clip also jumped out of the storyline.

4 In the Timeline, drag to insert the **Split-Screen Composite** clip between **IMG_6493** and **DN_9503**.

NOTE ▶ If you need to adjust a clip inside a compound clip or add additional clips to a compound in a project, double-click the compound to open it in its own Timeline, ready for editing.

You've completed the first enhancement pass. As was stated earlier, your project may not require any of these techniques, or your project may need all of them. Hopefully, you discovered some Final Cut Pro features that you'll have at the ready for your next editing job.

▶ **Creating Compounds in the Browser**

You can start a blank compound in the Browser and edit within the compound without opening a project. Press **Option-G** in the Browser and complete the necessary dialog information. When you create a compound in this way, the dialog will look much like a new project dialog asking for video format information. Once created, double-clicking the compound opens it for editing in the Timeline.

NOTE ▶ As you create more compounds, they will add up in the Browser. Don't forget that you can create a Smart Collection to group them in the event using "Type is Compound" from the Add Rule pop-up menu.

▶ **Checkpoint 6.5.1**

Refer to **Appendix C** for details on reviewing a Checkpoint.

Lesson Review

1. Which interface items allow access to the Custom Speed window?

2. You have manually set the retiming rate for a clip; however, at this rate, the clip is too long for the time slot in the project. Which interface item allows you to trim the clip without changing the playback speed?

3. Which retiming command was used to create the speed segments shown in the following figure?

4. How do you access an effect's parameters to adjust the look (or sound) of that effect?

5. What are the steps to reset an effect's parameters, disable the effect, and delete an effect from a clip?

6. What does the red bracket indicate in the following figure?

7. Referring to the previous figure, describe two ways to create the media handles necessary to apply a one-second transition.

8. Which of the following images displays that you are ready to adjust the transition's duration?

A   B   C

9. How do you replace a project transition with a different transition from the Transitions Browser?

10. Which Viewer interface element can you use to activate the onscreen Transform controls?

11. Describe the difference between Paste and Paste Attributes.

12. How do you access the individual components of a compound clip?

Answers

1. Retime pop-up menu and Retime Editor

   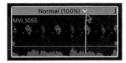

2. Ripple edit changes the clip's duration without changing the set speed rate.

3. The Blade Speed command from the Retime pop-up menu

4. First, the effect must be applied to a project clip. Second, the clip must be selected or the playhead cued over the clip to access the parameters in the Inspector pane.

5. Reset the parameters by clicking the effect's Reset button (the hooked arrow). Disable/enable an effect by clicking the effect's checkbox. With the effect's title bar selected, press the Delete key to delete an effect.

6. The starting clip does not have an adequate media handle to apply a transition.

7. Use the slip edit tool and drag left on the starting clip; or using the Roll trim tool, drag the edit point right to create a media handle prior to the clip's start point. The use of either method is dependent on available media handles on the opposite point: the end of the starting clip and the end of the ending clip, respectively.

8. C

9. You may drag the new transition to the existing transition, similar to performing a replace edit; or with the existing transition selected, double-click the new transition in the Transition Browser.

10.

11. Paste applies the copied clip and its attributes, similar to a replace edit. Paste Attributes allows you to select the desired attributes of the copied clip—such as a particular effect, or a specific parameter such as speed—to apply to another clip.

12. Double-click the compound clip.

Lesson 7
Finishing the Edit

You're now ready to embark on the finishing stage of the edit workflow. At this point, you'll be adding fun elements such as titles and graphics, but you also have some hefty, tedious issues to finally address, such as audio levels that are a little too loud, or B-roll that needs sound effects. This part of the workflow is all about dotting the i's and crossing the t's.

For Lifted Vignette, it's time to add text-based graphics, such as a **title page** and a **lower third**, which will name your soon-to-be finished piece and identify Mitch as the pilot. You also need to examine lots of audio details to mix the final audio into a cohesive soundtrack. And then you may need to perform color correction to resolve white balance issues and establish a visual consistency from clip to clip. You have a lot of work to do in this lesson, but the finished result is in sight.

Reference 7.1
Using Titles

Informational graphics answer one or more of the basic questions of who, what, when, where, or why. Whenever a project needs to present information, you have several ways to do so using a title.

- ▶ Add and modify a lower third
- ▶ Add and modify a 3D title
- ▶ Split edit audio and video
- ▶ Keyframe audio
- ▶ Use Audio Roles for organization and selection
- ▶ Differentiate the Luma and Chroma controls
- ▶ Correct an image using the Color Board, Color Wheels, or Color Curves
- ▶ Use the Balance Color options

A title page at the head of the project establishes a context and, you hope, entices the audience to sit down and watch. Lower thirds can identify who's who (or what's what) as the project unfolds on the screen. Finally, your project may need closing credits to acknowledge its participants and creators. Informational graphics are often the best way to convey details quickly and concisely.

Final Cut Pro utilizes the real-time design engine of Motion to add graphics to projects. Motion provides an assortment of high-quality templates inside the Final Cut Pro interface to get you started, even if you don't have Motion installed. If you download Motion from the Mac App Store, you can customize the supplied templates or redesign a new look from scratch. And with a growing user community, a plethora of third-party templates are available for use in Final Cut Pro and Motion.

Exercise 7.1.1
Adding and Modifying a Lower Third

When you started adding B-roll to this project, you held out a window of time for Mitch to appear on-camera. To help the audience identify with Mitch, you can insert a graphic to tell the viewer about him.

> **NOTE ▶** As you are starting a new edit pass for titles and graphics, practice good habits and snapshot your Lifted Vignette project before proceeding.

1   In Lifted Vignette, cue the playhead to the first frame of Mitch on-camera, at roughly 12 seconds.

> **NOTE ▶** Your "Add a title" marker may exist elsewhere on **MVI_1055**.

2   On the Browser sidebar, click the Show Titles and Generators button.

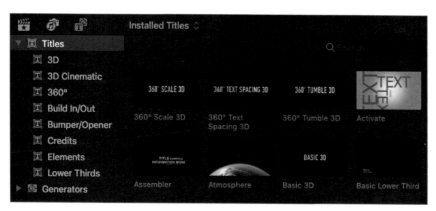

The Titles and Generators sidebar in the Browser area is similar in layout to the other browsers you worked with previously. The title templates are organized by category in the left sidebar. The Titles Browser also includes subcategories, where applicable, that group titles by theme as assigned by the title's artist.

3 In the sidebar, select the Lower Thirds category; and in the News subcategory, locate the Centered title.

4 Select the Centered lower third, and then press the Spacebar to preview it.

A preview of the lower third plays in the thumbnail and in the Viewer. You'll customize this title with Mitch's name and the company name. To customize a title, you first must add it to a project.

5 With the playhead still cued at the first frame of Mitch on-camera, double-click the Centered title to perform a connect edit.

The title appears as a connected clip at the start of Mitch's on-camera appearance. Depending on your B-roll edits, your centered title may be snugly wedged between the two connected storylines or overlapping the second connected storyline. Right now, let's change and format its text.

7.1.1-A Modifying Title Text

You have two methods of entering text into a title: using the onscreen controls or the Text inspector. You'll start by using the onscreen controls method, which allows you to enter text and also perform some spatial manipulation.

1   In the project, double-click the Centered title clip.

When you double-click, several things happen. The clip is selected, the playhead is cued to the first frame that clearly displays the text, and the first line of text is selected in the onscreen controls.

2   The text in the Viewer is automatically highlighted, so enter *Mitch Kelldorf H5 Productions*, and then press Esc to exit the text field.

The alternative method of text entry is to use the Text inspector.

3   In the Inspector area, select the Text inspector.

The Text field already displays the text you entered. Let's make a small change to the title, this time in the Inspector.

4   In the Text field, insert *Pilot,* (with comma) before the "H5 Productions" text.

When working with two text elements on the same line, creating a visual distinction between them improves viewer comprehension. You have a short opportunity in which the viewer will see this lower third.

NOTE ▸ Spell check will underline questionable words and suggest replacement words.

5   In the Viewer, place the mouse pointer over the title.

A bounding box appears around the text, and the Select tool icon changes to a Move tool. Dragging within the bounding box at this point would reposition the title.

6   Leave the title in place for now, but select Mitch's first and last names. Double-click to select his last name, and then, as in a word processor, drag across the text to select both his last and first name.

To visually differentiate his name from his job, let's change the text colors. Two parameters are associated with text color for this title template, and one of them is found in the Text inspector.

7   In the Text inspector, scroll down to the Face section.

By default, the Face parameters are active, but hidden from view.

8   With the mouse pointer on the Face section header, click the Show text button that appears to the right.

The Face parameters controlling the text's font face are displayed.

NOTE ▸ Alternatively, double-clicking an Inspector section's header shows/hides the associated parameters.

For the Color parameter, you'll find two color controls: the color well and the pop-up color palette. You can click the color well to open the macOS Colors window, or click the downward arrow button to open the pop-up color palette.

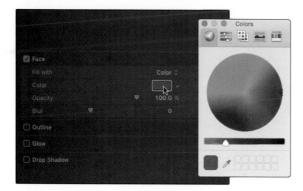

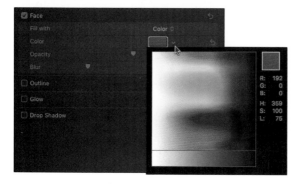

9   Using either the color well or the pop-up color palette, click a black color sample to display Mitch's name in black. Click the text in the Viewer, then press Esc.

The text color changes to black. It looks good, but you could add some flair by changing the font for the job position and company.

10 In the Viewer, select the "Pilot, H5 Productions" text. In the Text inspector, set the Style pop-up menu to Bold Italic. Press Esc.

The title looks great now because we have a difference between the two elements. It adds clarity to the storytelling without getting in the way. There is one technical change to consider, however: how long the title appears onscreen.

One common formula states that if the editor can read a lower third (or any onscreen text) at least twice but no more than three times, that's an appropriate duration to allow a viewer to see, read, and process it. In Lifted Vignette, you already created a short time slot between B-roll clips for this lower third; you should adjust the title's duration to fill that slot.

7.1.1-B Extending an Edit

Instead of dragging a clip's start or end point to shorten or lengthen a clip, you can use an extend edit to speed up the process. An extend edit rolls the selected edit point to the playhead or skimmer.

1   In the Timeline, select the end point of the title clip.

   By selecting this point, you've identified the edit point to extend edit to the skimmer or playhead. You'll now cue the skimmer to indicate when you want the title clip to end.

   NOTE ▶ Although your title may extend above the following storyline or may be short of filling the gap, the following steps still apply.

2   Cue the playhead to somewhere within the title clip.

3 Press **Shift-X** to extend the selected point to the playhead's position.

You need to extend the end point of Mitch's title clip to the start of the next B-roll clip.

4 Cue the skimmer to the start of **DN_9455**, and with the title's end point still selected, press **Shift-X**.

Like the trim start, trim end, and trim selection you learned earlier, the extend edit is another efficiency to speed up the editing process.

▶ **Replacing Title Text**

Depending on the number of interviews, locations, or open captions in your project, you may add many titles, and sometimes a spelling error may occur across multiple titles. For example, you may have used lower thirds with the text "Inside the H5 Hangar," "Outside the H5 Hangar," and "Returning to the H5 Hangar," but had misspelled "hangar" as "hanger." The "Find and Replace Title Text" command is your quick-fix solution. Choose Edit > "Find and Replace Title Text," and then use the Find and Replace fields to locate the incorrect text and replace it with the corrected text.

Reference 7.2
Creating 3D Titles

Sometimes a project may benefit from a title with a little simulated depth. You probably noticed the 3D and 3D Cinematic categories earlier when accessing the Title Browser. These 3D text templates allow you to leverage Motion's 3D Text capabilities within Final Cut Pro.

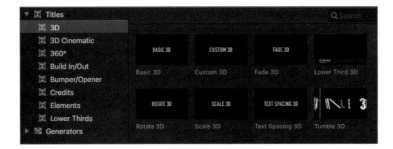

The 3D title templates include prebuilt text animations such as tumbles, slides, rotations, and tracking that are ready to be applied to your project. If you need something tailored to your project, you can create a custom template and modify the previously listed animations by tweaking a few more parameters to produce customized entry and exit animations.

In addition to the Inspector controls for animation, a 3D title contains many controls that modify the look of the 3D text. You'll find controls for setting the size of the text, its lighting, and the material makeup of each **glyph**'s multiple **facets**.

You'll also find controls for setting the depth and direction of the 3D extrusion, the weight of the front and back faces, and the style of the front and back edges.

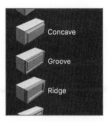

But wait, there's more. A special onscreen control exists for manipulating a 3D title in 3D space directly in the Viewer.

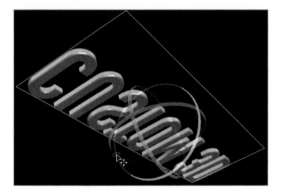

Let's create a 3D title using a Custom 3D Title template. You will set up the lighting, the look of the 3D text, and the animation behavior...in just a few clicks.

▶ **Converting a Lower Third from 2D to 3D**

A title may be transformed from 2D to 3D (and back) at any time. Selecting the 3D Text checkbox in the Text inspector immediately transforms a flat 2D title into a title with added dimension.

Mitch Kelldorf *Pilot, H5 Productions*

A 2D lower-third title

Mitch Kelldorf *Pilot, H5 Productions*

The same lower-third converted to a 3D title

Exercise 7.2.1
Exploring 3D Options

The 3D titles included with Final Cut Pro are great launching points for adding the power of 3D text to your project with only a little time and effort. In this exercise, you'll quickly create a title page for the beginning of the Lifted Vignette using a Custom 3D template.

1   In the Titles and Generators sidebar, select the 3D category, and then skim the Custom 3D template.

The results are neither very exciting nor very 3D at the moment. So let's place the 3D title in the project and then change the perspective of the text.

2   With the Timeline active, press the Home key to jump to the start of the project.

Currently, the project starts with the hangar door opening reflected on the helicopter's nose. The 3D title should start over black before this action in clip **DN_9488**. Furthermore, the 3D title should remain visible while **DN_9488** fades in under the title. To create this look, the entire project must be pushed down the Timeline. A quick way to do so is to insert a gap clip at the start of the Timeline.

3   With the playhead cued to the start of the project, press **Option-W**.

A three-second gap clip is inserted at the project's start, and the existing clips are pushed down the Timeline. Now let's add the Custom 3D title to the project.

4   With the playhead still cued to the start of the project, in the Titles browser, double-click the Custom 3D title.

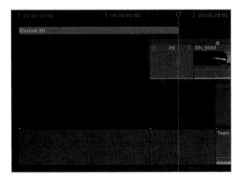

5   Option-click the Custom 3D title in the project.

Option-clicking a clip automatically selects the clip and cues the playhead over the clip. You're ready to manipulate the text in 3D space.

7.2.1-A Transforming Text in 3D

Earlier, you used the onscreen Transform controls to create the split-screen view of Mitch looking for traffic while flying around the cliff. These controls allow image manipulation for positioning in the X and Y axis and for rotation (also known as *bank* or *roll*) in the Z axis. The 3D onscreen controls enable rotation around the X axis and Y axis, which allow you to see the depth of each text glyph.

1   After Option-clicking the text to select the title and cue the playhead over the title, the title appears in the Viewer. Click the title once in the Viewer.

Six controls are available for manipulating the text in 3D space:

- ► Red arrow: Move the text left or right (X axis)
- ► Green arrow: Move the text up or down (Y axis)
- ► Blue arrow: Move the text near or far (Z axis)

- ▶ Red circle: Pitch the text forward or backward (X axis)
- ▶ Green circle: Spin the text left or right (Y axis)
- ▶ Blue circle: Roll the text clockwise or counter-clockwise (Z axis)

2 Using the 3D onscreen controls, manipulate the text to inspect all sides of the title.

3 Press **Command-Z** as necessary to undo your changes and return the title to its default orientation.

NOTE ▶ If you undo too many times, press **Command-Shift-Z** to Redo and revert to previous states.

The text has depth with sides, edges, and backs for each glyph. Each of these elements are customizable individually or as a group by using simple presets or detailed controls.

To clearly see the results when applying presets and using controls in the next exercise, let's adjust the title's position and the Viewer settings.

4   If necessary, set the Viewer's Display pop-up menu to 100%.

5   Using the 3D onscreen controls, drag the blue arrow control to the right to bring the text closer to you along the Z axis.

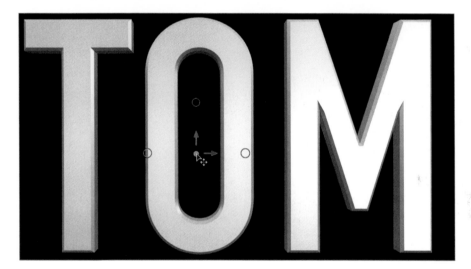

6   Drag the left rotation handle, the green circle, to the right to spin the text counter-clockwise.

7 Adjust the 3D controls as needed to position the text as shown in the following figure.

With the text positioned for close observation, you'll now explore the 3D customization options.

7.2.1-B Adjusting the Shape of 3D Glyphs

All the 3D title templates share the same parameter set, found in the Text inspector, for adjusting the look of 3D text. Because you'll later be resetting the title, feel free to experiment during this exercise.

1 Choose View > Toggle Inspector Height to display the Inspector at full height, if necessary.

2 In the Text inspector, locate the 3D Text heading, and click the Show button to view the parameters.

3   Drag the Depth slider to the right to a value of about 30 while observing the results in the Viewer.

The glyphs' depth thickens. By default, that thickening originates from a center Y axis in the glyph. The Depth Direction pop-up menu allows you to relocate that depth change from the center of the glyph to forward or backward from the front face.

4   Drag the Weight slider left and right while watching the results. When you're finished, set a value of 2.

The next four edge controls offer a variety of options for creating unique results.

5 Before experimenting with other parameters, reset the 3D Text settings by clicking its Reset button.

▶ **Lights!**

The Lighting parameters include two pop-up menus that preset the lighting placement around the text and set the environment reflected by the glyphs. For information about these controls, see the <a href="http://help.apple.com/finalcutpro/mac/10.2/?lang=en#/vere54ac6d03">Final Cut Pro X Help website</a>.

7.2.1-C Refining the Look of 3D Glyphs

You have many more parameters for customizing your 3D titles. In this exercise, you'll explore a few of them while creating the opening title for your Lifted Vignette project. Earlier, you changed the shape of the glyphs—their depth, width, and edge types. The Material settings give you granular control over several aspects of a glyph's faces or facets. Let's start by looking at the default, single-facet setting and its options.

1   With the Custom 3D title in the project still selected, look at the Material section of the Text inspector.

By default, the Custom 3D title composes all facets of the glyphs from one material, plastic. You can color that plastic using the Color parameter.

2   Next to the Substance: Color parameter, from the palette pop-up menu, choose white as the plastic color to be applied to the glyphs.

That's some bright plastic text! As you are creating the vignette's title graphic, you may decide that plastic is not the right surface type. Let's change the glyphs to an aluminum surface, similar to the helicopter.

3 In the Material section, from the Substance pop-up menu, choose Metal. Verify that the Type pop-up menu is set to Aluminum.

NOTE ▶ The light reflections will vary depending on the text's position relative to the simulated lighting and its environment. Adjust the position of the title using the 3D Transform controls in the Viewer to observe the changing reflections.

You can further customize the facets by controlling their type of paint and surface finish by adding Layer options to the facets' material. Let's make the paint reflective and add a polished look to create glyphs similar to the text and logo on the H5 helicopter.

4 To the right of the Material Options, from the Add Layer pop-up menu, choose Paint > Reflective Paint. Also from the Add Layer pop-up menu, choose Finish > Polish.

The Reflective Paint changed the paint color of the glyphs. Let's return it to white.

5   In the Paint Color parameter under the Reflective Paint category, choose white.

That's not bad looking, but more controls are available. You may want to mimic the SaberCat logo on the side of the helicopter by altering the individual facet groups of the title.

6   In the Text inspector, next to the Material category, click the Single pop-up menu, and choose Multiple.

The Facet controls are now grouped by edges, sides, backs, and back edges. Selecting a group control changes the Options parameters displayed for that group's settings. Currently, you are controlling the Front facets because the Front group is selected. Since you have already customized the front, let's proceed to the Side and Front Edge facets.

7   In the Material category, click the Side facet group to display that group's parameters.

8   In the Paint section for the Side facet group, set the Paint Color control to black.

9   In the Material category, click the Front Edge facet group, and set the Paint Color control to red.

You're now ready to create your title. You'll need a lighter font for the opening animation, which requires that the title be positioned at the center of the screen. Rather than guessing at the centering, you'll save the style settings applied to this draft title, refresh the title, and then apply this same style to the new copy of the custom 3D title.

10   At the top of the Text inspector, from the Preset pop-up menu (currently set to "Normal"), choose Save Appearance Attributes.

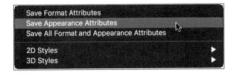

The Appearance Attributes include parameters such as paint colors and facets. The Format Attributes include settings such as font and font size.

11   In the Save Preset dialog that appears, type *Lifted Title*, and click Save.

12   With the Custom 3D title selected in the project, in the Titles and Generators browser, double-click the Custom 3D title.

As easily as that, you've refreshed the Custom 3D Title in your project. Now, let's choose a lighter weight font before reapplying the saved style.

13 Option-click the refreshed Custom 3D in the project.

14 In the Text inspector, from the Font pop-up menu, choose Zapfino for the title. Set the Size to 150, and from the Preset pop-up menu, apply the saved Lifted Title style.

15 Using the Text field in the Inspector, change the text to *Lifted*.

That Zapfino font may be a little too light weight, so let's use the 3D Text's Depth, Weight, and edge controls to add a more robust appearance.

16 In the 3D Text category of the Text inspector, set the following:

- ► Depth: 15
- ► Weight: 0.5
- ► Front Edge: Round
- ► Front Edge Size: 4

You have explored several parameters for creating and styling a 3D Title. In the next exercise, you'll animate the text using presets.

7.2.1-D Animating a 3D Title

You've styled the opening title. Now, you'll animate the title with a vertical movement similar to the helicopter's take-off. The Custom 3D title contains several animation parameters to create simple or complex entry and exit animations. In this exercise, you'll animate the title to rise from below while rotating into position in the center of a blank screen. After a brief pause (until the first video clip appears under the title), the title will resume vertical takeoff and rotate out of the frame.

1   With the Custom 3D title still selected in the project, go to the Title inspector.

The Title inspector contains additional parameters (borrowed from Motion) that enable you to alter title settings beyond what is available in the Text inspector. For this Custom 3D title, these additional parameters cover a wide range of animation options. Let's make the title start out of view.

2   In the Title inspector, from the Move In pop-up menu, choose Up. Cue the playhead to the start of the title clip, and play the Timeline.

You may have a sliver of the "f" glyph's terminal is visible at the start of the animation. A fade-in adjustment will hide it.

3   In the Title inspector, drag the Fade Duration In slider to 80 and play the Timeline.

Next, you'll add a rotation to the glyphs to make them move as if they each were a helicopter rotor.

4   From the Rotate In pop-up menu, choose Left.

One small change to that rotation—let's rotate and lift each glyph individually with a rippling effect. Two controls make this change possible: Animate By and Spread. Animate By sets the animation parameters to animate an entire line of text, individual words in the text, or individual characters. The Spread parameter controls the percentage of the animated items that should be animated.

5   In the Title inspector, set Animate By to Character and Spread to 40. Play the title.

The entry animation cascades similar to a wave from glyph to glyph. Now, you need to animate the title's exit.

6   Set the following parameters to the following values:

- ▶   Direction Out: Forwards
- ▶   Move Out: Up
- ▶   Rotate Out: Left
- ▶   Fade Duration Out: 80

7 Finally, extend the end point of the title for a duration of 5:21. Play the title to review your work.

You've added a customized 3D title to the beginning of your project that rises over the blank screen and reveals the helicopter as the hangar door rises. As the music starts, the title lifts into the air rotating like helicopter rotors, thereby thematically foreshadowing the takeoff as the music lifts into the chorus. (Or maybe it just looks cool.)

▶ **Checkpoint 7.2.1**

Refer to Appendix C for details on reviewing a Checkpoint.

Reference 7.3
Working with Audio

Until now in your workflow, the audio mix hasn't received the full attention it deserves, but for a good reason. Through Lesson 6, the project timing was altered as clips were inserted or removed. Individual clips also changed duration as they were ripple trimmed, speed manipulated, or slipped. And most recently, you composited effects and applied transitions that affected the timing and added elements that still require audio attention. Because of these inevitable duration changes, time spent mixing your audio early in the workflow could be time wasted. By attending to your audio design at this point in the workflow, you can refine some not-so-smooth edits once and for all, and really catapult your project to the next level of excellence.

You should begin working with audio at the clip level. Does every clip have audio? That standard question is often overlooked. If you want to make your sound design very detailed, you may ask an additional question: Is every content element of the image, visible or implied, represented by audio? Take a moment to listen to your current environment. What do you hear? The faint whirring of a computer fan? Cars going by outside the window? A clock ticking nearby? A plane crossing overhead? A conversation in the next room? All of these audio elements define the who, what, where, and even why of your surroundings.

Furthermore, those elements have a pecking order in your consciousness. If the conversation in the next room gets louder, you will conclude that you either moved closer to it; it moved closer to you; or it turned into a full-blown, full-volume argument. If you hear no change in the volume of that conversation, it will recede in your awareness and your attention will turn to other sounds. All of these changes in perception can be reflected in the audio mix to more fully involve your audience in the storytelling.

In Lifted Vignette, you've kept a general lookout for the level and mix. The audio mix favored Mitch's comments throughout the project, with the B-roll and music taking a secondary place. Primarily, you kept the audio level below 0 dB, but now your full attention should go to the project's audio on a clip-by-clip, clip-to-clip, and project-wide basis. You'll start with the clip-by-clip focus to ensure that every clip has a source of audio. You will then slide into a clip-to-clip focus of blending the audio of one clip into the next clip—the natural sound of one clip merging into the natural sound of the next clip. This task expands further to blend the clips vertically. Interweaving the music, sound effects (sfx), natural sound, and sound bites creates the project's audio mix.

Exercise 7.3.1
Adding Sound to a Clip

Sometimes the natural sound recorded with a clip is too low, too noisy, or just not usable. An example of this can be heard in the first clip in the project. The clip was reversed to create the hangar opening shot, which also reversed its audio content. But even if you reverted to normal audio playback, the clip's sound would still need help. Adding a sound effect will greatly improve its impact.

1   If necessary, reset the interface by choosing Window > Workspaces > Default.

2   In Lifted Vignette, cue the playhead to the start of **DN_9488**.

That motor sounds weak because it was recorded on a distant ambient microphone. You want that motor to sound stronger as it opens the hangar doors and your story. Let's search the Photos and Audio sidebar of the Browser to find a more power-ful sound effect. The Photos and Audio sidebar provides centralized access to your iTunes library and playlists, including more than 400 iLife sound effects and musical clips (if installed), and over 1,300 sound and foley effects that are part of the Final Cut Pro Sound Effects collection.

3   In the Browser area, click the Photos and Audio sidebar button, and choose the Sound Effects category.

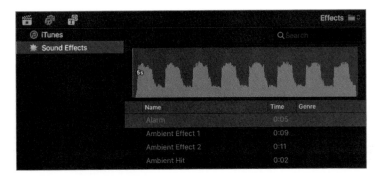

NOTE ▸   If the Sound Effects category is not available or is empty, choose Final Cut Pro > Download Additional Content to acquire it.

4   In the search field at right, enter *garage*. Three results are returned.

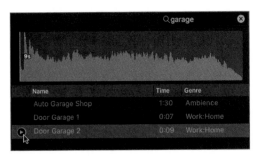

5   To audition the sound effects, click the preview buttons.

Door Garage 2 sounds about right for the hangar door.

6   Press **Q** to connect edit the sound effect starting at the head of **DN_9488**.

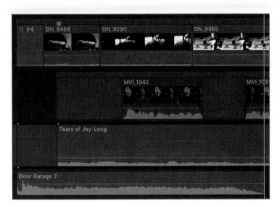

The sound effect is a little too long, but here's the great thing about that: The hangar door continues opening in the second clip, **DN_9390**.

7   Trim the end of **Door Garage 2** to stop at the end point of **DN_9390**.

You can trim the audio clip using one of the various methods you've learned. Try out each of the following, pressing **Command-Z** between methods to reset to the sound effect's full length:

▶   Using the Select tool, drag the end point of the sound effect clip left until the point snaps to the end of **DN_9390**.

▶   With the sound effect clip selected, skim to the end of **DN_9390**, then press **Option-]** (right bracket) to trim the end of the clip to the playhead.

▶   With the end of the sound effect clip selected, skim to the end of **DN_9390**, and press **Shift-X**.

As you've done with the other clips, you need to set the overall volume of **Door Garage 2** so it sounds as if the viewer is not standing immediately next to the motor.

8   With the Select tool active, move the mouse pointer over the volume control for **Door Garage 2**.

The control currently reads 0 dB because you just added it to your project. All clips come into Final Cut Pro with a volume level of 0 dB, which indicates that Final Cut Pro will play the clip at the level it was recorded.

9   Using the Select tool, drag the volume control down until the level reading displays –8 dB.

That takes some of the edge off of the motor's initial loudness while maintaining some presence. Let's move on to another clip that needs audio work.

▶ I Need More Waveforms

Dragging the volume control in the default view may be a little challenging because of its size. The Timeline's Clip Appearance settings allow you to change the displayed height of Timeline clips. Drag the Clip Height slider to make clips easier to drag. You'll adjust these settings further later in this lesson.

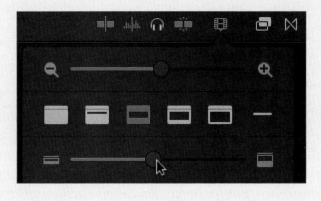

10 In the Timeline Index and under the Tags pane, click the "Show incomplete to-do items" button.

Listed at the top of the Tags pane is the first Add SFX to-do marker you placed to remind you of the audio fix you just performed. That's one to-do down.

11 Select the checkbox for the Add SFX to-do marker to convert it into a Completed marker.

The marker is removed from the to-do list.

12 Because you have also added Mitch's title to the project, you can select the checkbox for the "Add a Title" to-do marker because you completed that task when you added the lower third to identify Mitch.

The next to-do marker is the "Speed and SFX" marker. This clip shows the rotors starting to turn, powered by a little shot of jet fuel, so you need to add some jet-powered audio to support the visual. Unlike the "garage door" scenario you just completed, you already have audio content suitable for the helicopter's engine starting up and running. Rather than getting a helicopter sound effect from the Photos and Audio browser, you will use sound recorded on location.

7.3.1-A Retiming Borrowed Audio

For this edit, you will edit only the audio from a clip into the project and time it to match existing video in the project. You could choose from several B-roll shots that contain the sound of the helicopter's rotors turning, but one clip, **DN_9457**, depicts the rotor startup. You will speed up and copy its audio to match the dramatic visual in **DN_9452**.

1 In the Primary Media event, select **DN_9457**.

This is the rooftop clip of the helicopter starting up. The entire clip is 19:16 in length, but you need only a few seconds to cover **DN_9452** in the Timeline. Skimming the rooftop clip, you can simulate the sound of speeding up the audio for this clip.

2 Skim **DN_9457** swiftly but not too quickly.

You'll hear the "meat" of the sound effect. Around clip timecode of 02:28:32:00, the turbine's compressor kicks in and accelerates the rotor. Let's use that portion of the audio.

3 Mark a start point at around 02:28:32:00.

4 Leave the end point at its default for a total duration of about 13 seconds.

5   In the Timeline, select **DN_9452** to reveal a duration of approximately two seconds.

NOTE ▶   The duration of a selected Timeline clip appears at the top of the Timeline area.

That's the two seconds of audio you want to replace with a retimed version of **DN_9457**'s audio. First, you need to make an audio-only edit of **DN_9457** to the Timeline. Next to the four edit command buttons in the toolbar, a Source Media pop-up menu allows you to make standard video and audio edits or to limit an edit to audio or video only.

6   In the Browser, select **DN_9457** as the source, and from the Source Media pop-up menu, choose Audio Only.

The edit command buttons include speaker icons to indicate that the next edit is audio only. Now you need to make that audio edit and place the audio clip at the correct location in the Timeline.

7   In the project, cue the playhead to the start of **DN_9452**, and then press **Q**, or click the Audio-Only Connect button.

The audio from **DN_9457** aligns to the start of **DN_9452**, but is still about 10 seconds too long. That's OK because you will use that extra content while retiming the clip.

8 In the Timeline, select the audio clip **DN_9457**, and from the Retime pop-up menu, choose Custom.

The Custom Speed window appears above the clip. You know that **DN_9452** is two seconds long. You can use the Custom Speed window's Duration option to retime the audio clip to that desired length. As you did with the motor sound effect, you want to extend the audio of the turbine startup into the next clip. You are also going to overlap the preceding clip.

9 In the Custom Speed window, select the Set Speed: Duration option, and in the associated text field, enter 5. (five period). Press Return.

The audio clip shortens, not by trimming, but by increasing playback speed. Although the accelerated audio is shorter, it still overlaps the takeoff clip by three seconds. It would be great to also overlap the previous clip in which Mitch throws the switch.

10 Drag the start point of **DN_9457** left while monitoring the two-up in the Viewer.

The left image in the Viewer displays the video at the point the sound effect would start.

11 Continue dragging left until Mitch presses a toggle switch and the display screens change. The info flag will read approximately five seconds and 5 frames for the clip's new duration.

NOTE ▶ Disable snapping by pressing N, if necessary.

To refine the effect, smooth the edits into and out of this sound effect using the fade handles.

12 Drag both the start and end fade handles to add **ramps** of just over one second each. You'll add more blending to this sound effect in later exercises.

This audio previously was assigned the Natural Sound role. Now that you're using this audio clip as a sound effect, you should change the clip's assigned role.

13 In the project, Control-click the audio-only **DN_9457** clip, and from the shortcut menu, choose Assign Audio Roles > Effects-1.

14 Don't forget to select the to-do marker checkbox to confirm that you performed the speed and sfx fix after listening to the resulting edit. Oh, and you've already done the "speed to reveal," item so select that checkbox as well.

So now you've added sound effects to several clips, and even retimed one. Let's see what else needs some audio support.

7.3.1-B Splitting Audio with Another Clip

The aerial clips you added did not have audio, which isn't surprising because if a mic had been placed on that camera, it would have recorded pure wind noise. So you're going to need to add some audio to those clips. In the Takeoff storyline, two aerials are followed by the low-pass clip, **DN_9493**. Rather than borrowing audio, this time you'll share some audio from **DN_9493**. These types of edits are referred to as split edits. Sharing or splitting audio between clips starts with expanding a clip to reveal the video and audio as components of the clip.

1 In the Timeline, double-click the audio waveform of **DN_9493**.

The audio expands away from the video, which allows you to trim the audio and video contents independently while keeping them in sync.

2 Drag the audio start point of **DN_9493**, the low-flying helicopter pass, to the left, just past the start of **Aerials_11_02a**.

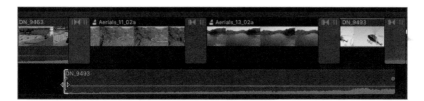

Extending the split audio a little into **DN_9463** gives you time to ramp and blend the split audio with the existing audio of the helicopter takeoff.

3 Drag the split audio's start fade handle to the right to blend into the audio by the transition's midpoint.

This split edit arrangement is known as a **J-cut** with the audio leading the video edit from the source clip. The opposite, an L-cut, has the audio lagging the video edit point. You'll perform more split edits in later exercises.

7.3.1-C Previewing an Audio Blend

You haven't yet mixed these clips, so the blend you performed using the fade handle will not be as smooth as it could be. Let's craft this one quickly so you can hear where we are going by adjusting all these audio details.

You want to realize a progressive, seamless audio transition from the helicopter starting up, taking off down the ramp, and getting airborne in the first aerial clip. This is going to require setting the volume levels of three clips along with some additional adjustments. As you can see in the sound bite storyline, this is the music chorus where you pause Mitch for a moment as the helicopter takes flight. You will not yet adjust the music.

1   The first volume level to set is the retimed startup sound in **DN_9457**. Change the volume level for this clip to –4 dB.

   NOTE ▶ Press the Command key while adjusting the volume level control to "gear-down" the control, allowing you to see every value rather than skipping values.

2   The takeoff clip, **DN_9463**, needs about a one-half second ramp in. Drag the clip's fade-in handle right to add the ramp.

3   Boost the volume level of **DN_9463** to –3 dB.

This boost is rather strong to pick up from **DN_9457**. That means you will also have to boost the split audio.

4   Raise the volume level of **DN_9493** to 3 dB and notice that the audio waveform peaks to red toward the end of the clip.

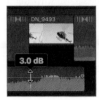

The higher level causes peaked audio waveforms at the end of the split audio. Let's mark that for attention.

5   Cue the playhead to the video portion of **DN_9493**. Press **M** to set a marker, and double-click that marker to open the marker window.

6   For the marker name, enter *Fix Audio Peak*, identify this as a to-do marker, and click Done.

7   Review the project beginning with the startup clip and continuing to before the video portion of **DN_9493**.

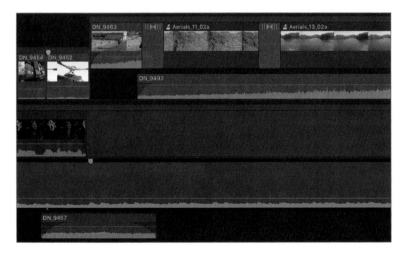

That's a nice audio transition from the ground into the air. You'll fix the peaked audio later when you complete the audio mix. For now, there are more clips that need additional audio before they can be mixed.

7.3.1-D Adding, Borrowing, and Splitting Audio

You don't need to look far to find the next split audio opportunity. **GOPR1857** has a nice, consistent cabin rumble sound. The next three clips, which were also shot inside the cabin, would sound more authentic with the GoPro's continuous audio underneath them. Audio continuity from clip to clip would also lessen distractions during Mitch's sound bites.

1   As an alternative to double-clicking the audio waveforms, Control-click **GOPR1857**, and from the shortcut menu, choose Expand Audio, or press **Control-S**.

2   With the audio of **GOPR1857** expanded, drag the end point right to just over one second into **DN_9503**. Then add a ramp out to the end of the split audio.

That rumble gives you a foundation of consistent cabin audio. This edit arrangement is an **L-cut** with the audio lagging the video edit.

Moving on to the Triple Aerial/Sunlight storyline, the silent aerial clips need sound because they have no usable audio. Unfortunately, the audio on **DN_9420** isn't long enough for a split audio edit. You're going to have to track down some additional audio. Fortunately, some is available. You could use the audio from **GOPR0009** or from two helicopter sound effects in the Photos and Audio's sidebar.

3   Edit in your choice of sound effect for at least the three aerial clips in the Triple Aerial/Sunlight storyline. Adjust the volume level and fade handles, as necessary. Refer to the following figure to see one approach to completing this edit.

Some clips at the beginning of the project have too much audio. **DN_9454**, in particular, has some off-camera chatter you should remove. Activating the Clip Skimming feature allows you to solo a clip without selecting or activating any keyboard shortcuts.

4   With View > Clip Skimming enabled, skim **DN_9454** to hear the off-camera audio.

Let's remove that extra chatter and share the audio from the previous clip to fill in the audio gap.

5   Expand and extend **DN_9453**'s audio under **DN_9454**, creating an **L-cut**.

6   Lower **DN_9454**'s audio volume level to $-\infty$ dB to remove it from the mix.

The same off-camera chatter mars **DN_9465**. You may borrow the audio from **DN_9470** by creating another split edit.

7 In the hangar storyline, create a **J-cut** of **DN_9470**'s audio underneath **DN_9465**.

8 Lower **DN_9465**'s audio to −∞ dB to remove it from the mix.

NOTE ▶ You may notice the "servo" sound at the start of **DN_9470**'s extended audio. You'll adjust for that later in this lesson.

You've now performed a clip-by-clip pass and started a clip-to-clip pass at the audio for Lifted Vignette. Every clip has audio content, whether it is native to the clip or added from another source. And some of that B-roll audio was achieved using split edits, sharing the audio from one clip to one or more clips.

Exercise 7.3.2
Adjusting Volume Levels over Time

So far, you've adjusted audio clip volume at a constant level. You lowered (attenuated) or raised (boosted) the volume level for an entire clip. However, using only this constant level adjustment has created a problem in the Takeoff storyline where you split the audio from **DN_9493** using a J-cut to the prior two aerials.

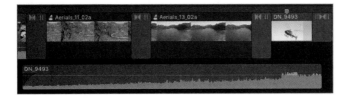

Take a look at the audio waveforms for **DN_9493**. They indicate that the audio is too loud. A good level should not have red peaks. This enhanced visual indicator is a great feature of the "live" audio waveforms for each clip. Without playing the clip, they help you identify clips with volume levels that are too high or too low. For **DN_9493**, the volume level needs to be higher to have the **nats** blend from the earlier nats of **DN_9463**, but the volume level should be significantly lowered later in the clip to address the peaks occurring during the middle of **DN_9493**'s video.

Varying volume levels within a clip involves setting **keyframes**. Keyframes are created using the Select tool and the Option key.

1 Visually scan the audio waveform of **DN_9493**'s J-cut.

You can see the helicopter approaching the microphone as the audio waveform creeps higher and higher. You can literally see the volume ramp up!

You can use keyframes to flatten that ramp-up and tame the loud helicopter at the end of the clip.

2 In the audio waveforms of **DN_9493** extended under **Aerials_11_02a**, locate the Select tool over the volume control after the start transition's midpoint.

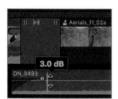

A level reading of 3 dB appears, and the mouse pointer changes to two arrowheads arranged vertically. This is where you will set the first keyframe so the level is locked-in-time at or before the fade handle completes the fade-in.

3 With the Select tool located over the level control after the midpoint of the transition, Option-click the level control.

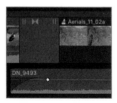

Your first keyframe is created, locking the volume control's setting at that frame. It takes a minimum of two keyframes to animate a volume control. Your single key-frame needs a second keyframe to determine whether the animation will raise or lower the audio level.

4   To set a second keyframe, position the Select tool over the volume control at the midpoint of the transition between **Aerials_11_02a** and **Aerials_13_02a**. Option-click the
volume control to create a second keyframe.

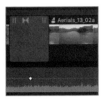

Keyframes may be adjusted after they are created. You may move keyframes laterally
to change their timing within a clip and/or vertically to change the volume level at the
keyframe. You are attempting to adjust the helicopter sound to set a consistent level
between the keyframes for this clip.

5   If you set the first keyframe at 3 dB, set this second keyframe to about –5 dB.

This clip needs a third keyframe at the midpoint of the third transition to further
tame the audio of the approaching helicopter.

6   Create the third keyframe at the midpoint of the third transition, and adjust it to flatten the waveforms for the second clip.

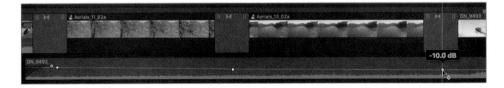

The third keyframe should be around –10 dB. The end of **DN_9493** will be louder to
emphasize the low pass of the helicopter before the start of Mitch's next sound bite.
The available time after the apex of the helicopter passes, but before the sound bite
starts, will determine the timing you assign to the next two keyframes. The goal is to
duck the helicopter sound under the sound bite rapidly, but smoothly enough so that

it doesn't stand out. Also, the level needs to blend into the audio of the next clip in the helicopter cabin.

7   Start by applying two keyframes to the end of **DN_9493**: one at the apex of the helicopter sound, and the second approximately 20 frames later.

8   Place the two keyframes at around −10 dB and −30 dB as the helicopter passes overhead.

9   To meld the three audio sources together, do the following:

▶   Lengthen the start of **GOPR1857** to align with the start of **MVI_1043**.

▶   Apply a one-second audio fade-in to the start of **GOPR1857**.

▶   Add a 12-frame audio fade-out to the end of **DN_9493**.

▶   If necessary, apply a quick ramp-up with the sound bite's fade handle.

You are now really taking control of your audio. Keyframes allow you to shape the audio within a clip, from clip-to-clip horizontally, and from clip-to-clip vertically. That's a lot of audio manipulation occurring within about 12 seconds. The range of time within which these three techniques shape the audio will become even shorter and more granular the deeper you get into sound design. You may be working with 6 or 10 clips vertically within a four-second span, for example, as you enrich and refine a project's soundtrack.

7.3.2-A Reading the Audio Meters

As you move into mixing clip-to-clip vertically, you'll want to hear the audio subjectively while viewing the audio levels objectively. As you listen to your project over and over, you will develop a perception of how loud those clips are within the mix. The Audio meters provide a visual confirmation, or reality check, of your perceptions.

1   If necessary, show the larger Audio meters in the Timeline by clicking the smaller Audio Meter button next to the timecode display.

The Audio meters appear on the right end of the Timeline. You may want to increase their size.

2   Drag the left divider of the Audio meters to the left to enlarge the meters.

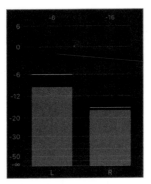

You already used the Audio meters to measure the peaks in the audio mix. The goal was to keep the audio from peaking at or above 0 dB. At this point in your workflow, however, you're focused on creating a dynamic mix in which the audio ebbs and flows with the sound effects, music, natural sounds, and the sound bites. These items must be mixed so they do not peak the meters, and remain within a **dynamic range**, the distance between the lowest and highest levels of the audio mix. The width of that range should be guided by the quality of your target audience's audio system.

In a movie theater, the speaker system is tuned to deliver very quiet sounds at pin-drop levels, followed by percussive, loud thunder as a storm overhead shatters the silence. To ensure that the audience feels the difference in volume, the mix is created with about 36 dB of dynamic range; that is, if the loudest sound is just shy of 0 dB, the quietest sound has a level of –36 dB on the meters. That is a very wide range and sounds awesome on a speaker system that can support such a dynamic range.

While that wide range works in a theater, the same dynamic sound is not possible, for example, on a smartphone. Delivering the same 36-dB dynamic-range mix to a mobile device will motivate the viewer to constantly adjust the volume level. An acceptable dynamic range for mobile devices and computers is 12 dB, so the average or nominal value of that dynamic range may be set to –6 dB. An average of –6 dB with 12 dB of range allows the loudest value to get close to 0 dB and places the softest sounds at –12 dB. That average value may be even lower for specific facilities or networks. Some facilities require a –12 dB average level, resulting in the loudest sounds at –6 dB and the softest at –18 dB. To test your mix, you can play a sample mix through a typical target platform to decide what average level and spread of dynamic range will be most enjoyable for your audience.

NOTE ▶ Use an average of –12 dB with a peak of –6 dB for these exercises. Later, you will adjust the entire mix to an average of –6 dB.

7.3.2-B Changing Channel Configuration

As you prepare to put the mix together, one more audio issue needs to be resolved. Mitch's sound bite audio was recorded split level, that is, with one channel louder, or "hot," and the other channel set to record the same microphone at a softer, or "cold," level. This is a common practice when recording with a crew of one (or no dedicated audio engineer). The practice is to use the "hotter" channel for editing unless the source gets "too hot." Then, the editor can switch to the "cold" channel momentarily to avoid overmodulation. The "hot" signal is more desirable to use because it records at a better signal-to-noise ratio than the "cold" signal (barring any other technical issue, such as AC hum or background noise). Because Mitch's audio level does not overmodulate, you will disable the second channel while redirecting the first channel to both left and right outputs. You'll start by selecting all of Mitch's sound bites.

In the Timeline Index, you have several ways to select just the sound bites (depending on the accuracy and depth in applying metadata to the clips):

▶   Using the Tags Index, search for clips with, at minimum, the interview keyword, and then select all clips in the listed results.

▶   Using the Clips Index, search for clips with the letters "MVI" in their name, and then select all clips in the listed results.

NOTE ▶   A third method is to Shift-click the sound bites directly in the Timeline. However, if your project was, for example, a two-hour documentary with many "slivers" of sound bites, selecting the sound bites by metadata could be safer.

1   Using the method you prefer, select all of Mitch's sound bites in the project.

2   In the Audio inspector, scroll down to the Audio Configuration section.

With the current configuration set to stereo, the channel 1 and channel 2 signals are treated as a stereo pair and linked together.

3   From the configuration pop-up menu, currently set to Stereo, choose Dual Mono.

The individual channels or components are displayed. Each component is automatically assigned a subrole.

4   Deselect the Dialogue-2 component to mute the channel, leaving Dialogue-1 as the only audio source for the sound bites.

5   Play the Timeline and notice that Mitch's voice is played in both speakers equally.

With Mitch's sound bites set to one balanced source, you can move on to the audio mix.

7.3.2-D Setting Volume Level by Role

Now that you have an understanding of the Audio meters, the average or nominal value of a dynamic range, and the dynamic range itself, look at the clip groups that make up the mix. In Lifted Vignette, you have four audio group clips: dialogue, music, effects, and natural sound. Earlier, you categorized these clips into roles. You may use these roles to solo a group using the Timeline Index. Soloing by role allows you to identify any errant clip within the role and to set consistency for a role's clips.

1   If necessary, open the Timeline Index, and click the Roles button.

The Roles Index lists the roles set for Timeline clips. You can mute multiple roles by deselecting a role in the index.

2   To hear only the Dialogue role, disable all the other audio roles by Option-clicking
the Dialogue role's checkbox.

You may find a few clips, probably natural sound clips, that have not had their roles
reassigned.

3   If necessary, select any unassigned or mis-assigned clip roles in the Timeline, and in
the Info inspector, reassign their audio to the correct role.

With the Roles Index set to play only dialogue clips, you may focus on setting the dialogue levels with the help of the Audio meters. Those clips were close to the desired
audio level for this project. The dialogue clips had an average peak of –12 dB with a
top peak of –6 dB. However, when you changed the Audio Configuration settings, the
measured level of output also changed.

4   Play the project, attenuating any sound bite that exceeds –6 dB or boosting any clip
that is not reaching –12 dB in the Audio meters.

As is typical for most people, Mitch alters his voice volume throughout the interview.
His sound bites need additional adjustments to equalize the volume levels of the
clips. To do so, you will manually add keyframes to adjust the level over time. For the
moment, however, almost every sound bite could be boosted by 4 dB. With the sound
bites adjusted, you'll re-enable all roles.

5   Return all roles in the index to enabled status.

You've set the volume level for the sound bites. Now you'll weave them together with
the sound effects, natural sound, and music.

7.3.2-E Ducking and Swelling the Sound Effects and the Music

The music clip drove the addition of several sound bite and B-roll edits in your project.
For a few of those edits, the music should be boosted to emphasize its importance. Music
and sound bites should work together to maintain the forward momentum of your project

and eliminate "holes" in the audio mix. In this exercise, you will use keyframes and the Range Selection tool to define when an audio element such as the music should **duck** under the sound bites and when the music should **swell** to drive the edit. To help you visualize these interactions, you'll take advantage of the visual benefits of roles.

1   If necessary, adjust your view of the Timeline to focus on the beginning of the project.

Because you are focusing on Timeline editing, let's remove possible information distractions and give yourself more room in the Timeline.

2   Above the Inspector, click the Hide Browser button.

3   Drag the Timeline toolbar up to create vertical space for your project.

NOTE ▶   For later use, you can save this or any custom arrangement of the main window by choosing Window > Workspaces > Save Workspace As.

So far, you've shifted major screen real estate to the Timeline. Now within that expanse, you'll gather your audio clips by roles, allowing you to focus on the audio mix without the video thumbnails blocking your view.

4   In the Timeline Index under Roles, click the Show Audio Lanes button.

Similar to the Expand Audio command you used previously, this hyper-expansion keeps each audio component synced with its respective video component, if applicable. The benefit here is that with a single click, audio clips are presented in grouped lanes based on their role metadata.

You can stay in the Audio Lanes view while creating the audio mix. Start with **Door Garage 2**. The sound effect should be strong at the start, and then get softer as the music and sound bites enter. You want to duck the sound effect under the music.

5 In **Door Garage 2**, create two keyframes: the first about one half-second before the music starts, and the second where **DN_9390** starts.

6 If necessary, adjust the first keyframe to –8 dB.

The second keyframe's level is dependent on the music clip's level. That level should currently be around –11 dB, although you will change that in a moment.

7 Set the second keyframe of **Door Garage 2** to –21 dB or lower.

Door Garage 2's audio will duck under the music's entry. The garage door sound effect literally cuts out at the end of the sound effect. You can smooth out the sfx's exit so its currently abrupt ending doesn't jar the audience.

8   Drag the fade-out handle left to align with the start of the sound bite.

The sfx quietly leaves rather than abruptly ending while Mitch is talking. The start of the music clip is weak in the mix. The music should make a stronger entrance, and then duck under as Mitch's sound bite plays.

9   In the music clip, set two keyframes: one before the first sound bite starts, and one about one half-second after the first sound bite starts. Adjust the two keyframe's values to –4 dB and –10 dB, respectively, so the music ducks as Mitch starts talking.

Setting keyframes is not always about ducking, or lowering, the volume as another clip starts. At times, keyframes are needed to raise the audio level as a clip progresses. As discussed earlier, Mitch's first sound bite starts strong, but then tapers off in volume. The clip waveform shows how his voice decreases. You'll need to add keyframes to bump up his volume.

10   Set a first keyframe in **MVI_1042** when Mitch says, "something." Set the second keyframe about mid-clip.

11   Using the waveforms as a guide, drag the second keyframe upward to align the audio waveform peaks to almost the same height, approximately 9 dB.

This will keep Mitch's voice strong while still exhibiting some fall-off.

12   Continue working through the remaining sound bites, adding keyframes to level out Mitch's voice during each clip.

As you review your changes, listen for the interaction between music, sound bites, and natural sound. The changes in audio focus should be neither too sudden nor too drawn out. You will need practice adjusting the keyframes vertically and horizontally to find the right balance of levels and timing.

7.3.2-F Using Range Selection for Keyframing

A little farther down the Timeline, the audio focus should return to the music when the helicopter takes off, the music goes to its chorus, and we hear the sound effect you added using **DN_9457**. To do so, you must swell the music and, if necessary, adjust the sound effects and natural sound clips' levels to suit the new mix.

Before setting the next two keyframes on the music clip, look down the Timeline to examine the upcoming sound bites. Rather than setting two keyframes at the start of the chorus and later setting two more keyframes to duck the music, you may use the Range Selection tool to set all four keyframes at once.

1   From the Tools pop-up menu, choose the Range Selection tool, or press **R**.

2   Using the Range Selection tool, drag a range within the music from before the sound bite **MVI_1055** ends to after the next sound bite, **MVI_1043**, starts.

Using range selection, you've defined a range where the volume control should swell and where the music should duck under.

3   To set the keyframes for this range, drag the volume control within the range to raise the level to 0 dB.

The marked range will set the four keyframes you will need to swell and duck the music as you raise the level within the range.

4   Click in a gray area of the Timeline to clear the selection, and press **A** to return to the Select tool.

You'll need to adjust the four keyframes for volume level (vertical) and timing (horizontal). A big advantage in making these changes is that at the start of **MVI_1043** the helicopter makes a low overhead pass. You'll be able to duck the music under the helicopter sound to make another smooth change in audio focus.

5   Adjust both pairs of keyframes, as necessary, and ask the following questions about the results:

  ▶   When the chorus starts at about 00:29 in the Timeline, do your music keyframes complete the music swell so the chorus is strong on its first beat?

  ▶   Does the music volume setting for the swell keep the audio mix below –6 dB when the helicopter does its low-pass fly-by?

  ▶   Are you taking advantage of the fly-by at the end of the swell section to conceal the music ducking?

6   You still need to complete three major edits to the music:

  ▶   Swell the music during **Aerials_13_01b**, and then duck under **MVI_1045**. Use the Range Selection tool.

  ▶   Swell the music during **DN_9420**, and then duck under **MVI_1046**.

  ▶   Using the Select tool, at the end of the music clip, perform a brief swell and fade-out.

7   Review the project for additional edits that may benefit from interweaving the music and sound bites.

You have an opportunity at the start of the project to swell the music between **MVI_1042** and **MVI_1055**. However, **MVI_1042** needs repositioning to widen the gap for that musical swell. Because the sound bites are in a storyline, trimming the gaps to move the sound bites will misalign the sync you set up between the sound bites, music, and natural sound later in the project. Using the Position tool avoids destroying your prior synchronization.

8   From the Tool pop-up menu, choose the Position tool, or press **P**.

9   Drag **MVI_1042** to the left –1:12.

The end of the first sound bite now fits snugly against the musical phrase at just over eight seconds into the project. Let's now swell the music between the first two sound bites.

10   Using the Range tool, draw a range that slightly overlaps the end of **MVI_1042** and the start of **MVI_1055**. Then raise the volume level control within the range to –2 dB. Click outside of the range to deselect it.

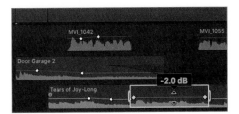

With the sound bite moved earlier in the project, the first music duck needs realignment. You can move both keyframes simultaneously to attenuate the music.

11   Locate the Select tool between the first two keyframes in the music, and drag the volume control left to position the keyframes before and after the start of **MVI_1042**.

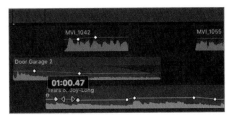

You're now ready to focus on the overall mix. But remember that a good audio mix takes time.

12 Add and adjust keyframes and fade handles for the entire project, summing all audio elements on the meters around –12 dB average, –6 dB peak.

Remember, you want to hear what you see, comprehend foreground over background, and let the audio roles interweave with one another to sustain the momentum of the project. And don't be afraid to trim a clip or two, or alter a transition's duration.

7.3.2-G Adjusting the Volume Level and Keyframes of One or More Clips

As you start to finalize your audio mix, you may find that a role is too loud or that the overall mix is too soft. You need to change levels, but the techniques you've learned so far would be tedious to implement if you'd already set keyframes on your clips. A more efficient method is to use the **Adjust Volume Relative** command.

1 With the Timeline active, press **Command-A** to select all the clips.

Currently, your audio mix is centering around –12 dB with peaks to –6 dB. You will use the Adjust Volume Relative command to raise the whole audio mix by 6 dB.

2 Choose Modify > Adjust Volume > Relative.

The timecode display changes to the relative adjustment display. Enter the number of decibels to boost the volume level of the selected clips relative to their current levels. If a clip's level is keyframed, the keyframes value will increase by that number. To lower the volume level, enter a negative number (that is, a minus sign followed by the value).

3 Type 6, which then appears in the timecode display, and press Return.

The clips' volume levels increase by 6 dB. Most likely, a few spots within the project are now too loud. You can use the Adjust Volume Relative command to attenuate your entire mix by 2 dB.

4 If necessary, press **Command-A** in the active Timeline to select all clips.

5 This time, press **Control-L** to activate the timecode display controls for the relative audio adjustment.

6 Type –2, and press Return.

The volume levels and keyframes of the selected clips decrease by 2 dB. The overall volume is now at a higher level than when you started this exercise, but you still have a little headroom to avoid peaking at or above 0 dB.

▶ **Adjust Volume Absolute**

The alternative to the relative command is **Adjust Volume Absolute**, which sets the volume levels of selected clips to a specified value. Regardless of the volume level value (keyframed or not), the Volume Absolute command resets the current values, including any volume level keyfra mes, to the dB setting you enter in the timecode display. The timecode display indicates when you are making a relative or absolute level adjustment. **Control-Option-L** is the Adjust Volume Absolute keyboard shortcut.

You've done quite a bit of editing while working on this audio mix. Take another two or three passes at playing the Timeline, while listening to the mix and timing of the sound bites in relation to the music, and the sound bites compared to the natural sound and sound effects. Evaluate whether they compete against one another, and then listen to the ways in which they work together, interwoven to carry your story forward. Animating the volume control requires a minimum of two keyframes. You can and should use more.

Always remember that you should spend as much, if not more, time on the audio edit as on the video edit. And be aware that your audio edit did not start in this lesson. Your audio edit actually began when you first selected sound bites in Lesson 3. Although beautiful visuals are important, audio refinement makes the difference between competence and excellence.

> **Checkpoint 7.3.2**
>
> Refer to Appendix C for details on reviewing a Checkpoint.

Reference 7.4
Understanding Audio Enhancements

Final Cut Pro includes audio enhancement features you can use to repair errors in recorded audio. Acquiring the audio correctly the first time makes these features unnecessary, but correctly acquired audio is not always available. These analysis and correction features are found in the Audio inspector. Here are the three areas of analysis and correction:

▶ Loudness: This analysis evaluates if a clip's volume is too low. The correction it offers is to boost the volume without over-modulating or peaking. The Amount parameter controls how much gain to boost the signal, while Uniformity compresses the range of loudness between the softest audio and the loudest audio.

▶ Background Noise Removal: Identifies and removes a constant noise within a clip (such as an air conditioner or the rumble of traffic).

▶ Hum Removal: Identifies electrical noise present in the audio signal. Select the appropriate AC Ground Loop frequency and Final Cut Pro will remove the hum. In the U.S., the AC frequency of a standard 110v outlet is 60 Hz.

You can activate Audio Enhancement analysis to take place during import, by clicking the Enhancements pop-up menu below the Viewer, or by clicking the Enhancements button in the Audio inspector's Audio Analysis row. If it detects a serious problem, the suggested repair is flagged with a red warning sign. If a slight-to-moderate problem is detected, the analysis feature flags it with a yellow caution triangle. A green-circled checkmark indicates that no enhancement is needed or an enhancement has solved the issue. You may alter or disable each repair by selecting or deselecting the feature's checkbox and adjusting the parameters associated with repairing the detected issue regardless of analysis state.

> **NOTE ▶** Non-retina displays may be challenged to reveal all the Inspector's available parameters without requiring scrolling. You can expand the Inspector vertically by choosing View > Toggle Inspector Height.

Reference 7.5
Recording a Voiceover

The Voiceover tool allows you to record audio directly into your project using an external microphone or a built-in FaceTime mic. One use for this tool is to quickly record a portion of the voiceover script. When editing the rough drafts, the script may not be locked in. Rather than paying for the ongoing services of voiceover talent, you may wish to record yourself for free. This is not intended to secure your 15 seconds of fame. Rather, even a roughly recorded test soundtrack can help you acquire a better sense of timing and pacing for your edit. This type of voiceover recording is often referred to as a *temp* or **scratch** track. Although this is a common application for the Voiceover tool, don't be fooled by the term "scratch." This tool records high-fidelity audio, and may even be used to record the actual voiceover for your finished edit. (The audio quality will depend entirely on your source microphone and recording environment.)

Exercise 7.5.1
Using the Voiceover Tool

For this exercise, you will record a scratch track of yourself adding a tag line to the Lifted Vignette project. To complete this exercise, your computer must have a built-in microphone, or you must supply and connect a microphone recognized by macOS.

1   In your Lifted Vignette project, cue the playhead to after the helicopter has passed overhead in the last shot, the helicopter flying off into the sunset.

2 Choose Window > Record Voiceover.

The Record Voiceover HUD appears. Looking at its basic settings, you may choose only to name the next recording using the Name field, test your mic level using the Input Gain slider, and then click the Record button to record directly into the Timeline. However, let's explore the advanced settings.

3 In the Record Voiceover HUD, click the Advanced disclosure triangle.

The Advanced settings present additional controls for recording your voiceover, including:

▶ Input: Choose the source device, and the desired mono or stereo channels. Examples include the Built-in Input (which is a line-in jack on the computer), FaceTime camera, or a USB audio input converter.

▶ Monitor: Enable/disable hearing the input specified in the headphones or other device set as the Output in System Preferences while recording.

▶ Gain: Adjust the level of the audio input presented to your audio output during audio monitoring. In other words, set how loudly you hear yourself while recording. The default $-\infty$ mutes your voice during recording while allowing you to monitor the project audio.

▶ Countdown to record: Display a pre-record timer.

▶ Mute project while recording: Disable project audio output during voiceover recording.

▶ Create Audition from takes: Compile the project's voiceover recordings into an audition clip.

▶ Event: Select the destination event for the voiceover's audio clips.

▶ Role: Assign an audio role to the recorded clips.

4   From the Input pop-up menu, choose your available audio source.

With any source, it is important to verify that you are choosing the desired input format because many sources give you the option of selecting mono or stereo. The setting also determines the recorded channel configuration: Mono In=Mono Clip, or Stereo In=Stereo Clip.

5   Deselect "Mute project while recording," but leave the other two options selected.

6   Choose Primary Media for Event and Dialogue-1 for Role.

7   In the Name field, type *Vignette Tag*, and press Return.

You are now ready to record a tag line for the vignette.

8   In the upper-left of the HUD, click the red Start Recording button.

The countdown appears in the Viewer and beeps in the headphones.

9   When the countdown ends, say into your microphone, *Visit H 5 productions dot com for more information.*

10   Click the square Stop Recording button to end this voiceover take.

The take appears as an audition clip with the playhead cued to the start of the clip. You could click Play and review the take, but you want to record a second take.

11 Click Record again, repeat the tag line, and then click Stop.

Now that you have two or more takes to compare, you may use the features of the audition clip to select the best one. You can access your takes by clicking the spotlight icon on the clip.

> ▶ **Mixing from Multiple Takes**
>
> Auditions present each take as a complete clip, but sometimes you may want to mix and match from different takes. You can use the Clip > Break Apart Clip Items command to view each take separately, which allows you to use, for example, the first phrase of the voiceover from take 3, the middle from take 1, and the rest of the voiceover from take 2.
>
>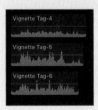

Reference 7.6
Correcting the Image

An editor's dream is to always have clips that are perfectly white balanced and ready for editing, but that isn't always what's recorded in the field. That's when the Final Cut Pro color correction tools earn their keep. A wide range of scenarios lead to an editor needing to know something about color correction. The deluge of raw material—from easy-to-use HD sources such as GoPros and iPhones edited alongside DSLR, ARRI, and RED material—can be overwhelming. The task of trying to give a scene a consistent look with that diversity of source material is not an easy one.

A common color correction problem occurs when a camera is **white balanced** at the start of a recording session, but due to shifts in the lighting temperature or setups during the day, the clips shot later in the day have a color cast: an unwanted color tint. The correction tools include a balance color feature that can effortlessly fix this type of color error.

Using balance color neutralizes any detected color cast or improper exposure within an image to create a color-balanced image. Final Cut Pro attempts to create an image in which shadows are clean blacks and highlights are clean whites without color casts. Balance color also attempts to optimize the image's **contrast**. During import, you can automatically analyze one or more clips for color balance, or do so later in your editing or finishing stages. In the following exercises, you'll learn how to use the automatic balance, but you will also discover how to manually adjust an image while acquiring a deeper understanding of the color correction effect set.

7.6-A The Color Correction Effects

Final Cut Pro includes four color correction effects: Color Board, Color Wheels, Color Curves, and Hue/Saturation Curves. These effects give you manual control over a scene's appearance. Each effect offers an increased level of control compared to the previous effect; although, you needn't use them in that order. One clip may require using only the Color Board to remove a color cast from fluorescent lighting; whereas another clip might require two Color Curves effects to remove a localized, fluorescent light problem caused by a mixed-lighting environment.

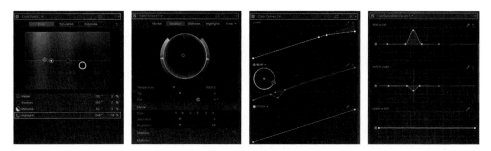

The four Color Correction effects.

In addition to fixing color balance or exposure errors, you can use the color correction effects as color enhancement tools to paint a look onto an entire scene or a portion of a scene. The color correction effects have built-in color and shape masks with which you can limit how an individual effect alters an image, as when you confined a blur effect to a roof in a previous exercise. Because you retrieve these effects from the Effects browser, the stacking order of the color correction effects, as well as any additional effects, in the Video inspector may result in visual harmony or disunity.

Rearranging the effect order.

This section of Lesson 7 takes a blended approach to exploring three of the four color correction effects. You'll learn foundational methods for controlling luma and chroma using the Color Board. Then, you'll switch to the next color effect, comparing the controls and the increased granularity of those controls. The color theory doesn't change, but the tools become more precise and thus more powerful.

7.6-B Video Scopes

Before you dive into color correction, you should know that your eyes and brain will try to fool you throughout this process. Unless you're trained as a colorist, your untrained senses tend to lead you to make more corrections than are really necessary. To supplement your subjective perceptions (and misperceptions), Final Cut Pro provides **video scopes** that display an objective representation of the values you are adjusting.

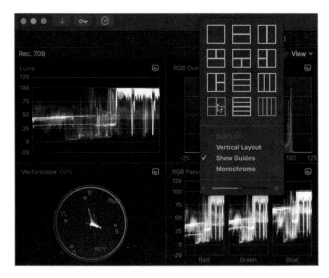

Several display arrangements are available for the scopes.

The video scopes measure the **luma** and **chroma** values of the pixels in the image. When you're working on projects destined for television broadcast, the scopes also act as measurement tools for verifying broadcast specification compliance.

Exercise 7.6.1
Exploring the Color Correction Tools for Luma

To experiment with color correction, you'll create a new project using the luma controls within the Color Board, Color Wheels, and the Color Curves effects. You'll also employ the video scopes to understand how they display clip changes made in the Color Correction effects.

1   Create a new project in the Primary Media event. Name the project *Color Correct*, and apply the custom settings shown in the following figure.

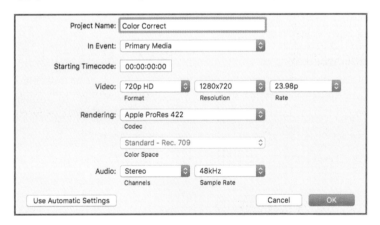

Your first edit utilizes a generator. Because some generators function independent of resolution and rate, Final Cut Pro needs you to define the frame size and frame rate for your project. If you fail to define the project settings, Final Cut Pro will prompt you to define those settings with your first edit.

2   In the Generators Browser, locate the **Grey Scale** and the **Gradient** generators.

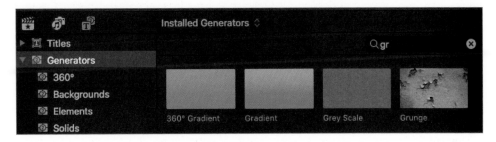

NOTE ▶ To filter the list, type *gr* in the search field.

3   Append edit the **Grey Scale** generator into the Color Correct project twice, followed by the **Gradient** generator.

With these generators placed in the project, you'll need to apply some quick adjustments to ready the clips. You'll need to configure the second **Grey Scale** as white and the **Gradient** as a grayscale gradient.

4   In the project, select the second **Grey Scale**, and in the Generator inspector, set the Level to 100%.

Although you could adjust the color settings for the gradient, you can achieve the desired grayscale gradient using an effect.

5 From the Effects browser, apply the Black and White effect to the **Gradient**.

NOTE ▶ The **Gradient** thumbnail may not update to reflect its grayscale contents. You can verify that the effect was applied by skimming the generator.

An additional clip is needed in this project. Let's add the helicopter clip with the knowledge that it needs some color correction before we can proceed.

6 From the Primary Media event, append edit clip **DN_9287** to the project.

As you explore these color correction effects, you will need to create duplicates of this project. Making a snapshot immediately is a good idea so you'll have an unaltered, original version to make future snapshots.

7 In the Primary Media event, locate the Color Correct project you created at the start of this exercise. In the Browser, right-click the project, and from the shortcut menu, choose "Duplicate Project as Snapshot".

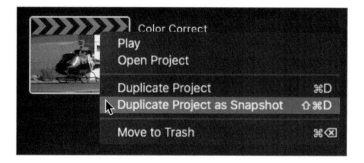

A duplicate of the Color Correct project appears in the Browser.

8 Click the snapshot project's name, and rename it Color Correct MASTER.

9 Rename the current project Color Board to match the effect that you will be using.

After you complete the exercise for one of these color correction effects, you'll reset the project using a new snapshot of this master before applying the next effect. To make the color correction tool set work for you, you'll need to set up the interface to display the video scopes. A workspace preset for color correction is available that does so.

10 From the menu bar, choose Window > Workspaces > Color and Effects.

With a color correction layout and project set up, let's start by reading luma and chroma information in the scopes.

7.6.1-B Reading the Luma Value of a Clip

Many perceived color issues in video are resolved by first adjusting the **contrast** of the image because the human eye is very sensitive to areas of contrast.

Contrast is measured as levels of brightness or illumination for each pixel. That **luma** information is separate from the color or **chroma** information. These terms will make more sense to you as you proceed with this exercise.

1 In the Color Board project, cue the playhead over the first **Grey Scale** generator.

Notice that only three of the four video scopes display data using lines known as **traces**. Those three scopes—the "Luma" Waveform, the RGB Overlay, and the RGB Parade—indicate that the first **Grey Scale** clip has pixels illuminated just below 50% brightness. Let's advance to the next clip and see how the video scopes respond.

2   In the Timeline, press the Down Arrow key to advance the playhead to the start of the second **Grey Scale** clip. Observe the changes in the video scopes.

The traces in three of the video scopes jumped to 100%.

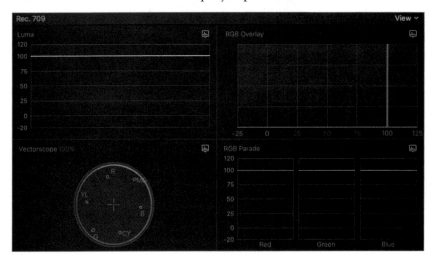

NOTE ▸ If you missed seeing the difference, press the Up Arrow key followed by the Down Arrow key to jump between the two Grey Scale clips.

Again, the Vectorscope does not return a measurement of chroma information for the grey scale clip. Every pixel in color video has three chroma channels: Red, Green, and Blue. Although chroma values are present in the first and second clips, the three color channels are of equal brightness.

3   In the RGB Parade video scope, notice the Red, Green, and Blue labels along the lower edge of the scope.

The three channels are illuminated at equal brightness for each pixel. Because video is an additive color system, adding the three channels together equally produces white pixels. Let's give the Vectorscope something to display.

4   In the Timeline, press the Down Arrow key as necessary to cue the playhead to
DN_9287.

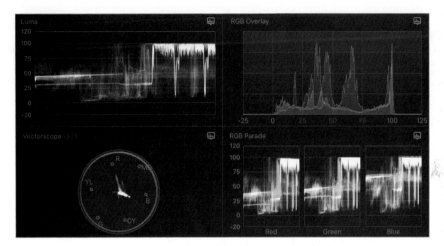

Yes, this clip definitely has chroma information. The Vectorscope has come alive with
traces indicating the hue and saturation values in the image. Watch what happens if
you change this image to a grayscale image.

5   From the Effects Browser, apply the Black and White effect to clip **DN_9287** in the
project.

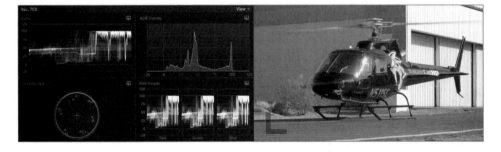

The effect suppresses the chroma in the image, and the Vectorscope traces reflect the
resultant loss of color.

6   Press Command-Z to undo the previous effect.

Next, you'll use the Color Board effect to modify the luma channel of these clips.

7.6.1-C Adjusting Master Luma Using the Color Board Effect

The Color Board effect enables you to control the luma and chroma data within a clip. Three sets of controls in the effect adjust the luma and chroma: Exposure, Color, and Saturation. First, let's adjust luma and contrast using the Exposure controls.

1   In the Color Board project, select all four clips.

2   In the Effects Browser, double-click the Color Board effect.

    The effect is applied to the selected clips.

    NOTE ▸ Using its default value, the Add Default Video Effect shortcut, **Option-E**, applies the Color Board effect.

3   In the Timeline, cue the playhead over the first **Grey Scale** clip.

4   In the Video inspector, notice the Color Board 1 effect.

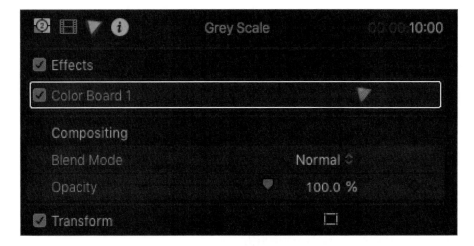

Similar to the effects you worked with earlier, the Color Board may be

▸   Reset or enabled/disabled

▸   Reordered amongst other effects; possibly yielding a different look

▸   Limited to affect a specific color or area of the image

A unique addition to the Color Correction effects, compared to other effects, is the presence of the Color inspector.

5 To the right of the Color Board label, or at the top of the Inspector, click the Color inspector button.

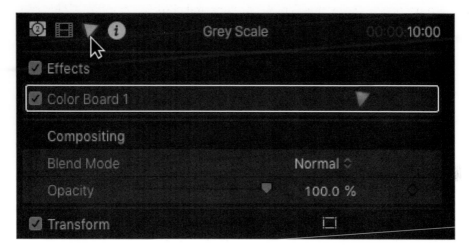

The three tabs across the upper edge define which aspect of the image the controls below the tabs adjust. Let's start by adjusting Exposure.

6 Click the Exposure tab to view the luma controls.

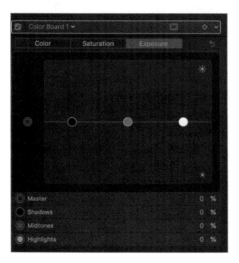

The Master slider at left affects the luma of the entire image.

7 Drag the Master slider to its full extent up and down while observing the results in the Viewer and the video scopes.

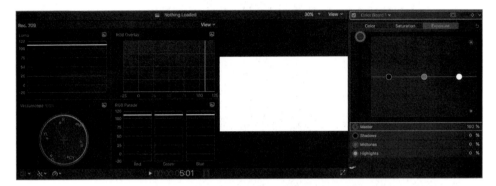

With the slider at its highest setting, the Grey Scale clip is a bright white. The measured luma value exceeds 100 on the scopes. This brightness level is referred to as "super-white."

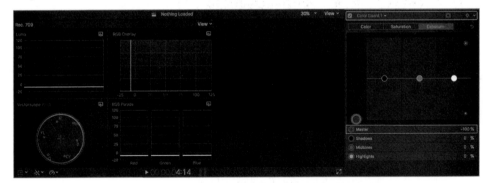

The Master slider at its lowest setting produces a dark black. The luma value drops below 0 on the scopes. This level is known as "super-black."

These two extremes exceed the broadcast specification for broadcast television. Non-broadcast cameras can acquire media at these levels even though they are not permissible in material intended for broadcast. When outputting broadcast-ready content, you can apply an additional effect to confine these levels to the broadcast spec.

8 From the Effects Browser, apply the Broadcast Safe effect to the first **Grey Scale** clip, then drag the Master slider to its full extent while watching the scopes.

The luma is **clipped** at 0 and 100. This is not an ideal color correction solution because luma data is lost in this process, but this effect does render the clip with these luma settings to be broadcast safe. Let's take a quick look at what data is lost in the helicopter clip.

9 Cue the playhead over **DN_9287** and apply the Broadcast Safe effect to the clip.

10 Drag the Exposure Master slider slightly upward.

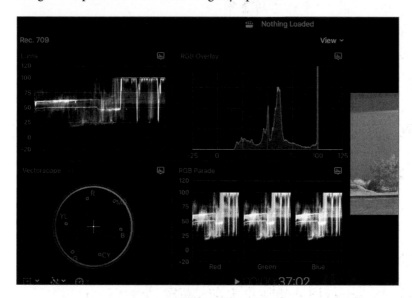

The highlight details in the hangar doors are quickly lost as if the image were overexposed.

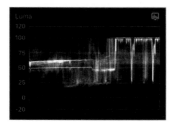

The measured luma confirms this result because the traces are clipped at 100. Traces that existed at the higher end of the scale are now bunched up at 100. Those highlight details are, in essence, deleted from the image. The same is true of the shadow details if you drag the Master slider down.

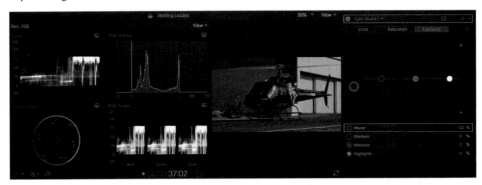

The Master slider is obviously not the only available exposure control. You'll dig deeper into the other Exposure controls next.

7.6.1-D Adjusting Grayscale Luma with the Color Board Effect

The Master control sets the luma values of all of an image's pixels. The Exposure tab also includes controls to adjust the grayscale luminance of each pixel according to its luma value.

Exposure Controls of Pixel Grayscale Luminance

Control	0–100	0–70	30–70	30–100
Master	X			
Shadows		X		
Midtones			X	
Highlights				X

All the controls overlap the grayscale values of other controls, which results in smooth blending across the image (unless extreme adjustments are set). This broad-based coverage also means that adjusting one control may require you to tweak another control to remove the grayscale change in a different part of the image. Let's explore these luma controls using the third clip, **Gradient**.

1   Cue the playhead to the **Gradient** clip.

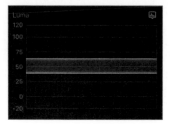

The luma values of this clip range below and above 50.

2   Drag the Master control to manipulate the luma values in the scopes.

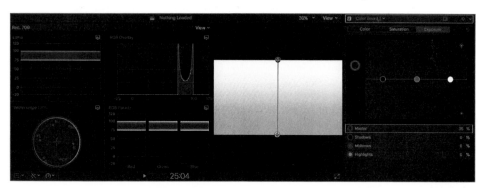

The range spread stays the same because the values are shifted higher and lower. You can reset the control by pressing Delete.

3   With the Master control selected, press Delete to reset the control to 0%.

The three grayscale controls allow you to increase (or decrease) the range spread of the gradient, thereby increasing the contrast of the image.

4   Drag the Highlights control upward until the Luma waveform scope indicates that the top of the range measures at 100.

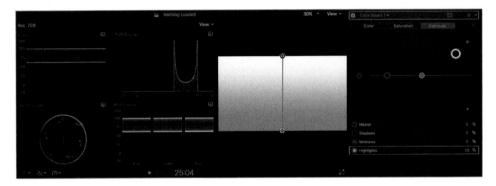

The entire range still shifts upward, but did you notice that the spread between the highest and lowest values increased? You will definitely notice it as you adjust the Shadows control.

5   Drag the Shadows control downward to its lowest setting.

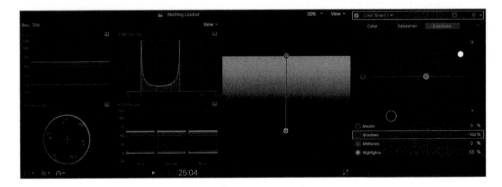

The contrast within the image expanded as the luma range increased. Because the controls cover a wide range of grayscale values, dragging the Shadows control to its lowest setting has also affected the brightest pixels, and the image no longer has the brightest possible highlights.

6   Drag the Highlights control to its highest setting.

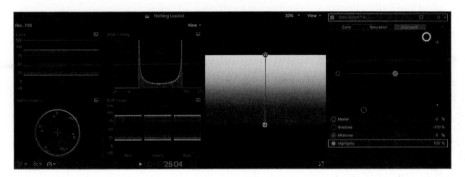

You've expanded the contrast of this gradient to the limits of the applied effects. Let's switch back to the helicopter clip and see how far you can expand its contrast.

7   Cue the playhead over **DN_9287**. In the Exposure tab, select the Master control, and press Delete.

Doing so resets the Master slider to 0. The Luma waveform scope indicates that the black paint of the helicopter is not a true black because no traces are registering at 0. Adjusting the Shadows control may change that situation.

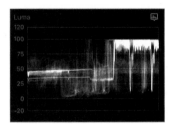

8   Drag the Shadows control down slightly until some traces touch 0 on the Luma waveform.

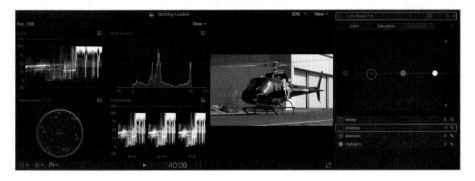

9 Continue dragging the Shadows control downward while observing that black portions of the helicopter lose details such as rivets and reflections.

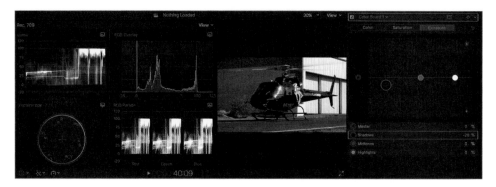

The Shadows control, used in conjunction with the Broadcast Safe effect applied earlier, is **crushing** the shadows at 0. Let's recover those shadow details.

10 Drag the Shadows control up until the lowest traces register 0 on the scopes.

With the previous adjustment completed, you've expanded the contrast in the helicopter clip. You've controlled the luma channel of a clip, and adjusted the exposure and contrast within an image using the Color Board effect. Now, while adjusting exposure, let's look at the next level of color correction control: the Color Wheels effect.

7.6.1-E Adjusting Grayscale Luma with the Color Wheels Effect

The next level of color correction control is found in the Color Wheels; however, because you are altering only the luma values in this exercise, the results will not differ from those you achieved with the Color Board. The goal here is to compare the Color Wheel effect's controls and functionality. As you use these correction effects, you will quickly recognize their similarities and also their individual differences. To begin, let's create a snapshot of the master project.

1 If you switched to the Color and Effects workspace, above the Inspector, click the "Show the Browser" button to show the Browser.

2   In the Browser, right-click the Color Correct MASTER project, and choose "Duplicate Project as Snapshot".

3   Rename the new project Color Wheels, and open the project into the Timeline.

> **NOTE ▶** You may hide the Browser to horizontally expand the Viewer and video scopes.

In the previous exercise, you applied the Color Board effect to all four clips at once. You could do the same using the Color Wheels, but let's try another method. In the Color inspector, you can directly apply any of the color correction effects to a clip.

4   In the Color Wheels project, Option-click the third clip, Gradient, to select the clip and cue the playhead to the clip.

5   If necessary, select the Color inspector as the active inspector.

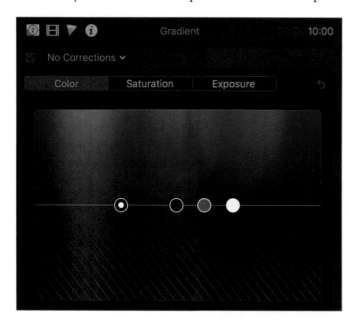

You may notice what appears to be a Color Board applied to the clip, but not quite. Look carefully at the top of the Inspector. The pop-up menu indicates that no corrections have been applied. You may change that status by using the pop-up menu to apply the Color Wheels effect.

6 At the top of the Color inspector, from the pop-up menu, choose +Color Wheels.

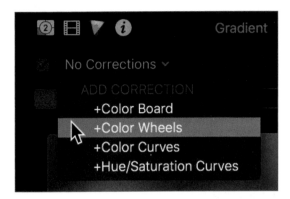

7 The four color wheels appear as Color Wheels 1. Each wheel represents the grayscale range that wheel affects in the clip: Master, Shadows, Midtones, and Highlights.

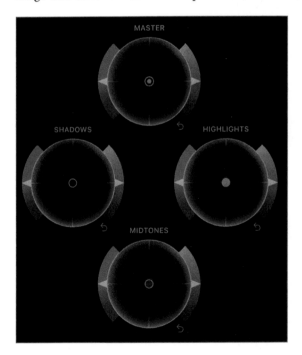

NOTE ▶ Set the Inspector to full height by double-clicking the Inspector's title bar (which currently reads "Gradient„).

For this exercise, you are dealing with image luma values. To the right of each wheel, the Brightness control manipulates the luma values. As you did with the Color Board's four Exposure sliders, you'll manipulate the four Brightness controls to see the results.

NOTE ▶ The Broadcast Safe effect is not applied, so you can see the full range of the effect.

8   In the Color inspector, drag the Master wheel's Brightness control toward its full extents while observing the results in the Viewer and video scopes.

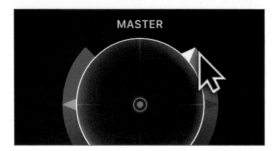

As you may have anticipated, similar to the results of dragging the Color Board's Master Exposure slider, the Color Wheels' Master Brightness control shifts the entire gradient's luma values up and down, while the range of luma values did not expand. You'll next expand that luma range.

9   Click the Master wheel's Reset button.

10 In the Color inspector, drag the Highlights wheel's Brightness control upward, and drag the Shadows wheel's Brightness control downward until you have expanded the luma range of the Gradient clip from 0 to 100.

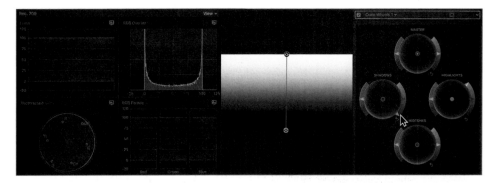

If you drag both controls to their full values, you went too far. You can use another color correction tool that will alert you to adjustments that exceed the broadcast-safe luma values of 0 and 100.

11 In the Viewer's View pop-up menu, under Range Check, choose Luma.

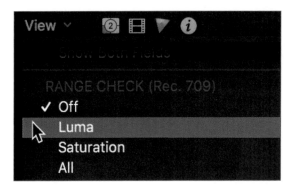

If your Brightness controls are at full deflection, zebra stripes will appear over the gradient in the Viewer. The zebra stripes indicate pixels that exceed the broadcast-safe values of 0 and 100 on the Waveform scope.

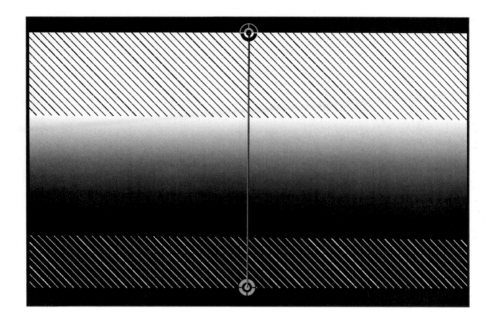

12 Adjust the Brightness controls until no zebra stripes are visible while maintaining the controls at their highest (and lowest) possible settings.

13 In the Viewer's View pop-up menu, under Range Check, choose Off.

Now that you are familiar with the luma controls of the Color Wheels effect, let's try out some curve-based controls.

7.6.1-F Adjusting Grayscale Luma with the Color Curves Effect

Don't be fooled by the simplistic look of the curve controls. These are precision controls that require considerable attention to detail, and you haven't even touched the chroma half of color correction! That said, don't be intimidated by them, either. You'll quickly grasp the concept of the curve controls in this exercise.

1 If you previously hid the Browser, above the Inspector, click "Show the Browser".

2 In the Browser, right-click the Color Correct MASTER project, and from the shortcut menu, choose Duplicate Project as Snapshot.

3 Rename the new project Color Curves, and open the project into the Timeline.

NOTE ▶ You may hide the Browser to horizontally expand the Viewer and video scopes.

Now, you'll add a Color Curves effect to the gradient clip, and discover the power of curves.

4 Option-click the Gradient clip to select it and cue the playhead to the clip.

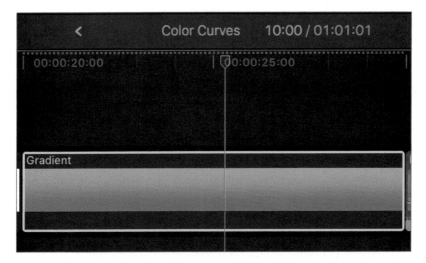

5 From the Color inspector's pop-up menu, add a Color Curves effect. Notice the top curve labeled Luma.

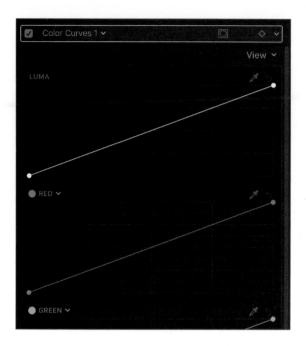

That's different. The Color Curves effect handles luma more precisely than the Board and Wheels. The vertical, or Y, values of the Luma curve graph are like the vertical values of the Color Board's Exposure controls and the Brightness controls of the Color Wheels—dragging upward increases the value and dragging downward decreases the value. The increased power and refinement of the Color Curves effect becomes apparent when adjusting the horizontal, or X values, in the curve. The grayscale values are not controlled by the fixed ranges of Shadows, Midtones, and Highlights. Rather, an eyedropper allows you to identify a specific grayscale value that you may then center a range upon.

6 In the Luma curve, click the eyedropper.

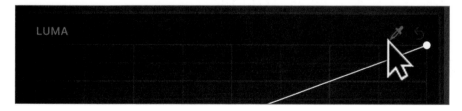

The eyedropper highlights and is ready for you to identify the luma value of any pixel you select in the Viewer.

7 With the Luma curve eyedropper active, move the eyedropper over the Viewer, and click in the gradient approximately one-third down from the upper edge.

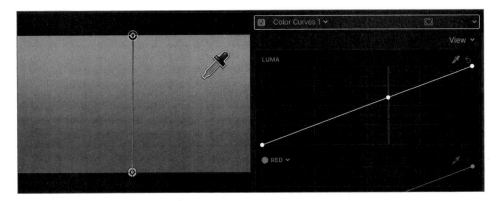

A line appears in the Luma curve with a control point at the intersection of the vertical line and the diagonal control line. The vertical line indicates where on a grayscale value—the X-axis of the curve—the selected pixel is measured.

A control point, like an audio keyframe, enables you to adjust a parameter value at a specific point (time, coordinate, grayscale value). In the Luma curve, a control point enables you to adjust the brightness value (Y-axis) of a specific grayscale pixel value (X-axis).

8 In the Luma curve, drag the control point created by the eyedropper upward along the vertical line.

The entire range of gradient is shifted upward. As with audio keyframes, the control point by itself creates the center of a range that extends to the next control point or the start/end of the curve. Dragging that one control point within the clip affects the entire curve.

9   Press Command-Z to undo the Luma adjustment, thereby returning the curve to a straight, diagonal line.

10 In the Luma curve, on the diagonal control line, click on each side of the control point at the vertical line to add two more control points.

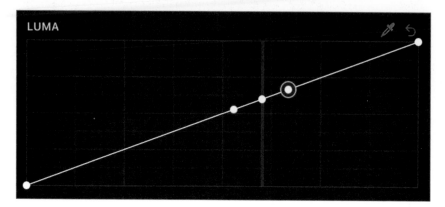

11 Among the three control points, drag the center control point slightly upward.

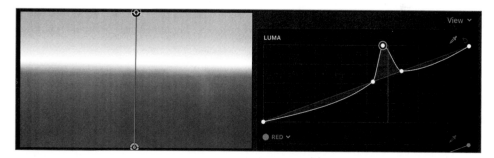

A brighter line of pixels appears in the gradient. The control points on the curve allow you to zero in on, or target, exactly the grayscale values you want to change.

Let's put this into use on the DN_9287 clip.

12 In the Color Curves project, Option-click the DN_9287 clip.

Those hangar doors are a bit bright. Let's use the Color Board to set the contrast, and tweak the Color Curves to slightly dim the doors.

13 With the DN_9287 clip selected in the Color Curves project, add both the Color Board, and then the Color Curves effects to apply them.

14 In the Color inspector, from the pop-up menu, select the Color Board 1 that you applied.

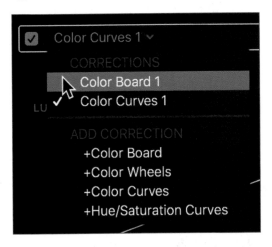

15 In the Color inspector, adjust the Exposure controls to set the contrast between 0 and 100 on the Waveform scope.

Now, you want to dim the front face of the hangar door panels and the header, leaving the side door faces as they are. To do so, you'll configure the Color Curves effect's Luma curve and its eyedropper to do the correction.

16 From the Color inspector's pop-up menu, select the Color Curves 1 you applied previously.

Rather than guess at the luma values of the doors and header, you'll use the Luma curve eyedropper.

17 In the Luma curve, select the eyedropper.

18 In the Viewer, drag the eyedropper over the hangar doors and header while watching the Luma curve.

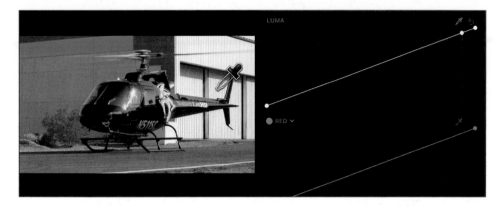

The Luma curve updates the vertical line as you drag. The door faces and header are in the 75–100 range (the right vertical quarter of the curve graph), except where the eyedropper touches the sides of the door panels (or obvious shadow areas). You'll create a control point at the 75% grayscale of the control line to adjust the doors and header.

19 In the Luma curve, click the control line around the X-axis' 75% mark two times, and drag down the control point at 100 to create a level line between the rightmost two control points.

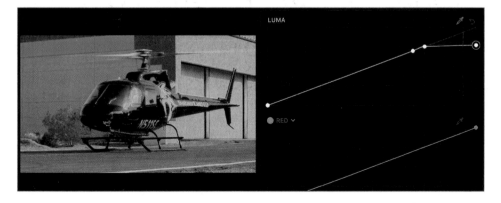

That may be dragging the point too far down. Remember to be subtle when applying any effect.

20 Drag up the rightmost control point to approximately halfway between its original start point and the level point where it was previously.

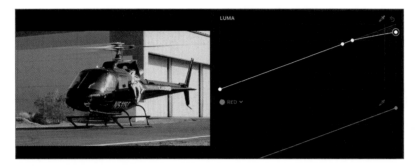

21 In the Color inspector, alternate between deselecting and selecting the Color Curves 1 checkbox to review your work.

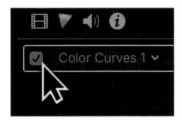

The Luma curve enabled you to make this narrow-range adjustment quickly compared to using the wide-range controls of the Color Board and Color Wheels.

Exercise 7.6.2
Exploring the Color Correction Tools for Chroma

Chroma is defined by two values: **hue** and **saturation**, each of which have separate tabs in the Color Board effect and separate controls in the Color Wheels. Let's start by adjusting Saturation because you will recognize its control layout in the Color Board. You'll start by creating a new snapshot of the Color Correct MASTER project.

1 If you previously hid the Browser, above the Inspector, click "Show the Browser".

2 In the Browser, right-click the Color Correct MASTER project, and from the shortcut menu, choose "Duplicate Project as Snapshot".

3 Rename the new project Chroma, and open the project into the Timeline.

NOTE ▶ You may hide the Browser to horizontally expand the Viewer and video scopes.

Now, you'll add a Colorize effect to the first, second, and third clips.

4   Click the first **Grey Scale** clip, Shift-click the Gradient clip, and in the Effects browser, double-click the Colorize effect to add it to the three selected clips.

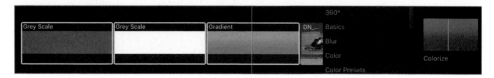

With the project clips readied, let's next modify the video scope layout for this color correction challenge. You can easily see the chroma-centered task using the Vectorscope and the RGB Parade.

5   In the Video Scope View pop-up menu, choose the 2-column layout.

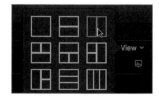

6   From the Scope Selector pop-up menu for each layout column, choose Vectorscope for one and Waveform: RGB Parade for the other.

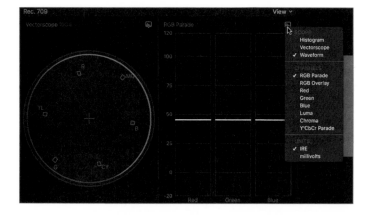

The video scopes are ready for the upcoming task.

7.6.2-A Desaturating a Color Cast Using the Color Board

The Colorize effect has overlaid a reddish tint to the grayscale. Let's remove the color cast that the Colorize effect created by utilizing color correction effects. You'll start by using the Color Board.

1 Cue the playhead to the first clip, and apply the Color Board effect to this first **Grey Scale** clip.

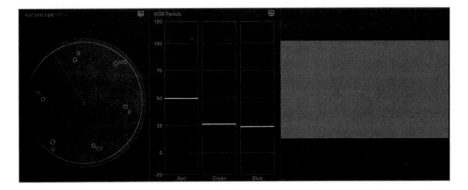

The Vectorscope indicates a reddish tint in the image, with the traces offset from the center of the scope toward the Red (R) target. In the RGB Parade, you can also see that the Red channel is generating brighter pixels than the Green or Blue channels.

You can easily desaturate this image to grayscale using the Saturation tab's Master control.

2 In the Color inspector, specifically the Color Board 1, select the Saturation tab, and drag the Master control to its lowest setting.

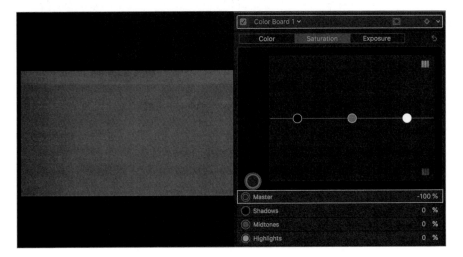

If you expected the image to desaturate to gray, you were correct; however, one detail in the Video inspector could prevent those results.

3 Return to the Video inspector, and look at the effect order.

The effects are processed from top to bottom. The Colorize effect created the color cast, and then the Color Board 1 effect desaturated the clip. What if the order of those two effects were reversed to place the Colorize effect at the lower position in the effects list?

4 In the Effect category, drag to rearrange the order of the two effects: Color Board 1 followed by Colorize.

Now that the color correction is processed before the Colorize effect, you are unable see the results of the master desaturation. Before you explore the grayscale desaturation controls, you should remove this desaturation effect.

5   In the Video inspector, from the Color Board 1 parameter pop-up menu, choose Reset Parameter, and then drag to rearrange the order of the two effects (the Colorize effect followed by Color Board 1).

Because television has been in color for decades, solving the color cast issue by desaturating the entire image is not the preferred method. In an upcoming exercise, you'll neutralize a cast without applying desaturation. But to complete this exercise, you need to explore desaturation within the Shadows, Midtones, and Highlights grayscale ranges.

6   Option-click the **Gradient** clip, and add a Color Board correction.

You already know what the Master desaturation will do, so let's experiment with the grayscale controls.

7   In the Color Board 1 effect's Saturation tab, manipulate each of the three grayscale controls, saturating and desaturating each individually and in combination, while monitoring the Viewer and the video scopes.

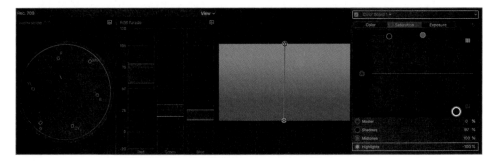

Saturating the Shadows and Midtones while desaturating the Highlights

As you probably anticipated, the saturation controls for the Shadows affected the darker areas of the image. The Midtones affected almost the entire image, and Highlights altered the lighter portion of the image.

8   Continue adjusting the Saturation Grayscale controls while observing the Vectorscope.

The Vectorscope represents the saturation or intensity of a hue in an image. As you increase the saturation of the Shadows, the Vectorscope's traces extend outward between the Blue and Cyan targets, which indicates that a surge of the hue will be visible in the darker areas of the image. As you desaturate, the traces huddle toward the center of the Vectorscope to indicate the absence of an individual hue: in other words, the image is black, grayscale, or white. Next, let's adjust the hue values of chroma using the Color Board.

► The Color Wheels Saturation Controls

The previous desaturating exercise may just as easily be completed using the Color Wheels. The following figure provides a visual guide to the respective controls.

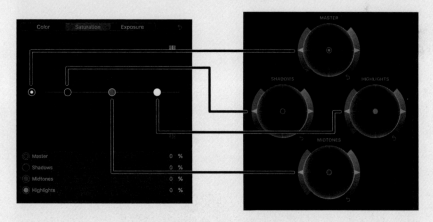

At the basic level, each Saturation control in the Color Board correlates to each Saturation control on the similarly named Color Wheel.

7.6.2-B Neutralizing a Color Cast with the Color Board

Typically, this task is necessary when a camera was not properly white balanced for its lighting conditions. This production error manifests itself as a *color cast*, or tint, usually in the Highlights or the Shadows ranges of the image. In additive color theory, adding its complementary color to another color will diminish an unwanted color cast. Let's force a color cast on the gray scale, and then use the Color Board to remove that cast. You'll stay in the Chroma project.

1   In the Chroma project, option-click the first **Grey Scale** clip.

2   If necessary, in the Video inspector, change the order of the effects to be (from top to bottom): Colorize, followed by Color Board 1.

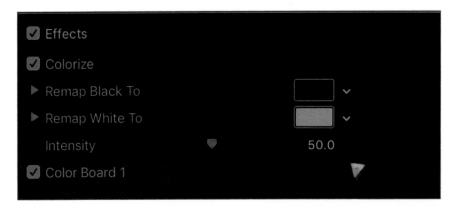

4   In the Video inspector, reset the Color Board by clicking the parameter pop-up menu, and choosing Reset Parameter.

5   In the Color inspector, verify that the pop-up menu is set to Color Board 1, and choose the Color tab.

The Color tab of the Color Board presents the same four controls that you worked with in the other tabs; however, all four controls move up and down and left and right to any color on the board.

6   Notice that the Vectorscope's traces are offset toward a reddish color.

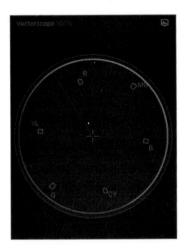

Because this color cast affects the entire image, you'll drag the Master Color control to neutralize the cast and return the clip to its original, gray look. You can do so using one of two methods with the Color Board.

You would first identify the hue in the Vectorscope; and then, do one of the following:

► Drag the control toward the negative of the hue.

► Drag the control toward the positive of the complementary hue.

Because the Vectorscope traces are going reddish, you may drag the Master Color control upward toward positive cyan or downward toward negative red.

7   Drag the Master Color control using one of these two methods until the traces align in the center of the Vectorscope.

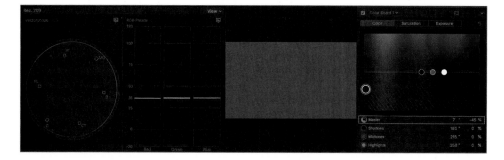

That was easy. Let's try combining the Luma and Chroma controls, and apply them to the helicopter clip.

▶ The Color Wheels Color Controls

The previous neutralizing exercise may just as easily be completed using the Color Wheels. The following figure provides a visual guide to the respective controls.

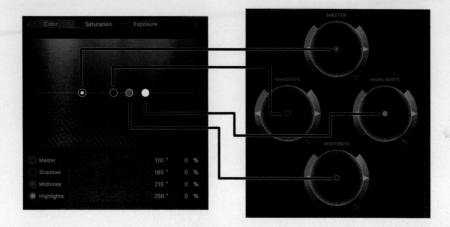

At the basic level, each Color control in the Color Board correlates to each Color control on the similarly named Color Wheel. The Color control inside each wheel represents a Vectorscope that accepts the complementary value of the tint. In the previous exercise, substituting the Color control of the Master Color Wheel for the Master Color control of the Color Board, you would drag the Master Color control towards Cyan to diminish the reddish tint.

7.6.2-C Color Correcting with Multiple Effects

In this exercise, you will apply both the Luma and Chroma tools. You have more than one way to achieve the desired look of a well-exposed, normal contrast, white-balanced image. Consider the following steps as a getting-started or first-attempt approach. Then, reset the color correction effects, and attempt a second correction using a different method.

1 Return the View Scope Layout to the 4-up layout configuration.

You should start by expanding the clip's contrast while remaining within the broadcast specification range of 0 to 100.

2   Option-click **DN_9287** clip, and then adjust the exposure to force the clip's lower shadows to touch 0 on the Luma waveform. You might use the Color Board or the Color Wheels to do so.

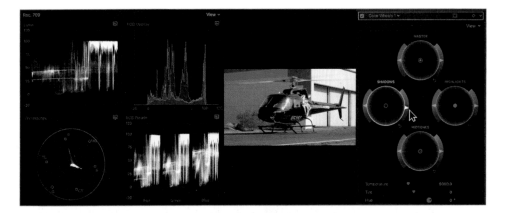

With more than one hue present in the image, the Vectorscope is difficult to interpret unless you have color correction experience. The RGB Parade scope helps you decipher that hue data.

3   In the RGB Parade scope, compare the three channels.

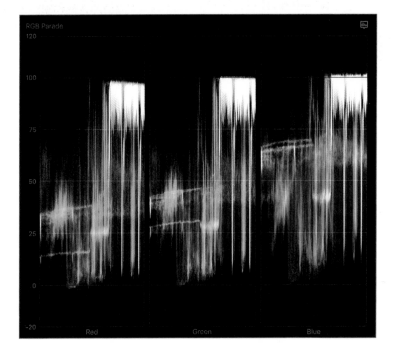

The blue traces are still above 0, which indicates a blue tint in the darkest areas of the image. Glancing at the Viewer, you can see that the black of the helicopter has a blue tint. That's exactly what the scope is telling you. To remove the blue cast in the shadows, you may adjust the Shadows control in the Color Wheel's effect.

4   First, drag the Shadows Color control towards yellow to remove the blue cast from the black areas of the helicopter. Be careful that you don't add too much yellow.

5   Continue fine-tuning by dragging the Midtones and Highlights controls. Because of the overlapping and interactive nature of these controls, you may find that the results of some controls will extend into other hues. In some cases, you may be adding rather than subtracting hues. Changing one control will usually require a change in at least one other control.

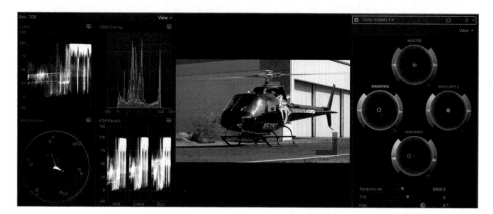

NOTE ▶   At the professional level, color grading is a meticulous art that requires a properly calibrated environment (neutral wall color and lighting), specially configured hardware (displays, Color Sync profiles, and external monitors), and eyes trained for the task. Your results may differ from those presented here if any of those elements are missing from your workflow.

▶ Hue/Saturation Curves

The Hue/Saturation Curves are an advanced color correction effect in Final Cut Pro.

You have already learned how the tools operate (the eyedropper identifies what you want to change, and the diagonal control line uses control points to make changes to some value). The key to adjusting these curves is to understand what the curve does by decoding the curve's title. For example, the HUE vs SAT curve could be understood by reading it as, "For pixels matching the eyedropper-selected HUE, change their SATuration." The eyedropper identifies on the curve with a vertical line and a range of control points. Dragging the center control point vertically alters the saturation of pixels that match the selected HUE.

7.6.2-D Using Auto White Balance

The Balance Color function really has two settings: Auto and White Balance. The White Balance lets you use the eyedropper to identify the pixels that should be white (or neutral gray).

1   Option-click the **DN_9287** clip, if necessary, to select the clip and cue the playhead.

To have the Balance Color effect neutralize the original image, you'll disable the previous adjustments.

2   In the Video inspector, deselect all effects currently applied to the **DN_9287** clip.

Notice the difference in the image as the Balance Color enhancement automatically white-balances the clip.

If you would like to manually define the reference point the Balance Color feature should use, you may do so in the Video inspector.

3   In the Video Inspector's Balance Color listing, set the Method pop-up menu to White Balance.

An eyedropper appears next to the pop-up menu, and the Viewer displays instructions to click or drag over an area that should be white. You should not select pixels that are overexposed. In this case, the helicopter's Saber Cat logo should suffice.

4   With the Balance Color's eyedropper active, in the Viewer, click the Saber Cat logo.

5   Continue clicking various parts of the logo until you achieve the white balance you desire.

6   Click the Balance Color's eyedropper to deactivate the selection.

The selected pixels are used as the reference white balance point. You may then apply color correction effects to further alter the image.

Color correction is an art, and you may have many ways to reach a visual goal. Different mixes of different colors may achieve similar results. Feel free to experiment with color. You can always click the Reset button and start over. Try one way of adjusting the controls, reset, and then try a different combination of control and curve settings. Experiment and reset, experiment and reset.

You've achieved a lot in this lesson. You started by adding and customizing a lower third and a 3D title. You then performed some detailed audio design exercises to create and enrich your audio mix. And lastly, you gained foundational knowledge of the color correction tool set in Final Cut Pro. In the next lesson, you'll share your work with the world.

Lesson Review

1.   What happens when you double-click a title in a project?

2.   What key should you press to exit text entry in the Viewer?

3.   What modifier key used with the Select tool will create audio keyframes?

4.   What command creates a split edit without creating an accidental sync offset in the Timeline?

5.   What function turns the skimmer into an "audio solo" skimmer?

6.   Where can you switch a clip's audio channels from stereo to dual mono?

7.   Your Timeline looks like the following figure, and not all the audio clips are audible. What should you do to hear and "see" all the clips?

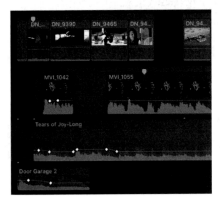

8.   What tool prepares a section of an audio clip to receive four keyframes at once?

9.   Which video scope, Waveform or Vectorscope, measures brightness (luma) based on the grayscale of the entire image?

10. Looking at a clip's image in the Viewer, the brightest parts of the image have a slight blue tint. How do you remove the tint?

11. Which color correction effect allows a luma adjustment to a narrow grayscale range without the use of a mask? Color Board, Color Wheels, or Color Curves?

Answers

1. The title is selected, the playhead cues to a frame where the text elements are visible, and the first line of text is automatically selected, ready for text entry.

2. Press the Escape key to exit text entry.

3. Option

4. Expand Audio/Video

5. Clip Skimming

6. With the clip selected, the Channel Configuration section of the Audio inspector

7. Look in the Timeline Index for roles that have been deselected (disabled).

8. Range Selection

9. Waveform

10. In the Color Board, drag the Highlights control toward positive yellow, or drag the Highlights control down toward negative blue.

11. Color Curves

Lesson 8
Sharing a Project

The two previous phases of the Final Cut Pro workflow—import and edit—led to this concluding phase: sharing. All your editing goes unrecognized if your project isn't made available to an audience, whether it is one person, a few hundred viewers, or millions. Craft doesn't become art until it is seen.

In Lesson 4, you exported an iOS-compatible file that would play in any recent OS and on most hosting platforms. In this lesson, you'll explore a few more export options. You will work briefly with a preset from Compressor, the Apple batch-transcoding application available in the App Store. We'll also discuss the powerful options available for exchanging a project with collaborators using third-party applications.

Reference 8.1
Creating a Viewable File

Sharing media from Final Cut Pro, also known as exporting, is a simple process, especially when sharing media in a commonly used format. The presets, called *destinations*, are named according to the target delivery platform. For example, if you needed to deliver a project to YouTube, you would select the YouTube destination. Or if you needed to deliver a sequence of JPEG or PNG images to a collaborator or archivist, you would add an Image Sequence destination.

GOALS

▶ Export to a media file

▶ Post media to an online host

▶ Create a bundle for multiple platforms

▶ Understand the XML workflow

▶ Integrate Compressor export options

A sample of the share destinations

No matter which platform you select, a compatibility checker confirms which devices will be capable of playing the shared file.

If the available destinations do not fit your needs, you can create custom destinations in the integrated Compressor app.

In this lesson, you will turn your attention to direct online hosting delivery and also learn how to create a high-quality archival master.

Exercise 8.1.1
Sharing to an Online Host

Final Cut Pro includes preset destinations for several online hosting services, including Facebook, Tudou, Vimeo, Youku, and YouTube. Each of these destinations, if you enter your login credentials into Final Cut Pro, can automatically upload files to the desired service following transcoding and the addition of metadata. Because all destination presets share similar options, you'll learn the sharing process in the course of preparing your media for one platform, Vimeo.

1   With the Lifted Vignette project open, press **Command-Shift-A** to deselect all selected items and clear all marked ranges.

  This keyboard shortcut is important to use because when a range is selected, Final Cut Pro shares only the range rather than the entire Timeline.

2   In the toolbar, click the Share button.

  The preset destinations list appears.

  NOTE ▶ The name of the destinations list is either Share Project to indicate that you are sharing a project, or Share Clip Selection to indicate that you are sharing a clip or range.

3   From the list of destinations, choose Vimeo.

The Share window appears with four main elements: a skimmable preview area to verify the content to be exported, Info and Settings panes, and a File inspector that summarizes the shared file's settings.

The Info pane displays the metadata to be embedded into the file. This metadata will flow into corresponding fields in the Vimeo file, if applicable.

4   To share the Lifted Vignette project, set the following metadata information:

▸   Title: *Lifted Vignette*

▸   Description: *A helicopter pilot and cinematographer describes his passion for sharing aerial cinematography.*

▸   Creator: [Your name]

▸   Tags: *aerial cinematography, helicopters, aviation*

NOTE ▸ To enter the tag "tokens," type the tag's text followed by a comma to close each tag.

5   After entering the metadata, click the Settings tab to modify the file's delivery options.

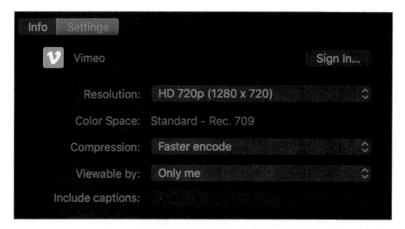

If you have not yet provided your online account's credentials, you may click the Sign In button to do so.

NOTE ▸ To maintain the security of your login information, do not enter your credentials on a public-use computer.

6 Enter your credentials, if applicable.

The preset options work perfectly for most initial uploads, but you should adjust them as needed. Also, you should always review the summary strip to perform a final check of what you will be uploading.

7 Because you will not be uploading this project, you should now click Cancel. If you intended to upload the project, you would click Next.

NOTE ► When uploading, a Terms of Service statement from the respective online platform appears. To continue, click Publish.

During the sharing process, the Background Tasks button lights up with a progress indicator. Clicking the button opens the Background Tasks window for more details on the sharing task.

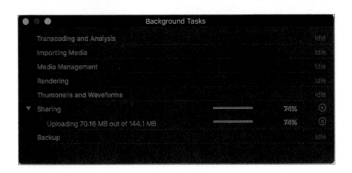

When sharing is completed (and your file is fully uploaded to the destination), a notification alert appears. The alert has a Visit button you can click to go directly to the video online.

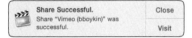

However, you have another way to see the video and determine where and when a video was shared to an online hosting service: You can select the project in the Browser. A simple way to do so is by using a keyboard shortcut.

8   With the project active in the Timeline, choose File > Reveal Project in Browser, or press **Option-Shift-F**.

The event containing the project is selected, along with the project itself. Information about the selected project appears in the Inspector pane.

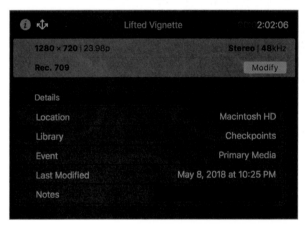

The Inspector pane for a selected project includes two inspectors, Info and Share. The Info inspector displays project metadata, such as when you created the project, the project's location, and the containing library and event. The Share inspector allows you to edit the Info pane's attributes that appear during the share process, and includes a log of shared instances.

9 Click the Share tab to open the Share inspector.

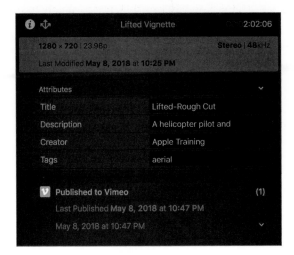

In this Inspector pane, when the project is published, an entry appears below the attributes. Click the pop-up menu to the right to view the options for the destination hosting service.

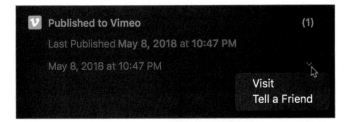

It's just that easy to post projects online. If you want to share to a hosting service not preset in Final Cut Pro, as long as the site accepts H.264 (AVCHD) format files, you should be able to post video files created with the Apple 720p or 1080p presets.

Exercise 8.1.2
Sharing to a Bundle

When you have projects to deliver to a corporate client who understands social media (which includes most of them these days), you may need to post those finished projects to more than one site. The bundling function available as a preset destination reduces this "distribute many" task to a one-click operation.

1 From the Final Cut Pro menu, choose Preferences.

2 In Preferences, select the Destinations pane.

You should start by creating customized destinations, if necessary. This involves dragging additional destinations to the Destinations list, selecting each one, and adjusting its preset's parameters.

You may reorder destinations in the list, and rename destinations to your liking. Once all the destinations to be bundled are placed and configured in the list, you can create the bundle.

3 Drag the Bundle preset to the left list, and position it as you choose.

4   Drag the desired presets from the Destinations list to the Bundle folder.

5   Click the disclosure triangle to display the bundle's contents.

Because you may create multiple bundles, give them descriptive names for future reference.

6   Click the bundle's name, and enter *Social Sites for Lifted*.

7   Close the Preferences window.

Let's select the "Social Sites for Lifted" bundle to see the options available in the Share window.

8   With the project active in the Timeline, from the Share pop-up menu button, choose the "Social Sites for Lifted" bundle.

The Share window opens as it did previously, with one exception. To the left, the name of the first social media site is displayed with a pair of navigation buttons.

9   Click the forward navigation button to review each website's video. This is your last chance to verify the general description and tags for all sites and the privacy and category settings for each destination site.

10 Click Cancel.

Edit once, distribute many. The Share command and customized destinations makes it fast and convenient to do so.

Exercise 8.1.3
Sharing a Master File

After making the distribution files, or even before, you should make a master file of your project. This is a high-quality media file of the final, edited project used for backup/archival purposes. You can't share a higher-quality file than this. Not only is the master ideal for your archivist, but it is also useful for sharing quick-turn transcodes in the future. Currently, H.264 is the preferred format for web delivery. Whatever future format may be required, however, if Compressor supports it, you may simply send this master file straight to Compressor to create a transcode, bypassing Final Cut Pro entirely.

1   With the Lifted Vignette project open, ensure that no clip or range is selected in the project by pressing **Command-Shift-A**.

2   In the toolbar, click the Share button.

3   From the list of destinations, choose Master File.

NOTE ►   If you placed the Master File destination into the bundle earlier, use Final Cut Pro > Preferences to re-access the Destinations preference. Control-click (or right-click) in the sidebar and choose Restore Default Destinations from the shortcut menu.

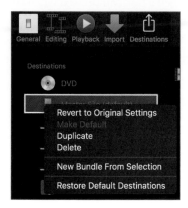

The Share window appears with the Info and Settings panes plus the summary data along the lower edge.

4   Set the following metadata information:

►   Title: *Lifted Vignette*

►   Description: *A helicopter pilot and cinematographer describes his passion for sharing aerial cinematography.*

►   Creator: [Your name]

►   Tags: *aerial cinematography, helicopters, aviation*

5   After entering metadata, click the Settings tab to view the file's delivery options.

The defaults produce a high-quality QuickTime movie file encoded in Apple ProRes 422 format. Because Apple ProRes 422 is the default render format and because it produces higher quality than most HD codecs, you should accept "Video codec: Source - Apple ProRes 422" as your preferred option. If you need a less-compressed video codec because you acquired with a higher-quality codec, you could consider choosing a codec such as Apple ProRes 422 (HQ), Apple ProRes 4444, or Apple ProRes 4444 XQ with the knowledge that these codecs will produce a larger master file.

When working with a third-party audio engineer or archivist, you will probably be asked to export **stems**, a submix of one group of elements, such as the sound bites or the B-roll's natural sound. These submixes may be set up for easy enabling/disabling using roles.

6   Click the Roles tab.

When delivering stems, you may choose to output them as a multitrack QuickTime movie or separate files. The multitrack and separate files options deliver practically the same thing. The difference is whether the audio is embedded in a QuickTime file or is bundled with, but external to, the QuickTime file.

7   From the "Roles as" pop-up menu, choose Multitrack QuickTime Movie.

All the active roles and subroles are listed.

You can insert or remove tracks, roles, or subroles to change the number of stems included in the QuickTime file.

8   Click one of the Channels pop-up menus.

Each of the audio roles may be set to Mono, Stereo, or Surround.

9   From the "Roles as" pop-up menu, choose QuickTime Movie to reset to the default format.

10   With the settings set for mastering as shown in the figure following step 5, click Next.

11   In the navigation dialog that appears, set the Save As name to *Lifted Vignette*, if necessary. Press Command-D to set the desktop as the destination, and click Save.

When the Share is completed, the file opens in QuickTime Player according to the default value chosen in the "Open with" pop-up menu in the Share Settings pane.

You now have a large but very high-quality file for your archives or future transcodes.

Reference 8.2
Creating an Exchangeable File

Several third-party applications take advantage of the robust XML (eXtensible Markup Language) files supported by Final Cut Pro. Other applications can read and write Final Cut Pro data in XML files, whether that data is related to an event, project, or library. This info can include which clips are in your event: the clips you used in the project; which events, projects, and associated clips are in your library; and the metadata for all three. Among the third-party applications that read/write Final Cut Pro XML data are Blackmagic Design's DaVinci Resolve, the various applications from Intelligent Assistance, and Marquis Broadcast's X2Pro. Visit the Final Cut Pro pages of apple.com for a listing of additional supported third-party software and devices.

> **NOTE ▶** Check with each software vendor to identify software requirements and any file preparation required within Final Cut Pro before you export or import an XML file to their product.

▶   To export an event, project, or library XML file: With the event, project, or library selected, choose File > Export XML.

▶   When exporting, you may select the format version and how much metadata, if any, to include in the XML file.

To import an XML file, choose File > Import > XML. When importing, you must identify which library will receive the imported data.

Reference 8.3
Utilizing Compressor

If you've created a customized preset in Compressor, you have two ways to access the preset when transcoding a project.

Exercise 8.3.1
Adding a Compressor Setting to the Share Destinations

You may access a customized Compressor setting within Final Cut Pro. As with other Share commands, when you start a share operation, it becomes a background process that allows you to continue editing, even including the project you are sharing.

1   In Final Cut Pro > Preferences, access the Destinations pane.

2   Drag the Compressor Setting preset to the Destinations list.

A Settings dialog appears listing the preset and custom settings from Compressor.

3   In the list, select your custom setting, and click OK.

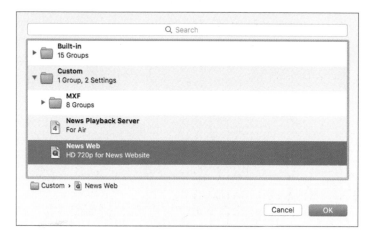

The Compressor Setting preset will take the name of the setting; however, you may rename it if you choose.

Exercise 8.3.2
Sending to Compressor

You can also take advantage of Compressor's distributed processing by choosing to "Send to Compressor" within Final Cut Pro.

1   With your project open and ready for sharing, choose File > Send to Compressor.

Compressor opens, and the project becomes a job in the center batch.

2   Click the "Show Setting and Locations" button to display the Settings options.

3   Drag the desired setting or settings to the job (your project) where it says "Setting."

You may customize the Location and Filename targets for the job's output file.

4   Control-click the Location in the target, and from the shortcut menu, choose a new location, such as Desktop.

5   Double-click the filename, and rename the file *Archive - Lifted Vignette*.

6   To start the export, click Start Batch.

The Compressor interface switches to the Active panel. Here you may monitor the progress of the export.

NOTE ▶ Click the Elapsed Time column header to display a time remaining column.

7   When the export is complete, close Compressor.

Compressor is not mandatory when using the Share Destination presets. But when you want to create custom destinations or take advantage of distributed processing with built-in Final Cut Pro integration, Compressor is just a click away in the App Store.

Congratulations, you have taken your raw video to a distributed, finished project with Final Cut Pro. As you have learned, Final Cut Pro provides a flexible approach to video post-production workflow. The magnetic timeline encourages experimentation, freeing you to audition different arrangements of your story by removing technical barriers and editorial apprehension. Although you can stay on the surface level of editing as the job allows, Final Cut Pro quickly lets you go deeper into your workflow when necessary.

If you are not a daily video editor, you are encouraged to find a small story to shoot and edit at least once a month. Even if your subject is your dog playing fetch as recorded on your iPhone, get in the art and stay in the art. The more time you spend with its tools, the more Final Cut Pro will work for you to tell your story.

Lesson Review

1.   Which Share window button do you click to display the compatible platforms for the current export settings?

2.   When sharing to an online host, which interface item displays details about the upload's progress?

3.   Where can you find a history of a project's shared instances?

4.   Which destination preset allows you to distribute to multiple platforms in a single share session?

5.   Which Master File Settings parameter allows you to export audio stems from inside a QuickTime movie?

6.   What export command outputs your project to a file format readable by several third-party applications?

7.   Name two export methods that utilize Compressor custom settings.

8.   Of the two export methods in the previous answer, which one uses Compressor's distributed processing capabilities?

Answers

1. The Share window's compatibility checker.

2. Click the Background Tasks button in the Dashboard to see details of the upload's progress.

3. With the project selected in the Browser, look in the Share inspector.

4. The Bundle destination preset

5. Roles as: Multitrack QuickTime Movie

6. File > Export XML

7. The Compressor Settings destination preset in the Share pop-up menu, and the File > Send to Compressor command

8. File > Send to Compressor

Lesson 9
Managing Libraries

Libraries provide a convenient way to manage, store, share, and archive one or more events and projects. In Lessons 1 through 8, you created a new library and imported files as referenced external media or as copied internal media into the library's events. This process of working within libraries occurs every time you start an editing job in Final Cut Pro. In this lesson, you'll experiment further with media managing a library.

Reference 9.1
Storing the Imported Media

Editors are creative control freaks. For a couple of decades, our workflows required us to cram information about a clip into its name and to create a precise, descriptive folder structure to store the clip's source media. The alternative was to bow to the demands of an editing application's rigid file structure. The external media management features of Final Cut Pro allow you to keep these habits (or scars), but apply an organizational structure in advantageous ways not currently available in other editing systems.

However, a few editors work a little differently. They are slightly (if not completely) disorganized when it comes to media management. Naming source media files is an afterthought, and storing source media files on the desktop is a standard procedure in their workflows. The internal media solution within Final Cut Pro can change these editors' habits in a positive yet not painful way. Let's look at how Final Cut Pro addresses each approach.

GOALS

- ► Differentiate external and internal media

- ► Import media as referenced and managed

- ► Move and copy clips within and between libraries

- ► Consolidate media files to one location

A library that includes both copied internal media
(left column) and referenced external media (right column)

The key to library management in Final Cut Pro is managing contained source clips. Because the clips inside a library may include both external and internal media, the choices you make when managing source media files will result in **media full** or **media empty** libraries, or a combination of both.

Internal source media files

A media full library contains all the source media files for all events and projects in the library. However, when all the source media files are stored inside that library, this library file may require a great deal of storage space.

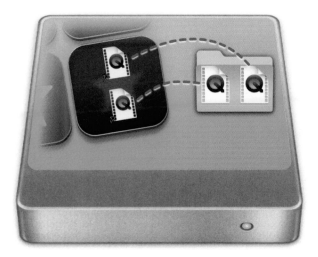

External source media files

When a library is media empty, the media files for the contained clips are **symlinks** to the external media files. An empty library has a small file size compared to a media full library.

Utilizing external media is a best practice for media storage in Final Cut Pro. Keeping the library media empty helps minimize the library file size, which allows you to easily pass a library to collaborators during the run of a job. The source media files may be stored in one centrally accessible location where they are available to multiple users. Sharing a media empty library file that references only external media enables efficient and cost-effective collaboration using just one set of source media files on a server. Furthermore, that one set of external files may be accessed by other applications, such as Motion or Logic Pro X, so compositors and audio engineers may also collaborate seamlessly with the editorial team.

Setting the import options to "Leave files in place"
creates external media files.

The media full internal solution works well for an editor who is working solo and/or prefers to have Final Cut Pro manage the media. Every imported source media file is copied into the library file. This may result in duplicate media files on the volume, but that's not necessarily a bad thing unless you are running out of available storage space.

Setting the import options to "Copy to library" creates internal media files.

NOTE ▶ Technically, the library file is a collection of files known as a bundle. Therefore, you should modify the contents of the library only within Final Cut Pro, and not change them directly in the Finder.

So far, our discussion here has been about internal versus external media—where in relation to a library are the source media files stored. There is another aspect to the storage location which is, how did the files get to that location? You've already heard these terms in earlier lessons: managed and referenced. As you've experienced media management in Final Cut Pro X, you could restate the storage methods as managed internal or referenced external. Managed internal was the media management method used with the GoPro clips. You instructed Final Cut Pro to copy the source media files into the Lifted library. For the other imported media files, you told Final Cut Pro to leave the files in place, which is known as referencing the existing media files external to the library.

The Library Properties inspector, in conjunction with your file handling settings in import options, sets the physical destinations for the imported media.

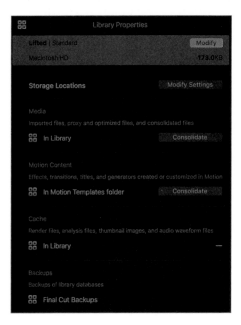

The Modify Settings button in the Library Properties inspector controls the Storage Location settings. These settings allow you to specify the library for an internally managed file or choose a folder for externally referenced media files.

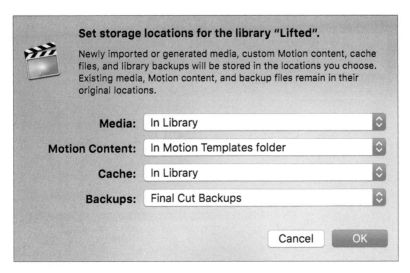

You can specify internally managed or externally referenced locations for imported media and generated media (renders, thumbnails, and waveforms).

That's right, the Storage Location settings allow you to set up an external location for copied files. Changing the Media pop-up menu to a location other than In Library directs Final Cut Pro to copy future imported media files to the specified location. This change to create externally referenced media is evidenced in the copy selection in the import options.

The following table summarizes the media storage location settings, the import options available based on that media storage location setting, and the resulting media status for the imported clips.

Library Management

Library Properties Inspector	+ Import Options	= Media Status
		Internally managed media
		Externally referenced media
		Externally referenced media

Left at its default, the Library Properties inspector lets the import options determine the internally managed or externally referenced state of the media files. Changing the Media storage location in this inspector allows copied media to become externally referenced. Let's see the three management methods in action.

Exercise 9.1.1
Importing Existing Files as Externally Referenced

The ultimate external media import option for the obsessive-compulsive editor is "Leave files in place" (the opposite import option of "Copy to"). "Leave files in place" references these existing, external files with no moving or copying of the imported source media files. Symlinks are created within the receiving library that point to the external files, wherever those files may be.

"Leave files in place" is the ideal choice when you need to share existing source media files in a collaborative environment, such as a high-bandwidth, low-latency network. Even if such a network is unavailable to you at the moment, you may still practice importing a clip with this option.

NOTE ▶ Choosing to "Leave files in place" virtually mandates that you organize your source media files before importing their symlinks into a library because moving, renaming, or deleting a source media file may cause the referenced clip to go offline in Final Cut Pro. When you decide that you will reference external media, then you are directly responsible for keeping Final Cut Pro abreast of any media management you perform outside of the application. See "Relinking Offline Clips to Source Media" in this lesson.

1   Choose File > New > Library.

2   In the dialog that appears, name the library *External vs Managed*, and for the purpose of this exercise, set the location to the desktop.

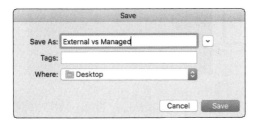

NOTE ▶ Outside the context of this lesson, you may set the location to any accessible, locally-available volume. This includes HFS+ and SMB3 volumes to which you have read and write access. Libraries shoud not be stored in locations under control of a cloud-based, file-synchronization application. That stipulation extends to use of iCloud Drive for your Desktop and Documents folders.

3   In the Libraries sidebar, rename the "External vs Managed" default event to *Event 1*.

For this event, you will import two of the aerial clips with "Leave files in place" chosen.

4   Press **Command-I** to open the Media Import window.

5   In the Media Import window, navigate to the FCPX Media/LV2/LV Aerials folder, and select **Aerials_11_03a** and **Aerials_11_04a**.

6   In the import options, ensure that "Add to existing event" is selected and that Event 1 is chosen in the pop-up menu.

Choosing the event here does not determine the external or managed state of a source media file. To be available for editing, every clip must be in an event. However, the actual media file does not have to be stored within that event's library. A symlink can stand in for the clip's source media file within the library. The choice of event within the pop-up menu defines only where the clip will appear in the Libraries sidebar. The physical location is controlled by a combination of settings here in the Files section of Import Options and the Library Properties inspector.

The "Leave files in place" option is literally an "edit in place" command. It produces no copies, and it does not move media. It just creates a reference to the existing source media file and adds it to the chosen event.

7   With "Leave files in place" chosen, deselect any other transcode, keyword, and analysis options, and click Import Selected.

The two aerial clips appear in Event 1's Browser and appear to be normal clips. When you look at the clips in filmstrip view, you'll see no indication that these clips are externally referenced. Let's continue importing internally managed clips, and then compare their storage locations.

▶ **Relinking Offline Clips to Source Media**

If you open a library, and instead of video thumbnails, discover red thumbnails with the very humbling text "Missing File," take a breath for a moment. The files go missing and the clips go "offline" when Final Cut Pro is unable to find the clips' source media files. In a worst-case scenario, the source media files were deleted, and the deleted files must be reimported. In a not-so-bad scenario where the source media files were moved, you may be able to point the offline clips toward the alternative source media files.

1   Select the event or library containing offline clips.

2   Choose File > Relink Files.

3   Choose to relink only missing clips or all clips.

4   Click Locate All.

5   Navigate to the folder containing the clips' source media files. Select the folder and click Choose.

6   In the Relink Files window, click Relink Files.

Exercise 9.1.2
Importing as Internally Managed Clips

For the editor who struggles with media management, handing the media management duties over to Final Cut Pro may save hours (or days) of frustration. A simple selection in Import Options creates managed media within a library. By allowing Final Cut Pro to take command, your struggles with media management are instantly diminished.

1 Reopen the Media Import window by pressing **Command-I**.

2 From the LV Aerials folder, select **Aerials_13_01b** and **Aerials_13_02a**.

For this exercise, you want to organize these two clips as internally managed, so you will create a new event for them in the import options.

3 Select "Create new event in," and from the pop-up menu of all open libraries, choose the "External vs Managed" library.

4 For the event name, enter *Event 2*.

5 In the Files section, select "Copy to library." Click Import Selected.

Choosing this option identifies the incoming clips as internally managed media. This setting is dependent on the Media Storage Locations setting in the Library Properties inspector.

Now that you have a library of events that contain both managed and external media, let's see how you can determine the difference between them in the Info inspector.

6   Select the "External vs Managed" library to display all clips in the Browser.

7   In the Browser, select **Aerials_11_03a**.

8   With the clip selected, look at the lower portion of the Info inspector to find the file information section.

This section lists the containing event for the selected clip. In this instance, **Aerials_11_03a** is stored in Event 1. Looking at the next info item, you'll find that the location is the volume where you placed the FCP X Media folder in Lesson 1. If your FCP X Media folder is stored on your desktop, for example, Location will display the volume's name because you imported this clip as "Leave files in place."

9   In the Browser, select **Aerials_13_01b**.

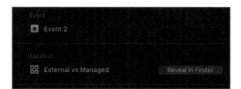

The Info inspector displays the location of this file as the "External vs Managed" library. This is an internally managed media file because it is stored in the library.

By making some simple choices during import, you are setting some important properties for your imported clips. These choices are not irreversible, but if you choose wisely during the first and subsequent imports, your workflow will move more smoothly.

▶ Importing by Dragging from the Finder

You may import source media files directly into an event in the Libraries sidebar by dragging them from the Finder or a supported application. While you drag, the pointer indicates whether you are importing the files as "leave in place" or copied media.

▶   A hooked arrow indicates that the file is imported as a referenced, "leave in place" media file.

▶   An arrow with a circled plus sign indicates that the file will be copied into the library as managed media, or it will be copied as referenced media into the external storage location specified in Library Properties.

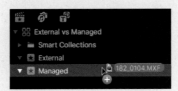

If you do not see the pointer you expect, try holding down the Option key, the Command key, or the Command-Option keys as you drag.

▶ No Duplicates

A library's database efficiently manages media in several ways. One efficiency activates when importing the same source media file...again. If the source media file **SMF1** exists (external or managed) in Event A of Library X, and you re-import **SMF1** to Event A or B, no duplicate source media file is created. **SMF1** is used as the source media file for the clip in Event A and Event B—two clips referring to a single source media file.

Exercise 9.1.3
Copying as Externally Referenced

This hybrid approach to media management is a combination of the two previously discussed media storage methods. The source media files you are going to import will be copied to outside the library (externally referenced). This management method allows you to easily share the source media files in a collaborative networked environment by copying the media files from camera cards, or another volume, to the shared location using just one import step. To begin, you change the Media Storage Locations setting in the Library Properties inspector.

1   In the Libraries sidebar, select the "External vs Managed" library.

2   In the Library Properties inspector, click the Modify Settings button.

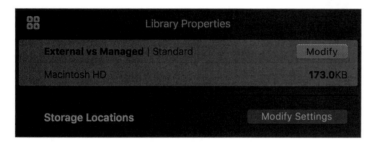

The storage location options dialog opens.

Here you may specify the storage locations for imported and transcoded media files either inside or outside the library. If you customize Motion templates, you may store the modified templates in a default location or inside the library. Additionally, you may redirect cache files such as render, analysis, thumbnail, and waveform to a location outside the library bundle—doing so allows you to set a different location for the library backup files. Keep in mind that these are backups of the open libraries' metadata, and not the source media files.

3   In the Media pop-up menu, click Choose.

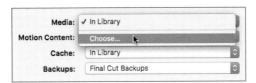

4   In the Finder window, navigate to the Desktop, create a new folder named *Externally Copied*, and select the new folder before clicking Choose.

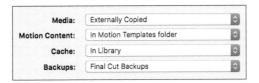

5   Click OK to close the dialog.

The Library Properties inspector lists the Externally Copied location as the media storage destination. Now, you will import two additional clips to this external location.

6   Reopen the Media Import window by pressing **Command-I**.

7   From the LV Aerials folder, select **Aerials_11_01a** and **Aerials_11_02a**.

8   Select "Create new event in," and from the pop-up menu of all open libraries, choose the "External vs Managed" library.

9   For the event name, enter *Event 3*.

10 In the Files section, select "Copy to Externally Copied."

A little more definitive than just "Copy to library," this setting reflects the change you made earlier in the Library Properties inspector.

11 Click Import Selected.

After the import is completed, take a look at these externally copied media files.

12 In the Dock, click the Finder icon.

13 In the Finder window that opens, in the sidebar, select Desktop.

14 Navigate the folder structure to reveal the two aerials clips inside the Externally Copied folder.

This hybrid file management method created external media files by copying them to the specified media storage location. If that location were a fast, shared network location, multiple users could access the media file simultaneously without interfering with one another's workflow.

15 In the Dock, click the Final Cut Pro icon to return to the application.

Exercise 9.1.4
Moving and Copying Clips Within a Library

Imagine a situation in which you want the same clip to appear in multiple events. Or perhaps you imported a source media file as a clip but placed it into the wrong event. To fix these situations, the Libraries sidebar allows you to drag a clip from one event to another event in the same library. However, "clip" is the operative word in the preceding sentences. Final Cut Pro manages the source media files (both internal and external) for the library while you simply manage the clips within the Libraries sidebar and Browser pane.

> **NOTE ▶** Media management within a library is best (and most safely) performed inside Final Cut Pro, not in the Finder.

1   To verify that Final Cut Pro is duplicating media files (or not), select the "External vs Managed" library, and then scroll down the Library Properties to the storage used section.

Notice that the Original media files on the volume total 389.9 MB, which represents all the files imported for this library so far. Let's start moving and copying clips to see what happens.

2   In Event 2, locate the **Aerials_13_01b** clip, and verify its managed media status in the Info inspector's file information.

This file is an internally managed source media file. The Location field displays the library into which it was imported.

3   Drag `Aerials_13_01b` from Event 2 to Event 1.

Notice that the pointer remains an arrow and does not change to a circled plus sign. This pointer icon indicates a simple clip move, the default behavior of dragging clips between events within a library.

4   In Event 1, select the added `Aerials_13_01b` clip.

The Info inspector displays the library where the file is stored, which indicates that it remains an internal source media file. If this were an external file, the Location field would display the volume that contains the referenced media.

5   In the Libraries sidebar, select the "External vs Managed" library, and then look at the storage used section of Library Properties.

As you may have expected, a move did not involve duplicating the media files. But what if you want the same clip to appear in both events? Then, you'll want to make a copy.

6   Option-drag `Aerials_13_01b` from Event 1 to Event 2. When the plus sign appears over the destination event, release the mouse button.

The Option key instructs Final Cut Pro to copy the clip to the second event. Let's check the aggregate size of the media files.

7   With the "External vs Managed" library selected, notice that **Aerials_13_01b** appears twice in the Browser. Now, let's inspect the storage used data.

The total storage occupied by the media files didn't change. Final Cut Pro created a **hardlink** for the copied clip that references the source media file of the original clip. You haven't wasted space by duplicating media inside a library. But what happens if the source media file is external to the library?

8   In Event 1, select and then verify clip **Aerials_11_04a** as external to the library with the Location displayed as a volume rather than a library.

9   Option-drag **Aerials_11_04a** to Event 2.

Again, holding down the Option key forces a copy so that the clip appears in both events. And guess what happened?

10 Check the storage space used by the library.

No change. Once again, Final Cut Pro created a space-saving copy of the file, thereby avoiding duplicate media files.

When you copy clips within a library, the library database keeps only one copy of the source media file. Additional instances of the clip in any event in the same library will reference the original source media file. Whether managed or external, Final Cut Pro strives to avoid storing duplicate source media files.

▶ **Using Clips Between Libraries**

You may not only drag clips between events within the same library, but also between events in different libraries. This feature is handy when you've created a library that contains stock footage because you may often add and copy clips to and from that stock footage library. Whenever you copy or move a clip between libraries, you should remember a couple of Final Cut Pro media management rules:

▶ Internally managed source media files are copied or moved to the destination library's media storage location. This location could be inside the destination library or in an externally referenced location.

▶ Externally referenced source media files are left in place.

A dialog reminds you of these management rules:

Exercise 9.1.5
Making a Library Portable

With a MacBook Pro and a Thunderbolt or USB 3 hard disk, an editor has a lightweight, HD-capable edit system to take on the road. In this exercise, we'll assume that you have a Mac Pro in the office where you usually edit; but for this client's job, you have to finish editing your project on-site. Final Cut Pro provides a built-in, two-step process that allows you to copy a library to wherever you have access.

NOTE ▶ In this exercise, you'll copy events to a new library. Alternatively, you could copy a project and all its media to a new or existing library; or duplicate a library in the Finder to a new location, and then perform the consolidation task described later in this exercise.

1   In the Libraries sidebar, select the "External vs Managed" library.

This is the library you want to use when editing remotely. You would want to leave everything on the Mac Pro system as it is, and just copy a subset of the library's contents to your portable volume. Let's start by creating a new library and designating the library itself as the media storage Location.

2   Choose File > New > Library. In the Save dialog, enter *On the Go*. Select Desktop as the save location, and click Save.

The new library appears in the Libraries sidebar with an empty, default event. You will delete the event's default name in a moment. With the library created, you're almost ready to copy events, but first you must set the media storage Location.

3   With the "On the Go" library selected, click Modify Settings to set the Media location to In Library, if necessary.

4   In the Libraries sidebar, select Event 1 and Event 2, and then choose File > Copy Events to Library > On the Go.

A dialog indicates that external media will be referenced, whereas managed media will be copied. Because you need to take a self-contained version of your project on-site, you need to copy all source media files to the "On the Go" library.

NOTE ▶ Ensure that you have selected only the two events, and not the entire library.

5   Deselect the "Optimized media" and "Proxy media" checkboxes, and click OK.

   If you were able to see it, the background tasks button briefly indicated that a background task was activated, but it was not activated long enough to copy all the source media files. Let's verify that not everything was copied.

6   In the Libraries sidebar, locate the "On the Go" library, and select Event 2. Select **Aerials_11_04a.**

7   In the Info inspector, verify in the File Information section that a volume (such as Macintosh HD) is listed.

8   Select a few more files, and note their individual file information details.

   A few files are listed with different storage locations. Because you want everything packaged for your on-site edit, you need to copy all the required source media files to your storage location.

9   With the "On the Go" library selected, choose File > Consolidate Library Media.

A dialog asks if you want to include optimized and/or proxy media. But notice that this dialog has a difference compared to the previous dialog. Notice the last sentence. It states that external media will be copied.

10 Click OK.

11 When the background tasks indicator returns to 100%, select at least one clip in each event of the "On the Go" library and refer to the clip's file information in the Info inspector.

All the clips are now located in the "On the Go" library and ready to edit separate from your office-based Mac Pro. You are ready to close the library to remove it from the Libraries sidebar.

12 Control-click (or right-click) the "On the Go" library, and from the shortcut menu, choose Close Library "On the Go."

By consolidating the media, your source files are packaged to one storage location. The library itself or some external folder may serve as that storage location. This one Final Cut Pro feature avoids many frustrating hours of hunting down stray media files to package for a complete project.

NOTE ►   To open an existing library, choose File > Open Library and select from the list of recently opened libraries, or select Other to select an unlisted library.

▶ Archiving a Library

Archiving a library basically follows the "portable library" creation process you just performed. When archiving, as when preparing a project "to-go," you want to consolidate
media after making the copy. If you don't, your archive library may be missing some
crucial source media files required to play that library's projects. Also, you should delete
the items that don't need archiving—such as render files, proxies, or optimized media—
to conserve volume space. Here are a few steps and tips to follow when archiving:

1   With the library for archiving selected, choose File > Delete Generated Library Files.

2   Select all three Delete options and All for Render Files.

3   Do not archive optimized or proxy media if you retained all the original source
     media files or their camera archive sources.

▶   As you did in the previous exercise, you may set the archive library as a man-
     aged media library to consolidate the final archived item into a single library file.

▶   In the Libraries sidebar, delete extraneous events. After quitting the application,
     you may use the Finder to delete the library from which you made the archive.
     You may also move the archived library (and external media folder, when appli-
     cable) to a different location, if desired.

▶   Don't forget to empty the Final Cut Pro internal trash can by quitting and
     relaunching the application.

▶   In the Finder, locate the camera archives separately, and store them in the same
     location as the archived library file.

▶   In the Finder, you can manually manage customized effects, transitions,
     themes, and generators by copying the Movies > Motion Templates folder.

▶ **Other Library Features**

The robust library architecture of Final Cut Pro allows you to perform powerful media management functions with just a few clicks. Here are a few additional notes on libraries and events:

▶ Final Cut Pro automatically backs up a library's metadata every 15 minutes (if the library file is updated). If you need to revert to a previous version of a library, select the library in the Libraries sidebar, and then choose File > Open Library > From Backup. A dialog appears with the date/time-stamped list of available backups.

▶ Rather than watching the mouse pointer to identify a move or copy function, you may move or copy events between libraries with the explicit "Copy Events to Library" and "Move Events to Library" commands chosen from the File menu.

▶ You may combine events to reorganize your library using the File > Merge Events command.

▶ If your original source media files were deleted for any reason, you may recover any camera source media files for which you still have the camera media (SD card, magazine, and so on) or for which you chose to make a camera archive during import. Do so by selecting the offline clips in the event, and then choosing File > Import > Reimport from Camera/Archive.

Lesson Review

1. Define and compare managed media and external media.

2. How is external media referenced in a library?

3. What media storage selection do you choose to define media as external?

4. How can you find the file information section shown in the following figure?

5. When archiving or preparing a library for transport, describe a few tasks you should complete.

Answers

1. Managed media files give Final Cut Pro the responsibility of storing your source media files inside the library you designate. Storing media externally saddles you with the responsibility of watching over the source media files. In either case, you determine where the media files are physically stored. The difference is who is responsible for tracking that media: Final Cut Pro or you.

2. External media is referenced inside the library through the use of symlinks.

3. The first answer is "leave files in place"; however, "Copy to" can designate an external folder outside a library, which would also result in external media.

4. With a clip selected in the Libraries sidebar, you will find file information in the Info inspector.

5. Consolidate the library as a managed library, and delete render, optimized, and proxy media files.

Lesson 10
Advancing Your Workflow

Regardless of the project, every editor follows the same general workflow: import, edit, and share. Source media files are ingested into Final Cut Pro, the edit is made, and the final video is exported. The individual workflow tasks or *sub-workflow* during each phase may vary depending on the project and the client. Furthermore, those three "primary" workflow phases may be assigned across a large team of collaborators, or fully completed by only one person.

The sub-workflows described in this lesson provide you with additional information and suggest steps you can apply to enhance the workflow you've followed throughout this book. You may never need some specific workflow techniques described here; however, these exercises also may contain some knowledge nuggets that will enhance your basic workflow.

GOALS

► Identify manual options for new projects

► Synchronize dual system recordings

► Create a chroma key

► Understand the multi-cam workflow

► Discover a 360° world

► Generate captions

Sub-workflow 10.1
Using Manual Settings for a New Project

Every project is defined by frame size (resolution) and frame rate. These two items are set in one of two ways when starting a new project:

► Automatically, by conforming to the first edit; the default setting

► Manually, by selecting "Use Custom Settings" in the Project Settings window

The Automatic setting is recommended for most projects and editors. Using the custom settings to manually set resolution and rate is required when one of the following is true:

▶ The delivery resolution and rate are known and differ from the source media files.

▶ A video clip of non-native resolution is used as the first edit.

▶ A nonvideo clip (audio only or still image) is used as the first edit.

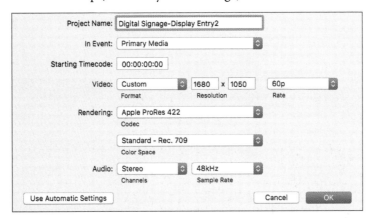

"Non-native resolutions" refers to a frame size not common to video formats. This resolution requirement has become more common with the growing use of video in nontraditional venues. Digital signage video is growing as businesses and advertisers compete to attract more eyeballs (compared to traditional static billboards, business advertising banners, and menu boards). These displays require non-native resolutions because many are "banner" layouts on custom displays or vertical "portrait" orientation. Other industries now exploring creative video display installations include museums and trade-show venues.

NOTE ▶ Although a project's resolution may be changed at any time, the frame rate locks after the first edit in the project.

This sub-workflow exercise exposes you to a project's manual settings. You will create a new project for this exercise that may be discarded later.

1 In the Libraries sidebar, Control-click (or right-click) the Lifted library, and from the shortcut menu, choose New Project.

The New Project window appears in which you can enter a project name and configure custom settings.

2 For Project Name, enter *Custom Project*. Set the In Event pop-up menu to Primary Media, and click the Use Custom Settings button.

The custom settings controls appear as the window expands. Here you'll find options with which you can manually configure the project.

In the Video settings, you can set the frame size (resolution) and frame rate. The Format pop-up menu filters the Resolution and Rate pop-up menus to the native, supported settings. However, at times you may need to set an uncommon frame size for a project.

3 To manually enter a resolution, from the Format pop-up menu, choose Custom.

The Resolution pop-up menu becomes two numeric fields in which you can enter a custom frame size. The Rate pop-up menu also changes to display an expanded list of supported frame rates.

4   For this sub-workflow exercise only, set the following values:

▶   Format: Custom

▶   Resolution: 1080 x 1920

▶   Frame Rate: 29.97

With the video parameters set, let's look at the "Audio and Render Properties" options.

5   Click the Audio Channels pop-up menu to see its two options: Stereo and Surround.

This control sets the number of audio channels you'll be working with in the project: two-channel stereo or six-channel surround.

6   Set the Audio Channels pop-up menu to Surround.

7   Click the Audio Sample Rate pop-up menu to view its choices.

Final Cut Pro supports a wide range of audio sample rates that determine how many times per second an audio signal is measured and recorded (sampled). The common sample rate for video production (and the default value here) is 48kHz, which means that the audio is sampled 48,000 times per second. The higher the sample rate, the more accurately the sample will represent the original source.

8   Leave the sample rate set to 48kHz, and then click the Rendering Codec pop-up menu.

When you added transitions, effects, and the title in previous lessons, a render bar temporarily appeared in the Timeline.

A render bar indicates the application will generate a media file to increase performance for that timeline section. You may not have noticed the render bar because the project played without rendering. When the application renders an element, the Rendering Codec pop-up menu determines the **codec** used to generate the rendered media file. When you are rendering HD video, stills, and graphics for your projects, the default Apple ProRes 422 is an excellent codec choice because it produces small media files of near-lossless quality.

NOTE ▶ Because Apple ProRes 422 produces higher quality than most HD codecs, you should utilize Apple ProRes 422 as your preferred option. If you need a less compressed video codec because you acquired with a higher-quality codec, you could consider choosing a codec such as Apple ProRes 422 HQ, Apple ProRes 4444, or Apple ProRes 4444 XQ with the knowledge that these codecs will produce larger-sized render files.

9 With Rendering Codec set to Apple ProRes 422, click OK.

Your project is created and opened into the Timeline. With the project selected in the browser, the Inspector displays the Project Properties. There, you can verify that the project's settings are 1080 x 1920, 29.97 fps, and Surround.

The project is now set to edit video and graphics for a digital signage installation that utilizes HDTV sets in vertical or portrait orientation and with surround sound.

Sub-workflow 10.2
Synchronizing Dual System Recordings

When shooting film it is common to use separate devices (camera and audio recorder) to record image and sound. With the proliferation of small, relatively inexpensive DSLR video cameras, this **dual system recording** workflow has found its place in the video world. When video and audio are recorded separately, it falls to the editor to reassemble those separate recordings into a single, synchronized clip for editing. In this exercise, you'll discover that Final Cut Pro simplifies this task. Let's try it by first importing some media.

1 From the FCP X Media folder, navigate to the LV3 folder, and import the Extras folder as a Keyword Collection into a new Lifted event, *Lesson 10*.

Select the Extras folder for import.   Choose to create collections from folders.

The Extras folder includes materials for use in this lesson's sub-workflows. The media you'll use here is in the Sync collection, which contains a video clip and an audio clip from Mitch's interview. Furthermore, the video clip comes with its own not-so-clean embedded audio that you'll need to synchronize with the separate audio clip.

2   To create one synchronized clip from the two clips, in the Sync keyword collection, select the two clips.

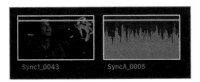

3   Control-click any one of the selected clips, and from the shortcut menu, choose Synchronize Clips.

A synchronization dialog appears that presents options similar to the project settings. You have the choice of using the automatic formatting settings, or you may choose to customize.

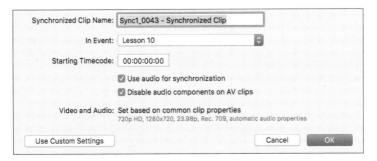

Two differing options include using the audio of the two clips for synchronization. The synchronization process starts by aligning timecode, if available, on the selected clips. If no timecode is available, Final Cut Pro attempts to use the content creation "time-of-day" of the selected clips. Whether or not those data points are available and match, with the audio option selected, the audio will be used to finalize the sync. The synchronization occurs faster as more of those items are available and conform. The second option instructs the synchronized clip to disable the camera's audio, utilizing the stand-alone audio file as the only desired clip audio.

4   With both options selected and the default name entered, click OK.

Final Cut Pro generates a new clip with the new name you provided and returns to the Lesson 10 event as active and the new clip selected.

Sub-workflow 10.3
Using Chroma Key

Until the recent increase of integrating LCD/LED displays everywhere on television news sets, the meteorologist presented the weather segment standing in front of a green or blue wall, commonly referred to as the "chroma wall." Still in use today, but for more than the weathercast, a chroma wall allows the editor to replace the wall color with a video clip or animation, transporting the person or object in the foreground to a different background location. A common use today (beyond weathercasts and movie visual effects) is to place talent or interview subjects on virtual sets or environments. And with portable chroma screens now available, formerly studio-bound chroma walls can now be used in the field. In this sub-workflow exercise, you'll start with a chroma key clip and superimpose the talent over a background graphic. You'll also use a mask to remove unwanted set items from the image.

1   In the Libraries sidebar, locate the Lesson 10 event's Chroma Key Keyword Collection.

Here you'll find **MVI_0013**, a short clip of an interview prep recorded in front of a chroma screen. This is your foreground clip. The workflow for chroma key is straightforward. You'll start by creating a project and placing the foreground clip into its primary storyline.

2 In the Lesson 10 event, create a new project named *Green Screen* and use the automatic settings to conform to the clip.

3 In the Browser, select **MVI_0013**, and then press **E** to append edit the clip into the primary storyline.

With the foreground clip in the project, let's apply the Keyer effect.

4 In the Effects browser, select the Keying category, and locate the Keyer effect.

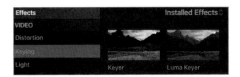

5 With the the foreground clip selected in the Timeline, skim the Keyer effect to preview it.

The Keyer thumbnail and Viewer preview the Keyer effect as applied to the selected clip, similar to the effects you previewed in an earlier lesson. The green background disappears from view.

6   Double-click the Keyer effect to apply it to the selected foreground clip.

The green background is replaced with an alpha channel, which currently appears black because no video clip is beneath the foreground clip to represent the background. You'll fix that next.

7   In the Generators Browser, select a background such as Grunge.

You may have some concern here as to where the background clip will connect. Performing a connect edit by pressing Q will stack the background clip into a higher lane, thereby hiding the foreground clip. Although you could lift the foreground clip out of the primary storyline and replace the resulting gap clip with the background clip, another option is to connect the background clip to the lane beneath the foreground clip.

8   Drag the **Grunge** clip below the primary storyline, snap it to the start of the foreground clip, and then release the mouse button.

The background clip replaces the empty background behind the interview. With a well-lit set, the Keyer effect does a great job of automatically keying out the chroma screen. You'll next remove the extraneous set items from view.

▶ **More Than Meets the Eye**

The generators within Final Cut Pro control access to parameters much like effects because only after you've applied a generator to your project can you access generator parameters. Grunge is not the only parameter available for that generator. After adding Grunge to a project, you can select the clip, and then alter the available parameters in the Generator inspector to apply a different texture and/or color tint.

10.3-A Masking Objects

Due to frame composition, lighting requirements, or location restrictions, some chroma key clips contain extraneous material that must be removed in editing. A simple way to crop these items from view is to use the Crop tool or a **mask** effect. You've already used the Crop tool, and you've explored the built-in shape mask available within effects. A third option is to draw a mask shape onto the green screen clip using the Draw Mask effect.

1   With the foreground clip selected in the Timeline, cue the playhead over the two clips so you may view the effect's results.

2   In the Effects Browser, select the Masks category, and double-click the Draw Mask effect.

3   Reposition the mouse to the Viewer, and observe the instructions that appear.

The Add Control Point tool is now active, ready for you to define the mask's shape. Everything inside the mask remains visible, while everything outside the mask is hidden.

4   Click in the Viewer to create a shape that retains the interview but removes the extraneous equipment and set items from the image.

5   To complete the mask's shape, click the first control point.

In addition to masks, you may use the Transform and Crop tools to further define the "keeper" parts of the image or the foreground's spatial relation to the background's contents.

10.3-B Manually Selecting Color Key Samples

Sometimes location, time, and equipment—or a combination of all three—do not allow a well-lit chroma screen. In that scenario, you may need to use a manual keyer in which you define the chroma key color. In this exercise, you'll switch the current composite to manual controls to define the keyer's setup.

1   With the foreground clip selected in the Timeline and the playhead cued over the clip, in the clip's Video inspector, locate the Keyer effect.

2   In the Keyer effect's parameters, change the Strength slider to a setting of 0%.

The Keyer is now in manual operation and the green background has reappeared. You will define which color from the foreground clip to replace.

3   In the Video inspector, locate the Refine Key's Sample Color button. This button activates a marquee-style selector to draw a selection rectangle around the color to be
replaced.

4   Click the Sample Color button, and then move the mouse pointer over the Viewer.

The pointer becomes a crosshair with a marquee box. You'll use this tool to identify
the green color within the image.

5   Drag out a marquee selection in the green chroma screen area of the image, while
being careful not to include the talent.

As you drag the selection, the green will begin to disappear.

NOTE ▶   You can select more than one color sample using the same tool.

6   Release the mouse pointer, and in the Video inspector, click the Sample Color button again. Drag the mouse pointer within the Viewer to select any remaining green areas of the chroma screen.

The residual selection rectangles are overlays that will not appear in your exports. And with a few clicks you've transported your talent to a new location.

NOTE ▶   Many additional parameters are available to fine-tune your chroma key composites. Refer to the *Final Cut Pro X User Guide* for additional information.

Sub-workflow 10.4
Working with Multicam

When more than one camera is shooting a scene simultaneously, you can use multicam as a powerful and efficient way to choose the best camera angle for any moment of the scene. Multicam effectively puts you in a live television director's chair, enabling you to monitor as many as 16 angles onscreen, and sync up to 64 angles. Practically speaking, most single disk volume configurations function best with no more than four streams of simultaneous video angles. However, when using high-bandwidth volumes connected by Thunderbolt 2, Final Cut Pro easily processes multiple simultaneous streams of HD or 4K+ video.

10.4-A Setting Up a Multicam Clip

As with other Final Cut Pro workflows, you begin a multicam workflow by importing and organizing media files from your multiple camera setup. For this exercise, you'll work with interview footage that was shot from two simultaneous camera angles. You imported the necessary files earlier in this lesson, so let's jump to the organizing part of the workflow.

1   In the Lesson 10 event, choose the Multicam Keyword Collection.

Four clips for the interview appear in the Browser, and Final Cut Pro has already applied some metadata to them. Let's add some more metadata that will help you create a multicam clip.

2   In the Browser, select clips **MC1_0** and **MC1_1**.

3   In the Info inspector's Metadata View pop-up menu, choose General.

The General view displays additional metadata about these clips. In this case, because you did not import this media directly from a camera card, metadata such as the camera name is missing. You'll want to have this supplemental metadata attached to these clips when creating a multicam clip because Final Cut Pro uses this metadata to automatically assign clips to the same multicam angle. You will also add a Camera Angle assignment that informs Final Cut Pro of the display order of the multiple cameras–Angle 1 and Angle 2.

4   For the two Browser clips from camera one, the MC1 clips, enter the following metadata:

▶   Camera Angle: *1*

▶   Camera Name: *MC1*

Next, you'll assign angle and name metadata to the MC2 clips.

5   In the Browser, select clips **MC2_0** and **MC2_1**, and assign the following metadata:

▶   Camera Angle: *2*

▶   Camera Name: *MC2*

With the four clips readied with the necessary metadata, let's create a multicam clip.

6   In the Browser, select all four clips in the Multicam Keyword Collection. Control-click any one of the selected clips, and from the shortcut menu, choose New Multicam Clip.

A multicam window appears, similar to the window you saw when creating a new project.

7   Enter *MC Interview* in the window's Name field, and ensure that the "Use audio for synchronization" checkbox is selected.

You'll be using the automatic settings for this multicam exercise. When clip metadata is less complete, however, you can help Final Cut Pro create multicam clips by defining in the custom settings how clips are assigned to angles, the sequencing of those clips for each angle, and how to synchronize the angles with each other. Let's try creating the multicam clip using the automatic settings and the existing clip metadata.

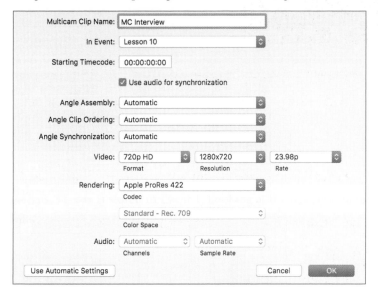

8   With the window set to use the automatic settings and audio for synchronization, click OK.

The multicam clip appears in the event represented by a "four square" icon. To review and evaluate the synchronization that Final Cut Pro performed, you can open the multicam clip into the Angle Editor.

9   In the Browser, double-click the multicam clip to open it into the Angle Editor.

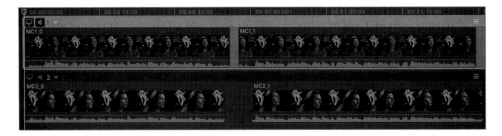

The Timeline displays the Angle Editor. To the left you'll find monitoring angle controls with which you can specify which angle or angles to see and hear during playback in the editor.

10   Click the speaker icon of both angles to monitor them both, and start playback.

You'll hear both angles while viewing the selected video angle.

11   Click the Video Monitor icon on each angle to switch between them.

You'll notice that the second angle has quite a bit of echo. With so much echo, the two angles could be a frame out of sync. You may nudge the clips inside an angle to check for sync between the angles.

12   Select the first clip in Angle 2, and then start playback while monitoring the audio of both angles.

13   Press the . (period) key once to nudge the clip right (later) by one frame.

Did the echo diminish or did you introduce a delay in the audio? You are listening for one voice to create the echo. When the clips are out of sync, will will hear two very similar voices speaking at once.

14 Press the . (period) key once more to move the clip one more frame to the right.

The audio should now clearly be audible as out of sync.

15 Continue nudging the clip, this time pressing the , (comma) key to nudge the clip to the left until the delayed second voice (but not the echo of the room) goes away. The second clip may not need any adjustment.

As mentioned, this multicam clip contains simultaneously shot footage from two different cameras. The source clips were created to simulate the cameras operating under a start/stop question-and-answer session. The pause between clips occurred when recording was paused. You will append this multicam clip into a new project and edit between the angles.

▶ **Set Your Camera's Date and Time**

The advanced multicam synchronization will sync multiple angles, even when camera operators stopped and started recordings at various times. When you're using clips in which the audio signal is degraded, Final Cut Pro augments the default audio synchronization process by accessing timecode information or the time/date stamp (content created). The multicam synchronization will even align still images to video angles in the multicam based on the content-created date/time stamp.

10.4-B Editing a Multicam Clip

The treat when editing with a multicam clip is the ability to make edit decisions in real time during playback. To do so, you'll use the Angle Viewer.

1 In the Libraries sidebar, Control-click the Multicam Keyword Collection, and from the shortcut menu, choose New Project.

2 Name the project *Multicam Edit*, use the default settings, and click OK.

3   Append edit **MC Interview** into the project, and then recue the playhead to the beginning of the Timeline.

You have a little more preparation before you can actually edit the multicam clip in the Angle Viewer. You'll need to open the Angle Viewer, which allows you to see several angles of the multicam clip at once. In the Settings pop-up menu, you can configure the viewer to display up to 16 angles at once (assuming that your media storage volume can play that many simultaneous streams).

4   From the View pop-up menu in the Viewer, choose Angles to open the Angle Viewer.

5   To open up more screen real estate for the Angle Viewer, hide the sidebar and browser using the button above the inspector.

By default, the Angle Viewer will cut and switch to the angle you click in the Angle Viewer. The cut will be placed where the playhead is located at the time of the click. Furthermore, that cut and switch will change both the video and the audio of the multicam clip. While this technique is fast and convenient, it can also lend itself to error until you become skillful with it. To see what can happen when using the Angle Viewer, let's make an edit in error.

6   Cue the Timeline playhead over the first third of the multicam clip.

In the Angle Viewer, one of the two angles is outlined by a yellow border to identify the angle that is currently visible and audible in the Viewer.

7   In the Angle Viewer, move your mouse pointer over the other angle, and notice that the pointer becomes the Blade tool.

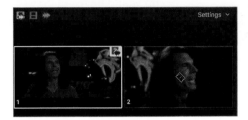

When used here, the Blade tool will cut the multicam clip in the Timeline into a new segment, and switch the active video and audio of the new segment to the newly selected angle.

8   Click the Angle Viewer with the Blade tool while observing both the Angle Viewer and the Timeline.

You cut the clip into two segments and switched to the other angle. This angle is now the active angle as indicated by the yellow outline in the Angle Viewer. The video and audio of this second angle are now active in the Viewer. This behavior reflects two facts:

▶   Clicking in the Angle Viewer without holding down a modifier key results in a cut and switch to the other angle at the playhead.

▶   A yellow outline indicates that the switch will include both the audio and video of the new angle.

9 This edit was intended only to demonstrate one edit command of the Angle Viewer, so press Command-Z to undo the previous edit and cue the playhead to the start of the Timeline.

Camera 1 recorded the good production audio while camera 2 recorded the not-so-great audio. The best strategy for using this multicam clip would be to cut between the video angles while playing the audio content of camera 1 throughout. Doing so requires a Video Only edit, which the Angle Viewer allows you to set up.

10 In the Angle Viewer, click the "camera 1" angle.

A yellow border appears around the angle to show that it is active.

11 In the Angle Viewer, click the Video Only Switching button, and then click the "camera 2" angle.

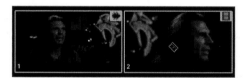

The "camera 1" angle's border turns green to indicate that its audio content is the active audio angle, while the "camera 2" angle's border turns blue to identify its video content as the active video angle.

The audio from camera 1 remains active across the edit.

12 Press Command-Z to undo the edit.

You're just about ready to finally edit the multicam clip. To do so, you will play the Timeline, and simply click the camera angle you want to cut to at any moment. The Angle Viewer, Viewer, and the multicam clip will all reflect your edits. After you stop playback, the Timeline clip's thumbnails will update to show your edit decisions.

13 With the playhead cued to the start of the Timeline, start playback, and in the Angle Viewer, click an angle each time you want to cut to it.

14 If you make a mistake, stop playback, and press Command-Z to undo the most recent cut. Recue the playhead, and resume playback and cutting.

The multicam feature makes editing between multiple cameras feel as if you're directing live TV. Seeing the multiple streams simultaneously allows you to see the alternate angles and, therefore, make better editorial decisions. The ability to use the Undo command means switching to the wrong angle is a mistake that is easily fixed, like directing live TV but with a free do-over.

10.4-C Fine-Tuning Within a Multicam Clip

The "live" playback and cutting between angles in a multicam clip is great for creating an edit very quickly. However, you may find that you cut to the wrong angle (when you have more than two available angle), or more likely, cut a little later or earlier than you intended. These errors are also easy to correct.

1 In the multicam clip, find a specific cut point (the perforated line that divides the clip into multiple segments) you want to move earlier or later in the clip.

2 When you locate the mouse pointer over a cut point, the Roll edit tool appears. Final Cut Pro assumes that you want to keep clips in sync, so it enables the only Trim tool you can use here without causing sync problems.

NOTE ▶ If you need to perform a different trim function, you can choose the Trim tool from the Tools pop-up menu.

3 Drag the cut point to the left about 10 frames.

If you accidentally cut when you did not intend to cut, whether to the same angle or a different angle, you may remove the cut.

4 With the Select tool, click a cut point to select it, and press Delete.

Before pressing Delete

After pressing Delete

The cut is removed, and the angle on the left of the cut is extended to the next cut point. This is known as a **join through edit**.

NOTE ▶ Traditionally, a join through edit occurs when the content is the same on both sides of the cut point. Technically, that remains true here because the content is the multicam clip container on both sides of the cut point.

▶ Switching Angles

When your multicam clip involves more than two angles, you may have cut to the wrong angle and just want to replace the angle. What you then need to perform is a modified switch, that is, a cut and switch without the cut. As with most functions in Final Cut Pro, if you need to perform an operation that is slightly (or radically) different, try combining the standard shortcut key with the Option key.

With your playhead cued over a multicam clip segment in the Timeline, Option-click the other angle in the Angle Viewer. The mouse pointer changes from the Blade tool to the Hand tool in the Angle Viewer. The clicked angle replace edits the segment angle in the Timeline.

Sub-workflow 10.5
Manipulating 360-Video

Working with 360° video clips in Final Cut Pro brings a new dimension to storytelling. As with multicam productions, editing with 360° source media files enables you to tell a story from several perspectives or fields of view. However, as the editor, you must be mindful that unlike multicam editing in which the editor determines the audience's field of view, interactive video players and VR headsets put the audience in the editor's chair. The editor may use audio or visual prompts to draw the audience to look in a specific direction, but the audience member makes the final determination of where to focus attention in a purely 360-video production.

10.5-A Importing a 360-Video Clip

Many 360° source media files must be processed by the camera or by camera-specific software to stitch the media files into a Final Cut Pro–compatible file before import. Final Cut Pro is compatible with 360-video clips in the equirectangular format, which represents the 360 sphere as a 2D rectangle. After you have stitched and formatted the 360-video file as necessary, you're ready to import the media as you would any media file. After importing, you need to verify some metadata.

1   In the Lesson 10 event, locate the 360 Keyword Collection, and select the clip assigned to the collection.

2   In the selected clip's Info inspector, verify that the 360° Projection Mode is set to Equirectangular, and the Stereoscopic Mode is set to Monoscopic.

Although you may assign the Projection Mode to other layouts, a 360-clip must be in and assigned to a equirectangular layout for editing within Final Cut Pro. A clip may be monoscopic or stereoscopic for editing within a similarly configured project. Let's create that project right now.

3   With the 360 Keyword Collection still selected in the Libraries sidebar, in the Browser, right-click the 360-clip, and from the shortcut menu, choose New Project.

The project settings dialog appears configured with the custom settings. As usual with a new, custom project, you will have a few options to verify.

4   Set the Project properties as shown in the following figure, and click OK.

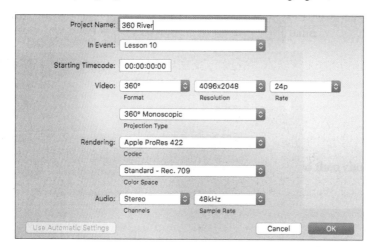

The project is created with the 360-video clip already placed in the Primary storyline.

10.5-B Previewing and Reorienting a 360-Video Clip

Depending on the camera setup and the stitching software, you may wish to establish a specific field of view to show the audience when the clip starts. Establishing a new, default perspective requires you to reorient the clip. However, you are unable to determine what that field of view should be until you've previewed the clip, right? A specialized 360° viewer allows you to preview a 360-video before you start editing.

1   From the Viewer's View pop-up menu, choose to show the 360° viewer.

The 360° viewer appears to the left of the Viewer. The 360° viewer is a live, interactive viewer in which you can manipulate the field of view.

2   Drag the image within the 360° viewer to experience the 360-video. You can drag left and right to pan the field of view. Drag up and down to tilt the field of view.

NOTE ▶   You may also roll the video as if you angled the camera over on its side. The easiest method is to use keyboard shortcuts, Control-Option-Command-[(left bracket) and Control-Option-Command-] (right bracket). To pan and tilt the 360° viewer, replace the bracket keys with the arrow keys.

Before you play the clip, let's reset the 360° viewer.

3   In 360° viewer, from the Settings pop-up menu, choose Reset Angle.

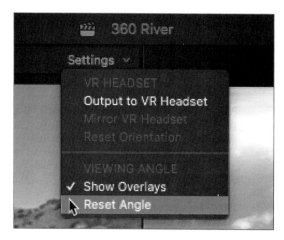

4   With the view reset, press the Spacebar to start playback. Continue dragging within the 360° viewer to look around and experience the clip's 360° contents.

Remember, the 360° viewer allows you to preview the clip, but does not alter its output. If you wanted to reorient the clip to start with a view that faces in the reverse direction, you would do so in the Inspector, or by using the Reorient tool in the Viewer. To prepare for that reorientation, let's reset the Viewer.

5   In the 360° viewer, from the Settings pop-up menu, choose Reset Angle. In the Viewer's View pop-up menu, deselect the 360° viewer to close it.

6   With the 360-video clip selected in the project, from the pop-up menu to the left in the Viewer, activate the Reorient tool.

7   With the Reorient tool selected, drag the image in the Viewer.

You may have noticed that dragging vertically does not tilt the camera as in the 360° viewer. Instead, dragging vertically rolls the camera. A handy horizon guide helps keep your 360-world on the level.

8   From the Viewer's View pop-up menu, choose Show Horizon.

9   Using the Reorient tool, drag again in the Viewer to set the default orientation while also adjusting the degree of roll according to the horizon.

10   In the Viewer's View pop-up menu, deselect the Horizon overlay to hide it; and in the Viewer, deactivate the Reorient tool by clicking Done.

You have a 360-video clip in a 360-project in which you've set metadata to tell Final Cut Pro how to interpret the clip. You've also set the default, or master, clip orientation to redefine the starting field of view for the audience. Next, you will work with an effect unique to 360° clips.

10.5-C Patching a 360-Video Clip

A major challenge with 360-video production is the lack of hiding places to keep the gear (and crew) invisible to your audience. A necessary gear item is the tripod, or sticks, on which the camera is mounted. Among several specialized effects for 360-video is a Patch tool. The 360° Patch effect allows you to sample a "good" area of the image and paste it to hide an undesirable portion, such as the tripod. You'll use this effect to hide the camera tripod in this clip.

1   With the 360-video clip selected in the project, in the Effects browser, locate the 360° Patch effect. Double-click the effect to apply it to the 360-video clip.

The 360° Patch effect has onscreen controls that you can activate in the Inspector.

2   Activate the onscreen controls by selecting the Setup Mode.

Two regions appear in the Viewer: The red target region covers the bottom of the image, which includes the tripod. The green source region is used as the paste-to-target region that will hide the tripod. You'll utilize a combination of the onscreen and Inspector controls to hide the tripod under the bridge.

3   Use the onscreen and Inspector controls to fill the target region with the source region's area of the bridge. Try to obscure as much of the tripod as possible and blend the patch into the original. Refer to the following figures for reference, but your settings may vary.

NOTE ▶ Because the 360° patch is an effect, you can apply it more than once to a single clip. However, be mindful to activate the Setup Mode for only one effect at a time.

▶ Share a 360° Project

Final Cut Pro automatically embeds the 360° nature of your project into your shared projects. The 360° metadata will flag your file as 360-video when uploaded to online sharing destinations.

Sub-workflow 10.6
Generating Captions

Projects destined for industries, governments, or specific delivery platforms may identify closed captioning as one of the delivery specifications. Final Cut Pro enables you to generate captions that conform to the CEA-608 (EIA-608) or iTunes Timed Text standards. You may create the captions directly in your project, import them as a source file into your project, or extract them from a CEA-608–embedded media file. Editing, timing, and arrangement of captions is performed in the Timeline and in the Captions inspector (where a validation indicator alerts you to any formatting issues with the chosen standard). The ability to export captions as a separate file or embed them within a project media file allows you to adhere to multiple specifications within one master project.

10.6-A Creating a Caption Clip

In this sub-workflow, you'll import a version of the Lifted Vignette project in the FCPXML format. The XML file already includes most of the captions. However, an additional caption is needed, and you will have to address some validation issues to successfully export the project.

1   In the Libraries sidebar, select the Primary Media event.

2   Choose File > Import > XML.

3   In the Finder window that appears, navigate to your FCP X Media folder, and locate the LV3 > Captions folder and its contents.

4   Select the Captions.fcpxml file, and click Import.

The FCPXML file is imported, thereby creating a new project, "Captions", in the Primary Media event.

5   Double-click the Captions project to open it in the Timeline.

You should recognize the Lifted Vignette project that you've been editing and also see some additional clips placed in higher lanes.

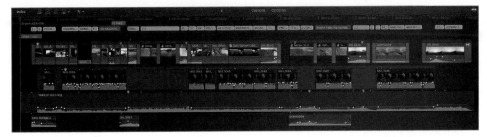

Captions are connected text clips that are synchronized to visually augment the audio content. Captions may differ from the titles you created in Lesson 7 because, whereas titles are part of the visual image and are visible every time the project plays, captions (applied here as closed captions) may be displayed or hidden by the end user. When captions are present in your project, you assign them to a language subrole of a Caption role. Final Cut Pro offers two Caption roles that represent the two supported standards: CEA-608 and iTT.

▶ Which Caption Role Should I Use?

CEA-608 (EIA-608) and iTunes Timed Text of these Caption roles are industry standards for caption delivery. Each standard provides slightly different formatting, character, and layout options. Which one of these Caption roles you should use depends on the delivery specification of the destination platform and the target audience. For general web delivery outside the iTunes Store, use the CEA-608 role.

Most of the captions for this project have already been placed. But you will need to create a caption for the end of Mitch's final sound bite. Also, you must fix the two caption errors that are indicated by the red caption clips.

6 In the Captions project, park the playhead at the start of DN_9424, and where the next caption should begin at 00:01:48:10.

You've cued the playhead at the point where Mitch starts delivering his last sentence. Let's create a caption clip here and associate it with clip **MVI_1046**.

7 To add a new caption clip, select the Timeline clip **MVI_1046**, and then choose Edit > Captions > Add Caption, or press **Option-C**.

An empty caption clip is created. The Caption inspector automatically opens if the Inspector is visible, and the Caption editor opens for text entry.

8 In the Caption editor, type "LOOK WHAT I SAW TODAY AND LOOK WHAT ADVENTURE I WENT ON." Do not press Return or Esc just yet.

NOTE ▶ If you close the Caption editor, you may reopen it by double-clicking the caption clip.

While you are in the Caption editor, you may need to compare the written caption text with its associated audio contents. Unfortunately, your trusty J, K, L, and Space-bar keyboard shortcuts are not available as usual. To use these playback keyboard shortcuts here, you'll need to combine then with the Control modifier key.

9   In the Timeline, press **Control-L** to start playback, and then **Control-K** to pause playback.

Using these combination key shortcuts allows you to modify the caption in the Caption editor while controlling the playhead.

NOTE ▶ With the Caption editor open, press **Command-Left Arrow** or **Command-Right Arrow** to open the previous or next caption, respectively, into the Caption editor.

10   Close the Caption editor by pressing the Esc key, or clicking outside the Caption editor.

10.6-B Modifying a Caption Clip

Now that you have completed the necessary captions, you may alter their timings and durations as you would in any other clip. However, you'll now explore a few functional quirks that are specific to modifying caption clips. Let's start by trimming a caption.

1   In the Captions project, park the playhead at 00:01:51:10 where Mitch's last sound bite ends.

Mitch's last caption should end here to sync the caption's duration with the audio content.

2   Select the End point of the final caption.

NOTE ▶ Slightly zoom the Timeline view in to the caption by pressing **Command-=** (equals sign), if necessary.

3   With the End point selected and the playhead cued to where the End point should be located, press **Shift-X**.

The extend edit command lengthens the caption duration to end at the playhead.

When you previously created this caption, you selected the **MVI_1046** clip before adding the caption clip. That simple selection connected the caption to the sound bite clip, but not to the music in the Primary storyline. This behavior differs from other connected clips, thereby allowing you to connect a caption to only the clip that requires the caption. So, if a project edit later alters the timing of the sound bites, such as delaying the last sound bite, the connected captions will move along with that sound bite. Let's verify this behavior and alter a caption's connection point using a keyboard shortcut you've already learned.

4   In the Captions project, select the **MVI_1046** clip, and press the . (period) key to nudge the clip to start one frame later in the Timeline.

An invalid caption error occurs, as indicated by the red captions.

5 If necessary, open the Inspector, and select the second red caption at the end of the project.

The Validation section of the Inspector identifies the error as overlapping captions. The overlap occurred because the second red caption was connected to the Primary storyline and not the sound bite, as with the other captions. To fix this, you'll undo the one-frame clip nudge, change the connection point, and try nudging the clip again.

6 Press **Command-Z** one time to return the sound bite and the captions to their original positions, thereby removing the overlap error.

7 With the caption that starts with "And in turn" selected, **Command-Option-click** toward the upper edge of **MVI_1046**.

The connection point moves from the music to the sound bite. Nudging the sound-bite a few frames without overlapping the attached captions would be poosible.

Another overlapping issue occurs earlier in the project, and it also needs repair. This time you'll have Final Cut Pro fix the error.

8 In the Captions project, press **Shift-Z** to fit the project within the Timeline.

At the start of the project, the first pair of red caption clips obviously overlap because one is stacked on the other.

9 Select the two overlapping captions, right-click either caption, and from the shortcut menu, choose Resolve Overlaps.

The captions no longer overlap.

NOTE ▶ If the "It takes" caption remains red, the resolution left the caption too close to the previous caption. With the red caption selected, nudge the red caption right using the . (period) key.

10 Scroll the Timeline to locate the last red caption. Then, Option-click the red caption to select it and relocate the playhead.

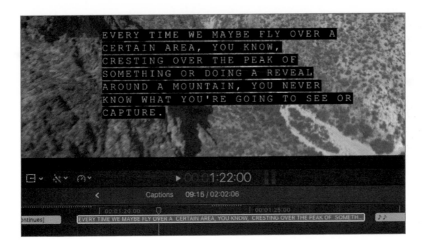

Yikes! That's a lot of caption. The CEA-608 standard limits a caption to four lines of 32 characters (which includes the control characters that are invisible to you). Here's one way to remedy this situation quickly without reentering text.

11 Right-click the red caption, and in the shortcut menu, choose Split Captions.

The caption is split into seven single-line captions; but they intrude vertically into the image, and their timing is off. You can solve these issues with a couple of steps. You'll start by rejoining lines as pairs starting with the last and next-to-last captions.

12 Select the "know" and "capture" captions, right-click either, and from the shortcut menu, choose Join Captions.

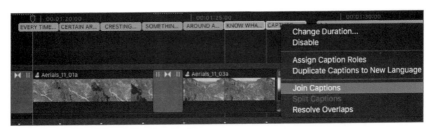

13 Repeat this operation by selecting the next pair and joining them; and finally, join the next pair, thereby leaving the "Every" caption as a single line.

As you joined the captions, they automatically moved to the bottom of the image. You'll need to manually configure the "Every" caption to reposition itself vertically.

14 With the "Every" caption selected, in the Caption inspector, in the Placement category, click "Move the caption to the bottom".

You still have a timing issue to fix. The transition from the first to second caption works, but the second to third needs adjustment. The captions are connected clips, that when adjacent, allow you to use the Trim tool to roll their edit points.

15 Press T to switch to the Trim tool, and click the edit between the "certain" and "something" captions.

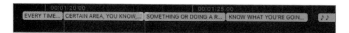

16 Play the project, and then park the playhead before Mitch says "something," which is where the third caption should start.

17 With the edit between the second and third captions still selected, press Shift-X to roll the edit to the playhead.

And now you need to adjust the transition between the last two captions.

18 Press the Down Arrow key as necessary to advance the playhead to the edit between the last two captions.

19 Press the \ (backslash) key to move the roll selection to the edit under the playhead.

20 Using the keyboard navigation shortcuts (J, K, L), cue the playhead to the right, between Mitch saying "never" and "know", and press Shift-X.

NOTE ▸ If you cue the playhead using the mouse, you might deselect the edit, causing the previous step to fail.

With no validation errors detected, the captions are almost ready for export. You did spell-check them, right? Spend a few moments checkimg accuracy and placement of the captions on the video.

▶ **Including Special Characters**

The CEA-608 standard supports a limited number of special characters, whereas iTT supports a wider range of non-Roman characters. The supported special characters are located in the Caption inspector's parameter pop-up menu.

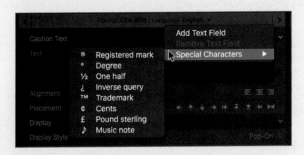

10.6-C Sharing Embedded and External Captions

When exporting, captions are shared as a separate file and/or embedded within the shared media file. In this exercise, you will employ options. The method that a project requires is determined by that project's delivery specifications.

1   With no range set in the project and the Select tool active, from the Share pop-up menu, choose the Apple Devices 720p destination.

2   In the Share window that appears, click the Roles tab.

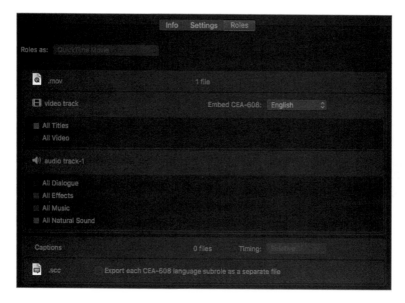

To the right of the video track listing, you'll find the Embed CEA-608 pop-up menu. This menu is set to the language subrole that was active when the project was shared. You may select a different subrole to export, if available, or choose not to embed the captions.

Additionally, you can export each caption subrole as a separate sidecar file by selecting the checkbox in the Captions section. The timing data may be configured as a relative or as an absolute value. Relative values reference a starting timecode of 00:00:00:00 regardless of the project's starting timecode. The Absolute values set the caption's starting time according to the project's starting timecode.

3 In the Captions section, select the separate files option, and from the Timing pop-up menu, choose Relative.

You've prepared the settings regarding closed captioning export. Now you'll return to the Settings tab to change how the destination file is processed.

4 Click the Settings tab.

5 If necessary, in the Settings tab, from the "Add to playlist" pop-up menu, choose "Do nothing".

6 Click Next.

7 Change the filename as desired, and select a save location (such as your desktop) for the file. Click Save.

8 When the Share Successful notification appears, click the Show button.

A Finder window displays the two shared files: an .m4v file for an iOS device and a .scc Scenarist caption file.

NOTE ▶ If the notification did not appear, click the Finder icon in the Dock to open a Finder window. Navigate to the save location you specified in step 7.

9 In the Finder window, double-click the .m4v file you shared.

10 When the file opens in QuickTime Player, start playback, click the SubTitles button, and choose the language subrole syou assigned to the captions during the edit.

When using CEA-608 captions, you may use Compressor to embed captions into additional media files for a variety of platforms. And, of course, you also can use Compressor and a separate iTT file (that Final Cut Pro can create) to prepare your media for iTunes Music Store Package distribution.

Lesson Review

1. Which project Video Properties parameter must be selected to edit in a non-native video resolution?

2. Identify the default render format in Final Cut Pro.

3. What command creates a compound clip that synchronizes a video clip and an audio clip recorded on separate devices?

4. In what vertical order should clips be placed for compositing?

5. In the Keyer effect, what parameter should you set to disable the auto-keyer and gain manual control over the settings?

6. Fill in the blank: Double-clicking a multicam clip opens the _____.

7. Which View pop-up menu option do you click to display a multicam clip's angles for monitoring and to choose the active angle during playback?

8. What do the three active angle colors indicate?

9. What 360° Projection mode for 360-video is supported by Final Cut Pro?

10. Which caption format is required when submitting an iTunes Music Store Package?

Answers

1. The Format parameter must be set to Custom.

2. Apple ProRes 422

3. Synchronize Clips

4. The foreground clip should be placed in a lane above the background clip.

5. Set the Strength slider to 0.

6. Angle Editor

7. Clicking Show Angles reveals the Angle Viewer.

8. Yellow indicates the active video and audio angle. Blue indicates the active video angle. Green indicates the active audio angle.

9. Equirectangular.

10. iTT.

Appendix A
Keyboard Shortcuts

Although Final Cut Pro includes over 300 commands, the tables in this appendix focus on the most commonly used keyboard shortcuts. You also may create or reassign Final Cut Pro shortcuts to your liking.

Assigning Keyboard Shortcuts

Final Cut Pro allows you to create and modify keyboard shortcuts in the Command Editor.

1   Choose Final Cut Pro > Commands > Customize to open the Command Editor.

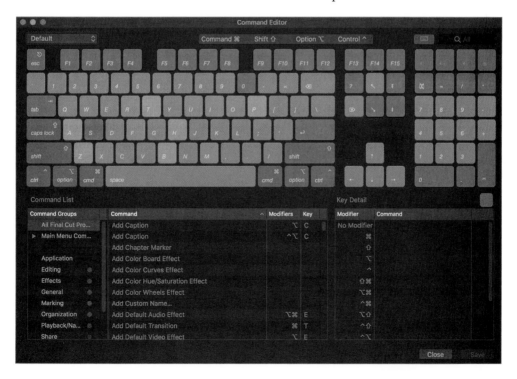

The Command Editor includes a keyboard, a search field, and a list of all available commands. These three elements provide multiple methods for manipulating commands and keyboard shortcuts.

NOTE ▶ When assigning new shortcuts, you will first duplicate the current command set. If you forget to set up a duplicate keyboard command set, Final Cut Pro will remind you.

2 From the Command Set pop-up menu, choose Duplicate.

3 Enter a name for the command set, and then click OK.

A-1 Using the Keyboard

Click a key on the Command Editor's keyboard. A list of that key's assignments appears in the lower right of the Command Editor. You may use this list in conjunction with the other two interface elements to assign commands to the selected key.

A-2 Using the Search Field

The search field allows you to search commands by name and description. For example, entering cut in the search field will return not only the Cut command, but also the Blade command because it "cuts" through clips.

The search field

Search results appear in the command list.

A-3 Using the Command List

Final Cut Pro completists may enjoy taking a scroll through the command list, which displays every one of the hundreds of assigned and assignable commands in Final Cut Pro. It's a great way to discover new commands.

Selecting a command list item displays a description at right.

Reviewing the Default Command Set

The following tables constitute a short list of default keyboard shortcuts.

General

Command	Shortcut	Description
Select All	Command-A	Select all items.
Deselect All	Command-Shift-A	Deselect all items.
Undo	Command-Z	Delete the most recent edit.
Redo	Command-Shift-Z	Redo the last command.

Copy/Paste/Remove

Command	Shortcut	Description
Copy	Command-C	Copy the selected item(s) to the macOS clipboard.
Paste	Command-V	Paste the contents of the macOS clipboard.
Paste Attributes	Command-Shift-V	Allow a specific selection of attributes from a copied clip to be pasted to other clip(s).
Remove Attributes	Command-Shift-X	Allow a specific selection of attributes to be removed from a clip.

Tool Palette

Command	Shortcut	Description
Select	A	Select a clip.
Trim	T	Ripple, roll, slip, and slide trimming functions
Position	P	Adjust positioning of clip or edit in Timeline without affecting others.
Range Selection	R	Define a segment of a clip or clips.
Blade	B	Split a clip into two segments.

Interface

Command	Shortcut	Description
Zoom to Fit	Shift-Z	Browser: Display one thumbnail per clip. Viewer: Display the entire image in the Viewer. Timeline: Display the entire project within the Timeline.
Zoom In	Command- = (equals sign)	Browser: Display more thumbnails in a filmstrip. Timeline: Stretch the time scale of the Timeline.
Zoom Out	Command- – (minus sign)	Browser: Display fewer thumbnails in a filmstrip. Timeline: Collapse the time scale of the Timeline.
Browser	Command-1	Make the Browser the active pane.
Timeline	Command-2	Make the Timeline the active pane.
Inspector	Command-4	Show/hide the details of one or more selected items.
Media Import	Command-I	Open the Media Import window.
Timeline Index	Command-Shift-2	Show/hide the Timeline Index.
Show Audio Meters	Command-Shift-8	Show/hide the Audio meters.
Increase Waveform	Control-Option-Up Arrow	Increase the waveform display size for Timeline clips.
Decrease Waveform	Control-Option-Down Arrow	Decrease the waveform display size for Timeline clips.
Workspaces: Default	Command-0	Arrange the interface in its standard configuration.

Interface *continued*

Command	Shortcut	Description
Workspaces: Color and Effects	Control-Shift-2	Arrange the interface for color correction and effects editing.
Hide	Command-H	Hide the application.

Navigation

Command	Shortcut	Description
Play	Spacebar	Press to play forward. Press again to stop playback.
Forward	L	Play forward. Press multiple times for fast forward playback.
Pause	K	Pause playback.
Reverse	J	Play reverse. Press up to four times for fast reverse playback.
Play Selection	/	Start playback at range start point, and stop at range end point.
Play Around	Shift-?	Cue the playhead to two seconds before its current position, play for four seconds, and then return the playhead to its original position.
Go to Start	Shift-I	Cue the playhead to the start of the selected range.
Go to End	Shift-O	Cue the playhead to the end of the selected range.
Previous Frame	Left Arrow	Cue the playhead to the previous frame.
Next Frame	Right Arrow	Cue the playhead to the following frame.

Command	Shortcut	Description
Up	Up Arrow	Browser: Cue the playhead to the previous clip. Timeline: Cue the playhead to the previous edit point.
Down	Down Arrow	Browser: Cue the playhead to the next clip. Timeline: Cue the playhead to the next edit point.
Go to Beginning	Home (Fn-Left Arrow)	Cue the playhead to the start of the project.
Skimming	S	Enable/disable the skimmer.
Audio Skimming	Shift-S	Enable/disable the audio skimming (skimming must be enabled).
Position Playhead	Control-P	Position the playhead by entering a timecode value or relative time value in the Timecode Display.

Clip Metadata

Command	Shortcut	Description
Set Range Start	I	Start a range at the skimmer or playhead location.
Set Range End	O	End a range at the skimmer or playhead position.
Set Additional Start	Command-Shift-I	Mark a start point for additional ranges within a clip.
Set Additional End	Command-Shift-O	Mark an end point for additional ranges within a clip.
Select Clip Range	X	Set range selection to duration of clip.

Clip Metadata *continued*

Command	Shortcut	Description
Clear Selected Ranges	Option-X	Clear one or more selected ranges (marked start and end points).
Skimmer Info	Control-Y	Show/hide the Browser clip's name, keywords, and timecode at the skimmer's location.
Favorite	F	Assign a selection a Favorite rating.
Unrate	U	Assign a selection an Unrated rating.
Reject	Delete	Assign a selection a Rejected rating.
Delete	Command-Delete	Move the selected clip or event to the Trash. Collection: Delete the collection, removing the keyword from all clips in the collection.

Audio

Command	Shortcut	Description
Expand Audio Components	Control-Option-S	Display the active, individual audio channels of a clip.
Create Audio Keyframe	Option-click	Create an audio keyframe on a clip's Volume control using the Select tool.
Gain +1 dB	Control- = (equals sign)	Boost the volume of the Timeline selection by 1 dB.
Gain −1 dB	Control- – (minus sign)	Attenuate the volume of the Timeline selection by 1 dB.
Adjust Volume Relative	Control-L	Boost or attenuate the volume of the selected Timeline clips by a specified value.

Command	Shortcut	Description
Adjust Volume Absolute	Control-Option-L	Boost or attenuate the volume of the selected Timeline clips to a specific value.
Solo	Option-S	Mute all nonselected audio items from playback.

Trimming

Command	Shortcut	Description
Trim Start	Option-[	Trim start point of clip to skimmer or playhead location.
Trim End	Option-]	Trim end point of clip to skimmer or playhead location.
Trim to Selection	Option-\	Trim start and end points of a clip to the marked range within the clip.
Duration	Control-D	In the Timecode Display, display and allow changes to the duration of the selected clip(s).
Blade	Command-B	Blade the primary storyline clip or one or more selected clips.
Extend Edit	Shift-X	Move the selected edge to the skimmer or playhead position.
Nudge Left	Comma	Clip edge selected: Trim the selected clip edge one frame to the left. Clip selected: Move the selected clip one frame to the left.
Nudge Right	Period	Clip edge selected: Trim the selected clip edge one frame to the right. Clip selected: Move the selected clip one frame to the right.

Editing

Command	Shortcut	Description
Append	E	Add the selected clip to the end of the primary or selected storyline.
Insert	W	Insert the selected clip into the primary storyline within the marked range, or at the skimmer or playhead location.
Connect	Q	Connect the selected clip to the primary storyline within the range, or at the skimmer or playhead location.
Overwrite	D	Stamp the selected clip on top of any clips for the duration of and within the Timeline range, or within the duration of a selected clip at the skimmer or playhead location.
Backtimed Connect	Shift-Q	Perform a three-point connect edit in which the Timeline and Browser marked end points are used to start the edit. Content is backfilled from the end points the duration of the Timeline marked range.
Snapping	N	Turn on/off snapping in the Timeline.
Select Below	Command-Down Arrow	With no existing selection, selects the clip in the highest lane under the skimmer or playhead.

Command	Shortcut	Description
Lift from Storyline	Command-Option-Up Arrow	Perform a lift edit, moving the selected clip vertically out of the containing storyline and leaving a gap.
Create Storyline	Command-G	Place the selected, connected clips into a storyline.
New Compound Clip	Option-G	Browser: Create an empty Timeline container for pre-edits/segments/composites. Timeline: Nest the selection into a compound clip.
Expand Audio/Video	Control-S	Display the embedded audio of a clip as a separate component allowing for independent adjustment of the start and end points of the audio or video.
Reveal in Browser	Shift-F	Display the Browser's selection for the current Timeline selection; match frame.
Reveal Project in Browser	Option-Shift-F	Display in the Browser the current project in the Timeline.
Duplicate Project as Snapshot	Command-Shift-D	Duplicate the selected or active project as a snapshot.
Set Marker	M	Press once to set a marker. When cued to a marker, press once to edit the marker's settings.
Clip Disable/Enable	V	Disable/enable a clip's visibility (or audibility).

Retiming

Command	Shortcut	Description
Retime	Command-R	Display the Retime Editor for the Timeline selection.
Hold	Shift-H	Create a zero-percent speed segment at the playhead.
Blade Speed	Shift-B	Create a speed segment at the playhead.

Gaps

Command	Shortcut	Description
Replace with Gap	Shift-Delete	Replace the selected clip with a gap clip. Also known as a "lift" edit.
Insert Gap	Option-W	Insert a three-second gap clip at the playhead or skimmer.

Connections

Command	Shortcut	Description
Override Connections	` (grave accent)	Allow connected clips to lock to time while the anchoring primary storyline clip is manipulated.
Move Connection	Command-Option-click	Click the connected clip to relocate the clip's connection point to the primary storyline.

Transitions and Effects

Command	Shortcut	Description
Add Default Transition	Command-T	Apply the default transition to the selected edit or clip(s) (plus audio crossfade, when applicable).
Add Default Video Effect	Option-E	Apply the default video effect to the selected clip(s).
Add Default Audio Effect	Command-Option-E	Apply the default audio effect to the selected clip(s).

Appendix B

Editing Native Formats

These tables list the native editing formats for Final Cut Pro. Native format editing does not require transcoding to another format. Final Cut Pro, macOS, and the Mac hardware have more than enough power to push today's formats. Whether you are using the MacBook Pro or the iMac Pro, the combination of pro hardware, macOS, and professional applications is ready to tackle UltraHD, 6K, and any future formats, all natively.

Native Video Formats

This table lists most of the SD, HD, and 1K+ formats. Some supported wrappers include .mov, .mts, .m2ts, .mxf, and .mp4 in addition to the native wrappers of the formats listed.

DV, DVCAM, DVCPRO/50/HD, HDV
H.264, MTS(AVCHD), AVCHD, AVCCAM, NXCAM
AVC-Ultra/Intra/LongG, XAVC S/L, XDCAM EX/HD/HD422, XF MPEG-2, XF-AVC
iFrame, Apple Intermediate
H.265, HEVC
Apple ProRes 4444 XQ, 4444, RAW HQ, 422 HQ, 422, LT, Proxy, Log C, RAW
REDCODE RAW (R3D)
Uncompressed 10-bit and 8-bit 4:2:2

Native Still-Image Formats

This table lists the native still-image formats used for photos and graphics, for example.

BMP
GIF
JPEG
PNG
PSD (static and layered)
RAW
TGA
TIFF
HEIF

Native Audio Formats

This table lists most of the audio file formats natively supported in Final Cut Pro.

AAC
AIFF
BWF
CAF
MP4
WAV

Appendix C

Checkpoints

Editing is a creative art. As you continue to edit with Final Cut Pro and perform the exercises in this book, you may also explore your own creativity and challenge yourself to learn more about the tools and features of the app. In doing so, your editorial choices may differ from the ones made by the author. Checkpoints are a feature of this book that allow you to sync-up with the author's edit.

Downloading and Relinking the Checkpoints Library

You can download the Checkpoints library from the Peachpit website in the same location where you downloaded the Lifted Vignette media files.

NOTE ▸ If you downloaded the Checkpoints library in Lesson 1, skip to step 5.

1   In a web browser, go to www.peachpit.com.

2   Click ACCOUNT SIGN IN and log in to your Peachpit.com account.

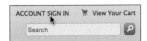

3   Locate the downloadable files on your Account page under the "Lesson and Update Files" tab.

4   Click the Checkpoints.zip link to download the file to your Downloads folder.

After downloading the zip files from the website, the file unzips itself, placing a Checkpoints library in your Downloads folder.

5   Drag the Checkpoints library into the FCP X Media folder you created in Lesson 1. Double-click the file to open this library in Final Cut Pro.

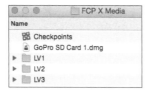

The Checkpoints library is a hybrid library of managed and referenced media. The GoPro clips, as well as the hangar door sound effect, are internally managed within this library, while the remaining library clips reference the source files you placed in your FCP X Media folder. Because this library is not linked to that folder, the externally referenced clips will appear offline or missing in the Checkpoints library in Final Cut Pro. You can relink these clips to your FCP X Media folder and return them to online status.

NOTE ▸   If your Checkpoints library clips are not missing or offline, you may skip to "Using the Checkpoints Library."

6   In the Libraries sidebar in Final Cut Pro, select the Checkpoints library. Choose File > Relink Files.

7   Choose to relink only missing clips.

8   Click Locate All.

9   Navigate to the FCP X Media folder that contains the clips' source media files. Select the FCP X Media folder and click Choose.

10   In the Relink Files window, click Relink Files.

All clips in the Checkpoints library now appear online and ready for use.

Using the Checkpoints Library

The Checkpoints library contains edits of the Lifted Vignette project at various milestones. These milestones are noted in the book as shown here:

▶   **Checkpoint 4.2.2**

Refer to **Appendix C** for details on reviewing a Checkpoint.

The Checkpoint's title shares the name of the corresponding project in the Checkpoints library.

The project represents the Lifted Vignette project's edit progress at that milestone in the book. You may compare the author's Checkpoint version of the project to your own Lifted Vignette edit. After comparing, return to your project to continue with the book's exercises. If necessary, you may drag a Checkpoints project from the Checkpoints library to your Lifted Primary Media event to continue with the book's exercises.

Index

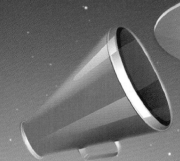

Get Apple certified.
Stand out from the crowd.

Get recognized for your expertise by earning Apple Certified Pro status.

Why become an Apple Certified Pro?

Earn more. Studies show that certified professionals can earn more than their noncertified peers.

Demonstrate accomplishment. With each certification, you get an Apple Certification logo to display on your business cards, resume, and website. You'll distinguish yourself from others.

Reach a wider audience. When you publish your certifications on the Apple Certified Professionals Registry, you can connect with even more clients, schools, and employers.

Learn the way you like.

Learn independently with Apple Pro Training Series books from Peachpit Press.

Learn in a classroom at an Apple-authorized training location with Apple Certified Trainers.

Visit training.apple.com to learn how to get certified on these Apple products:

macOS

Final Cut Pro X

Logic Pro X

"The Apple Certification is a cornerstone of my consulting business. It guarantees to our clients the highest level of dedication and professionalism. And above all, the trusting smile of a client when you mention the Apple Certification can't be replaced."

—Andres Le Roux, Technology Consulting, alrx.net, inc.

 Training and Certification